Automatism as a Defence in Criminal Law

Automatism is a notoriously difficult subject for law students, lawyers and judges. This book explores the science and medicine of sleep disorders and examines how the criminal process deals with such disorders when presented as a defence. It systematically examines the legal doctrines involved, and their implications for the use of the evidence key to establishing automatism, while also exploring the medical conditions that can cause automatism (particularly epilepsy, sleepwalking and diabetes). This book is a valuable resource for law students, lawyers, judges and expert witnesses.

John Rumbold is Senior Research Fellow at the School of Science and Technology, Nottingham Trent University.

Automatism as a Defence in Criminal Law

John Rumbold

Routledge
Taylor & Francis Group
LONDON AND NEW YORK

First published 2019
by Routledge
2 Park Square, Milton Park, Abingdon, Oxon OX14 4RN

and by Routledge
52 Vanderbilt Avenue, New York, NY 10017, USA

First issued in paperback 2020

Routledge is an imprint of the Taylor & Francis Group, an informa business

British Library Cataloguing-in-Publication Data
A catalogue record for this book is available from the British Library

Library of Congress Cataloging-in-Publication Data
Names: Rumbold, John, author.
Title: Automatism as a defence in criminal law / by John Rumbold.
Description: New York, NY : Routledge, 2018. | Includes bibliographical references and index.
Identifiers: LCCN 2018020018| ISBN 9781138701632 (hbk) | ISBN 9781351787833 (web pdf) | ISBN 9781351787826 (epub) | ISBN 9781351787819 (mobipocket)
Subjects: LCSH: Defense (Criminal procedure)—Great Britain. | Criminal liability—Psychological aspects. | Automatism.
Classification: LCC KD8358 .R86 2018 | DDC 345.41/05044—dc23
LC record available at https://lccn.loc.gov/2018020018

ISBN 13: 978-0-367-58564-8 (pbk)
ISBN 13: 978-1-138-70163-2 (hbk)

Typeset in Galliard
by Swales & Willis Ltd, Exeter, Devon, UK

Contents

Cases (from England and Wales unless otherwise noted)

Statutes

Acknowledgements

This monograph is partly on my doctoral thesis on the sleepwalking defence, although it will be apparent to the reader that is much material dedicated to other disorders.

I owe a big debt of gratitude to Professors Martin Wasik and Clive Hawkins, my joint supervisors, for their mentoring and supervision through the PhD process. I must also thank Dr Martin Allen (who was almost a third voluntary supervisor) and his colleagues, Ann Cooper and Nathalie Bryan, for teaching me about sleep medicine and sleep studies, and listening to my ideas about my research. The sleep expert community have been amazingly helpful – I have thoroughly enjoyed talking to so many enthusiastic and knowledgeable people, who have taught me so much about their special interest and given so generously of their time. This research would not have been possible without the help of those British and North American sleep experts. They were very willing to share and keen to learn about my results. Dr Renata Riha and Dr Ian Morrison have been extremely helpful in ensuring that the details on sleep disorders in this monograph are accurate, although any errors are of course mine alone.

In particular I must thank Professor Rosalind Cartwright and Dr Mark Pressman, Dr Jonathan Bird, Dr Irshaad Ebrahim and Dr Chris Idzikowski. I have had productive discussions and collaborations with Dr Renata Riha, Dr Ian Morrison, Dr Gethin Rees and Dr Cedric Gilson, and some of this has gone into my thesis. The latter two also provided some useful feedback on some parts of my thesis. I must also thank the members of the academic community with whom I've had illuminating and informative conversations – Professor Antony Duff, Professor E. Michael Coles, Dr Giuseppina D'Oro, Dr Simon Barnes, Dr (now Professor) Gerben Meynen, Dr Filippo Santoni de Sio, and the attendees of the Keele medicolegal seminar to name but a few. My thanks go to Professor Ronnie Mackay for doing me the honour of being my external examiner, and for writing a foreword to this work. I would also like to thank Chloe James and Melanie Marshall for their invaluable assistance with my first book, their patience was remarkable.

Last but not least my wife who has supported me through my magnum opus amid many hardships.

Medical and legal technical terms are defined in the glossary.

Foreword

How should we view those who claim unawareness of their antisocial behaviour because of automatism? This is a question which continues to trouble the criminal law. Recently, there have been several high-profile cases of the phenomenon known as "sexsomnia" where the defendant claims to have been in a sleep-related state at the time of an alleged sexual assault. In addition, there continue to be a number of driving-related episodes attributable to some form of automatism. In short, this is not just an academic or theoretical issue. Rather, it has emerged as a matter of continuing concern with ever increasing complexity of terminology. As an example of the latter, in the recent civil appeal case of *Dunnage (Terry) v. Randall (Kathleen Bernadette) & Anr* [2015] EWCA Civ 673 Vos LS remarked:

> We have been referred to numerous cases that consider what ought properly to be the position when a defendant "loses" control of his actions, "loses any power of choice", "ceases to know the quality and nature of his actions", "ceases to know that what he is doing is wrong", "loses any power to will his own actions", "ceases to act voluntarily", "loses consciousness" and "loses his personal autonomy", to name just a few of the possible linguistic formulations. These formulations emanate variously from the M'Naghten rules applicable to insanity as a defence in the criminal law, the defence of automatism in the criminal law, and from elsewhere. [28]

Some might argue that we should rid the criminal law of any automatism defence which allows the accused to be found "not guilty". Why should he or she walk free when the alleged offence is attributable to some form of condition which has produced an abnormal state resulting in a profound unawareness of what took place? These and other concerns have prompted the English Law Commission in its Discussion Paper of July 2013 to reconsider the role of automatism as a defence in its own right. The Commission's provisional recommendation is to abolish the common law rules on both the defences of automatism and insanity and to replace these with a new statutory defence of "not criminally responsible by reason of recognised medical condition". This new defence would include any (qualifying) medical condition which resulted in a total lack of capacity, so would include virtually all forms of automatism. In doing so the law would be made more logical as the complex distinction between sane and insane automatism would be eradicated as would the anomalous "external factor" doctrine which, by way of illustration, currently results in the diabetic who experiences automatism being adjudged "sane" or "insane" on the basis of whether the defence is primarily due to the diabetes (internal – insane) or to the insulin regimen (external – sane). To many, this new approach would be welcome but it comes at the expense of greatly reducing the chances of an ordinary acquittal which is presently available to a bona fide sane automaton. Rather, it ensures that such automatons would no longer walk free from court but instead would be subject to judicial disposal powers, including hospital orders and supervision orders. To remove a defence which the common law currently recognizes as permitting a "not guilty" verdict is a major step which must be closely scrutinized and for some, this might be a step too far.

These and many other matters are addressed by the author in this interesting monograph which charts the development of the defence of automatism in English common law and in other jurisdictions. In doing so it contains a comprehensive discussion of the medicolegal aspects of this complex but intriguing defence which is one that continues to trouble the courts, the legal and medical professions. Although solutions to many of the problems posed are hard to find, this monograph will be a useful resource for readers who wish to know more about the fundamentals of the plea. The author is, therefore, to be congratulated for his assiduous research and analysis of automatism, for the more we grapple with these problems the more likely we are to make progress in our understanding of a defence which, although formerly described by a Canadian judge as "intractable", may yet be more fully understood after reading Dr Rumbold's monograph.

Ronnie Mackay
Professor of Criminal Policy and Mental Health
Leicester De Montfort Law School
De Montfort University

1 Automatism

What is it?

Definitions of automatism

Automatism is the defence of the person who was not a moral agent; who was effectively an automaton at the time of the illegal act. Although it is a defence for all crimes, it is far from a panacea for the defendant. There are several limitations on the defence. Also, it is typically argued in circumstances where the defendant does not and cannot contend that the illegal act occurred. Automatism has been described by the courts as a

> quagmire . . . seldom entered nowadays save by those in desperate need of some kind of a defence.
>
> (Lawton LJ in *Quick*)

The doctrine of automatism has confused law students, lawyers, legal academics, and expert witnesses over the years. The humble aim of this monograph is to dispel some of this confusion, whilst simultaneously providing deeper analysis of the doctrine. This work arises from my doctoral research, which focused on forensic parasomnias and expert evidence (Rumbold, 2015). Sleepwalking is in many ways a paradigmatic example of automatism; the capacities normally associated with criminal responsibility are inhibited, but the capacity for potentially criminal actions are preserved. However, this work will deal with other causes of automatism too.

The terminology used plays a significant part in the confusion. Automatism has several different definitions in different contexts. Another source of confusion is the use of the term automatism to describe both non-insane automatism (*automatism simpliciter*) and insane automatism. Insane automatism is simply the insanity defence, and in this monograph that term will generally be used to avoid confusion. Medical automatisms are stereotyped, non-purposeful and repetitive behaviours, occurring during psychomotor seizures. They are most commonly oral (e.g. lip smacking or chewing) or manual (e.g. patting or fumbling). These behaviours would be unlikely to cause any difficulties for the court.[1] Legal automatism,

1 People with psychomotor epilepsy have reported difficulties with the police due to seizure activity; although inconvenient, these incidents rarely lead to further action.

however, is defined in English law as either total loss of voluntary control (non-insane) or by the *McNaughtan Rules* (insane), but there are a number of different formulations (see Chapter 2). The conflation of medical and legal automatism has caused issues for expert witnesses. In the case of *Clarke (Trevor Norman)*, the expert witness for the prosecution asserted that hypoglycaemia had never been reported as a cause for automatism.[2] This seems to be a fundamental misunderstanding of the nature of medicolegal automatism (and the application of evidence-based medicine in expert evidence).

There is some legal argument over whether or not total loss of control is required when the matter is not a motoring offence. This formulation came from the problematic case of *Attorney-General's Reference (No. 2 of 1992)*. Here it was alleged that "highway hypnosis" had produced a state of mesmerism where the lorry driver was able to make minimal adjustments to stay in his motorway lane, but unable to avoid the fatal collision in question. This case and the case of *Isitt* would arguably have been better decided on the basis of an inherent predisposition that must have existed, which would have been an insane cause of automatism. The 2010 *Crown Court Bench Book* (Judicial Studies Board, 2010) stated that:

> To be an involuntary act the loss of control must be complete. Deliberate and purposeful driving is inconsistent with involuntariness.
>
> (p. 315)

The requirement that there must be a complete loss of self control has been condemned across the board by leading commentators on the law as "harsh" (MacKay), "very harsh" (Smith, Herring) and "unduly harsh" (Ashworth) (Smith, no date; Mackay, 1995; Ashworth, 2009; Herring, 2010).

Wigley talks about "automaticity", the commonly recognized experience whereby we can automatically perform well-practiced tasks (Wigley, 2007). This phenomenon can be observed with all "overlearned" behaviours that arise from procedural memory rather than declarative memory. However, a car driver who is in automaticity (or on "autopilot") and thinking about other things whilst driving a familiar route will be brought out of his reverie when something untoward occurs. Likewise, a lorry driver would be alerted by hazard lights on the hard shoulder. This is fundamentally different from the person in a state of automatism, who cannot do this. Legal automatism requires automaticity in combination with unconsciousness (in the sense of unawareness).

It could be argued a total loss of control would render the individual unable to walk or perform any other motor activity. The bipartite formulation of Lord Denning in *Bratty* has some appeal:

> an act which is done by the muscles without any control by the mind such as a spasm, a reflex action or a convulsion; or an act done by a person who is not conscious of what he is doing such as an act done whilst suffering from concussion or whilst sleepwalking.

2 Details from solicitor's case notes, accessed with kind permission of Mr Clarke.

This inclusion of unconsciousness could be argued to include the denial of *mens rea*, rather than legal automatism per se. This confusion is partly down to the evolving understanding of automatism in the common law.

The early articles about automatism use phrases like "conscious volition" that demonstrate no separation between consciousness and voluntariness and often refer to a denial of *mens rea*. In *Quick*, the prosecution counsel commented that:

> When *mens rea* is required, somnambulance would be automatism, and the Crown would have to prove *mens rea*.

Viscount Kilmuir LC commented in the earlier case of *Bratty* that:

> if, after considering evidence properly left to them by the judge, the jury are left in real doubt whether or not the accused acted in a state of automatism, it seems to me that on principle they should acquit because the necessary *mens rea* – if indeed the *actus reus* – has not been proved beyond reasonable doubt.

This suggests that the denial of either the *actus reus* or the *mens rea* was considered the basis of automatism. However, in the case of *Sullivan*, it was commented that:

> The unusual feature of the present case is that the whole of the *actus reus* occurred within a period of unconsciousness.

This implies that automatism was still not seen as a denial of the *actus reus*.

Smart in 1987 stated that:

> The difficulty is that voluntariness of conduct is not invariably accepted as part of the *actus reus* but is sometimes thought to relate to *mens rea*. Another view enquires whether the doctrine of voluntary conduct is itself accepted [Glanville Williams].
>
> (Smart, 1987)

Automatism is seen differently in New Zealand, as the case of *Cottle* demonstrates:

> "automatism [is] a condition resulting in the doing of an act without conscious volition", that might occur due

(a) to a healthy mind as in somnambulism
(b) to a mind temporarily affected by a drug, an intoxicant or a blow
(c) to a mind where there is present an abnormal condition capable of designated a mental disease in which case the McNaughtan rules would apply.

(Gresson, P. in *Cottle*)

There is consequently uncertainty as to whether automatism is a denial of the *actus reus* or *mens rea* in New Zealand (Law Commission, 2013).

The conditions that cause states of reduced or absent consciousness can support three distinct defences, so in this monograph the term "medicolegal automatism" is used to describe these states. There are two main definitions that fit this concept.

Fenwick defined automatism as follows:

> An automatism is an involuntary piece of behaviour over which an individual has no control. The behaviour is usually inappropriate to the circumstances, and may be out of character for the individual. It can be complex, co-ordinated and apparently purposeful and directed, though lacking in judgment. Afterwards the individual may have no recollection or only a partial and confused memory for his actions. In organic automatisms there must be some disturbance of brain function sufficient to give rise to the above features.
>
> (Fenwick, 1987)

Another way to define medicolegal automatism would be mental absence, or the "missing defendant" as Eigen puts it – a defendant whose incapacity is not due to a partial delusion affecting their perception of their actions, but to a partial or total lack of consciousness resulting in their actions being both unintentional and involuntary (Eigen, 2003). In fact, non-common law jurisdictions often use the term "unconsciousness" to describe these states in their criminal codes. This is another term which causes difficulty for medical expert witnesses, who would understand something rather different as unconsciousness.

McSherry agrees with this formulation for automatism:

> While there have been some cases where automatism has been equated with a complete lack of consciousness, because automatism is related to the concept of involuntariness rather than consciousness, a degree of awareness or cognitive function is not necessarily fatal to automatism being accepted by the trier of fact.
>
> (McSherry, 2004)

The defendant at a criminal trial for a serious offence will be held criminally responsible where he has committed a guilty act (*actus reus*) with a guilty mind (*mens rea*) and without a relevant excuse (strict liability offences are more complicated; see further below). It is for the prosecution to prove that the offence is made out by proving the *actus reus* and *mens rea*, and they may have to prove the lack of a relevant excuse; that is, the prosecution has the burden of proof. Therefore, the legal defences that can be argued when the defendant has suffered an episode of medicolegal automatism are:

1 lack of the requisite *actus reus* (involuntariness)
2 lack of the requisite *mens rea* (unconsciousness)
3 insanity (lack of reason).

Figures 1.1 and 1.2 demonstrate the required elements for criminal liability and the basis for these three defences as per McSherry:

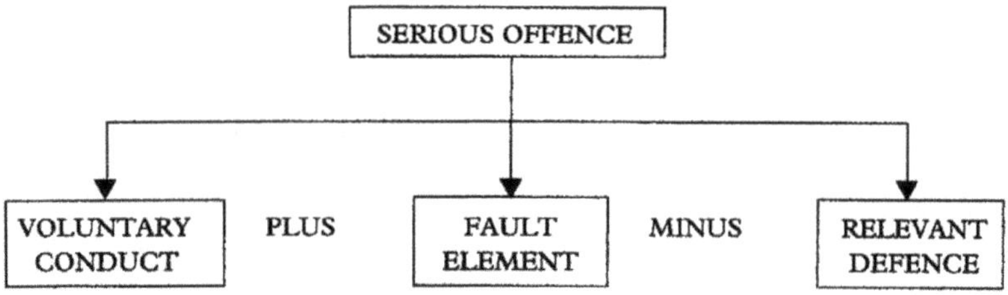

Figure 1.1 Required elements for criminal liability

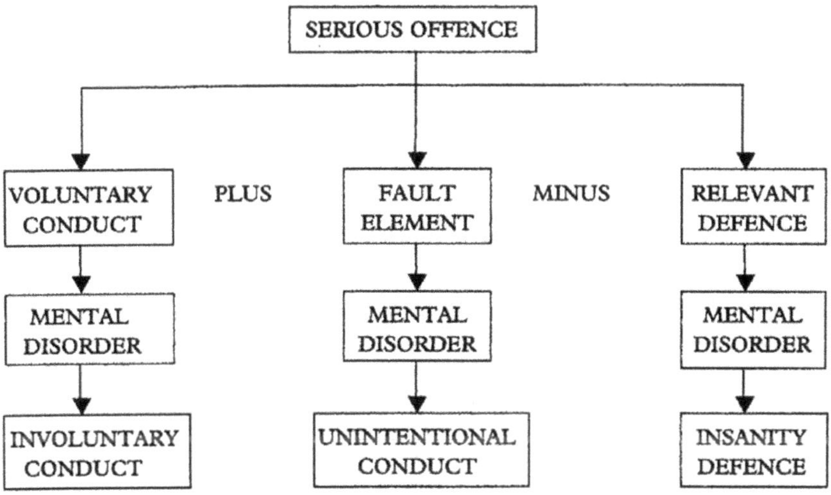

Figure 1.2 Mental condition defences

(Above figures from pp. 582 and 583 "Voluntariness, Intention, and the Defence of Mental Disorder: Toward a Rational Approach" by B. McSherry (2003), with kind permission)

Legal automatism, or *automatism simpliciter*, is strictly a denial of the *actus reus* (in English law at least). This requires a total loss of control (in the motoring cases at least). It does not mean that the physical act was not carried out (which would make the offence inchoate). The *actus reus*, or guilty act, involves more than the commission of the necessary physical act, it requires that the act be voluntary (or at least not involuntary). This means that for many so-called strict liability offences, there is an implied fault element. There is no advantage in arguing this rather than denial of *mens rea*, unless the offence is strict liability (and therefore has no *mens rea* requirement). It is for the prosecution to prove that the conduct was voluntary beyond a reasonable doubt, once the defence has satisfied the evidential burden. The evidential burden simply requires that the judge is satisfied that the jury needs to consider the issue. There are other defences available for many strict liability offences, such as duress for example.

Mens rea, or guilty mind, is the accompanying state of mind that renders the person culpable. Lack of the requisite *mens rea* is less demanding in practice than demonstrating lack of the *actus reus*. Generally, in cases where medicolegal automatism is in play, the illegal act has been either been demonstrated clearly, or is not being disputed by the defence. There are four main types of *mens rea*, listed in increasing culpability: negligence, recklessness, knowledge, and intent (direct or oblique). These terms have different definitions in different jurisdictions, and indeed may have different definitions in different offences.

Negligence is the lowest standard. This requires the actor fall below the standard of the reasonable person (sometimes referred to in English law as "the man on the Clapham omnibus"). This is an objective standard. This is also the standard for tort law, which is civil law.

Recklessness can be subjective or objective. Objective recklessness is where the reasonable man would have thought the act or omission was reckless. Subjective recklessness is where the defendant realized the act or omission was reckless (barring the effect of voluntary intoxication).

Knowledge can be knowledge about the object or the outcome; in the latter case, it is knowledge that the outcome is reasonably certain. For example, selling stolen goods requires that the accused know or believe that the goods were stolen.

Intent can be direct or oblique. Direct intent is the desire to produce a particular outcome. Oblique intent relies on the knowledge that a particular outcome is virtually certain. An example of oblique intent is *R v. Walker and Hayles*, where the defendants threw their victim from a third-floor balcony. He miraculously survived, but given that death was virtually certain, it was held that they had intended his death and so were convicted of attempted murder.

Confusingly, criminal intent is often used in the legal literature as a synonym for *mens rea*. Offences of general intent only require negligence or recklessness, whereas crimes of specific intent require knowledge or intent. Additionally, there will be *mentes reae* of statutory offences that do not fit neatly into these four categories. Drug possession for example does not require knowledge that the item possessed was an illegal drug.

Insanity is a general defence, although there is some debate over whether or not it is a defence to crimes of strict liability. In English law, there is a presumption of sanity. This is an exception amongst defences. The justification for this exception is that the defendant is the person best placed to provide of his mental state, therefore it is reasonable to place the burden of proof on the accused. In English law, this has to be proved on the balance of probabilities. In the USA, the standard of proof in Federal trials is that a clear preponderance of evidence supports insanity. The accused may opt to argue the insanity defence, or the judge may direct the jury to consider the insanity defence. The prosecution can only ask for the insanity defence to be considered when the defendant is pleading diminished responsibility.

The differences between these three defences can be seen in Table 1.1.

Table 1.1 Differences between the three mental condition defences

Type of automatism	*Non-insane*	*Insane*	*Lack of* mens rea
Burden of proof	Prosecution	Defence	Prosecution
Standard of proof	Beyond reasonable doubt	Balance of Probabilities	Beyond reasonable doubt
Definition	Total loss of voluntary control	M'Naghten Rules	Lack of *mens rea*
Cause	External	Internal	Either
Applicability to strict liability offence	Yes	Maybe	No
Verdict	Not guilty	Not guilty by reason of insanity	Not guilty
Disposal	Free without Restrictions	May be subject to supervision or detention	Free without restrictions

It can be seen therefore that the same state caused by the same medical condition can be dealt with different ways, which results in different outcomes for the acquitted person. Many of the cases described as automatism involve an argument that the requisite *mens rea* could not be formed. It has been argued that the requirement for a total loss of voluntary control only applies to driving cases. However, Herring comments:

> there is nothing in the judgment of the Court of Appeal in *Attorney-General's Reference (No. 2 of 1992)* that explicitly restricts their discussion to driving offences.
>
> (Herring, 2006)

The confusion probably arises from the use of the term automatism to describe a lack of the required *mens rea*, rather than just a lack of the required *actus reus*. This conflation occurs in much of the literature.

The defence of automatism has attracted controversy and press attention at times. In recent times, the press has reported with frank disbelief the actions of defendants attributed to sleepwalking. This disbelief has been entirely appropriate in some instances. Many of the reported sexsomnia cases involve alcohol in circumstances where simple intoxication is far more likely than parasomnia. In some cases, the issue is that doctors who do not specialize in the relevant areas have commented on cases. One such example are the comments by Dr Cosmo Hallstrom, Fellow of the Royal College of Psychiatrists:

> People do sleepwalk and they do strange things in their sleep, but it is usually no more complex than grinding the teeth or smacking the lips—at most they

> may get up and make a cup of tea. I would think it was extremely difficult to perform such a complex manoeuvre as having sexual intercourse while asleep—especially if the other person is unwilling.
>
> (quoted by Harry Cohen in Hansard, 2008)

This description would rule out all sexsomnic episodes. It must be noted that although Dr Hallstrom is a psychiatrist approved under Section 12 of the Mental Health Act, he is not a sleep specialist.

Harry Cohen, then MP for Leyton and Wanstead submitted an Early Day Motion proposing a change in the law which would have denied the defence of automatism to those accused of sexual offences. He commented "A rape is a rape and should be treated as such."

However, it appears he was happy for parasomnia to be argued as an insane automatism from his speech in the Commons where he stated:

> The expert medical opinion presented evidence that sleepwalking was a mental abnormality and could deem the defendant legally insane. The judge accepted that, but the series of more recent cases to which I have referred have overridden that decision as far as rape is concerned.
>
> (from Hansard, 2008, see further at Appendix A)

This is also suggested by his Early Day Motion which stated that he:

> considers that those are not proper defences for rape or murder which warrant walking free without any consequence and if they are now deemed to be so, represent a massive legal loophole; further considers that anyone who kills or commits rape cannot be considered completely safe to walk free in the community without much more extensive tests to check that they will not act in the same manner again and that the seriousness of the act should require detention for such tests in all cases.
>
> (Hansard, 2008)

This failure to impose social control measures has been criticized by other commentators.[3] The relevant case law does indicate that sleepwalking (and therefore sexsomnia) should be treated as an insane automatism. However, this precedent is apparently "more honoured in the breach than the observance", if the cases reported in the press are a reflection of all the cases heard.

The feminist critique of sexsomnia focuses on the discovery of yet another excuse for sexual assaults and the frequent association of alcohol with purported episodes. One blogger commented:

3 It should be noted that the Domestic Violence, Crime and Victims Act 2004 has already made it impermissible to make hospital orders for conditions not considered mental disorders under the Mental Health Act 1983.

> I allude to this story from Ontario in which a drunken asshole boor was acquitted of rape using the good old "sexsomnia" defense.
>
> What is sexsomnia, you ask? Why, it's a "sleep disorder." The symptoms include raping women while you're asleep. If you "suffer" from this disorder, as does the recently acquitted Jan Luedecke, and you live in Canada, your life's young dream of flitting from town to town sticking it wherever you please with nary a care in the world has been given the green light. Because although sexsomnia is supposedly a "disorder," it apparently does not rise to the level of a "mental disease," which designation would have had restrictive legal consequences for the somnorapist Luedecke. Although rapists already have it pretty good the world over, in Canada, the coveted sexsomnia diagnosis is a free pass to even the most reluctant pussy! It's a frat boy's dream come true!
>
> (Twisty, 2005)

In recent years, the condition of sexsomnia has attracted a great deal of media attention. In some cases, the defence of sexsomnia never reached the evidential burden (and so was not even considered by the jury). In the case of Stephen Davies, the expert witness, Dr Idzikowski, agreed that Davies did suffer from sexsomnia but testified that the episode in question was not sexsomnia. The press reports, however, stated that the expert witness supported the defence of sexsomnia. The newspaper misreporting of the case might be partly explained by its complexity, but probably arose because the court reporter was present for one part of the expert testimony, but not the crucial part. There were several later corrections, which stated that his defence was not sexsomnia but a plain denial of rape (*Daily Mail*, 2011). Davies's complaint to the Press Complaints Commission about *The Guardian* newspaper, on the grounds that his trial was misreported as sexsomnia, was upheld (Commission, no date). In fact, the defence was three-stranded and *did* include the defence of sexsomnia. The jury was apparently not sure that the defendant had no reasonable belief of the victim's consent, and so they acquitted him.

The case of *Jeal* was misreported in the press as a sleepwalking defence – he was a sleepwalker, but in fact he argued that he had made a mistake as to consent (Jamieson, 2008; Koster, 2008). He had been visiting friends and was going to be staying overnight in their spare bedroom. He had an argument with his wife, before falling asleep on the couch. His wife went home instead. The couple whose house it was also had an argument, and the woman then went and slept in the spare room. Mr Jeal woke up on the couch, and then went to the spare bedroom. Assuming the woman in the bed was his wife, he proceeded to have sexual intercourse with her. The jury acquitted on this basis – sleepwalking was not argued at all.[4]

4 These aspects of the case were not included in the press reports, but were related to me by the defendant's solicitor.

By contrast, the defence of automatism has been argued for several decades when diabetic drivers have suffered hypoglycaemic episodes behind the wheel. The required *mens rea* is different, because public safety considerations are foremost. The foremost global expert witness in this area Professor Marks reports that these defences usually fail on the issue of prior fault (personal communication, 2013). There is also the issue of lack of total loss of control, at least at some point during the continuing act of driving. The ability to drive safely within the expectations of society and the law is rather more demanding than the ability to drive at all. Thus, the latter ability should not be taken as evidence that the accused was physically capable of the former at the time of the alleged offence.

Parasomnia trials

It is impossible to get accurate numbers of cases where automatism was being argued. The statutory insanity defence, whether an example of insane automatism or the conventional defence, results in the special verdict if successful. This is not the case for automatism, where there will be a plain acquittal. Analysis of press reports of one particular cause of medicolegal automatism has shown a dramatic increase between 1994 and 2010 (see Figure 1.3) (Rumbold, 2015). Increasing awareness of sleep disorders, improved diagnostic tests and high-profile trials has seen the number of referrals to forensic sleep experts increase exponentially; Dr Idzikowski reports one enquiry per week. The proportion of referrals seen as bona fide varied between 10 and 80 per cent (Rumbold, 2015).

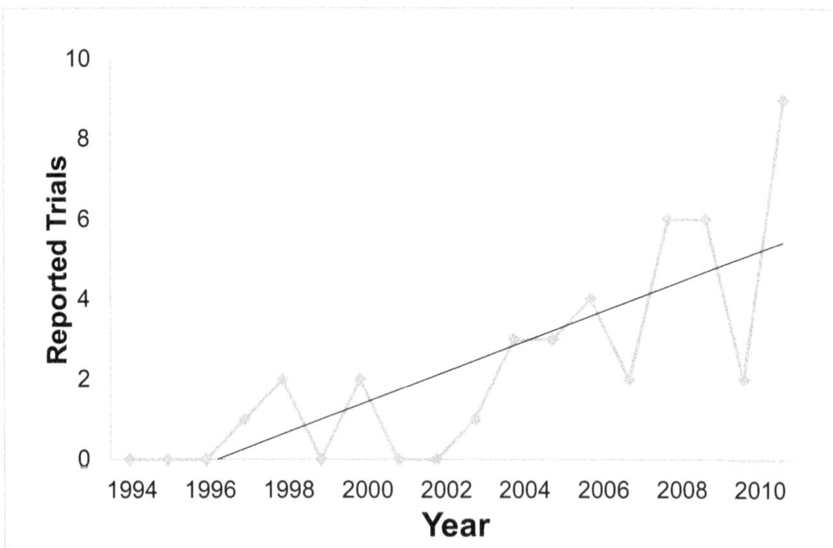

Figure 1.3 Press reports of forensic parasomnia trials 1994–2011

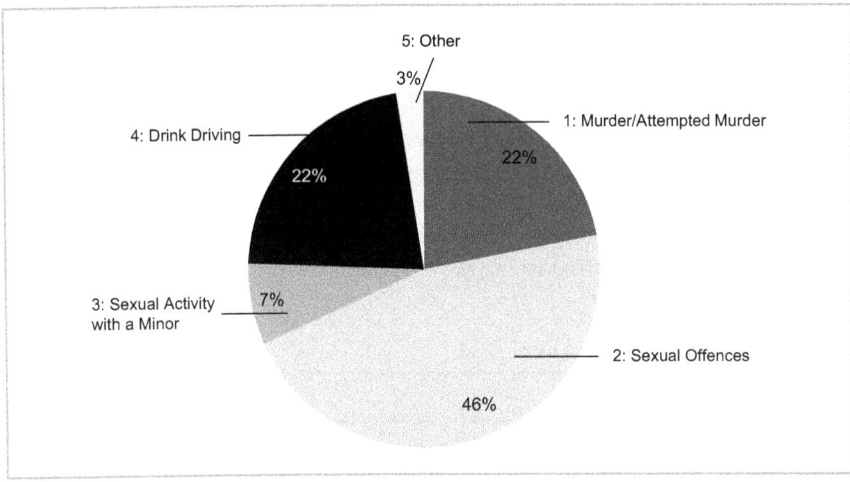

Figure 1.4 Type of offence

There are a number of possible reasons for this increase, including greater availability of sleep experts, greater awareness of sleepwalking amongst the legal profession, and greater media interest in the defence. The same analysis of press reports revealed the particular offences where automatism is most likely to be argued. They are generally serious crimes, or crimes of strict liability (such as drink driving – see Figure 1.4).

The offences charged were mostly sexual offences, homicide and drink driving (see Figure 1.4). The fact that the offences that go to trial are serious ones should be no surprise – there is anecdotal evidence less serious offences are either dealt with outside of the criminal justice system, fail to secure funding for expert opinions and sleep studies, or sleep studies are performed but the evidence is not tested in court.[5] It appears, for example, that nude sleepwalking is very common in hotels, but staff are trained to deal with it informally and sympathetically rather than treat it as a criminal act (*Telegraph*, 2007). Also, most of the acts are perpetrated towards family or friends. They are usually aware of the sleepwalker's condition, and so the criminal justice system is not involved.

The male preponderance in the press reports and in the literature may reflect the greater ability of males to inflict serious harm. Also, female sexsomnia is probably less likely to involve the police due to social and physiological differences – female sexual aggression is perceived differently and penetration would require active male participation (however, this author has been asked for expert evidence on the likelihood of a sexsomnic episode on the part of a victim of an alleged rape).

5 Personal communication from Dr Idzikowski.

Seven defendants currently, or had previously, served with the armed forces. Of these, two had been diagnosed with post-traumatic stress disorder (PTSD) and in another his experiences in the Gulf War were blamed for precipitating his parasomniac episode.

Other details of the defendant, the circumstances of the alleged offence, or his medical history were analysed with results in Table 1.2 (although the reporting of these details was very patchy). There were 41 cases in total. The average age of the accused was 37.1 years of age. The male: female ratio was 39: 2.

Some of the cases illustrate vividly the "desperate need of some kind of a defence" Lawton LJ referred to in *Quick*. Freaney, who was convicted of murder

Table 1.2 Features of reported cases

Parasomnia:	
Sleepwalking	20
Sexsomnia	9
Defendant changed plea before or during trial	**3**[6]
Confusional arousal	3
Miscellaneous	6[7]
Prior History of Parasomnia (where reported):	*Family History of Parasomnia (where reported):*
Yes **3**	Yes **22**
No **1**	No **5**
Precipitating event/factor:	*Consumption of alcohol before the episode (where reported):*
Yes **13**	Yes **28**
• PTSD **2**	No **2**
• War experiences **2**	
• Stress **5**	
• Medications **3**[8]	
• Sleep apnoea **1**	
No **4**	
Verdict:	
Convicted	**18** (44%)
Acquitted	**22** (54%)
Not guilty by reason of insanity	**1** (2%)

6 In two cases defendants changed their plea to guilty; in the other case the defendant maintained his innocence but changed the basis of his defence to erotic asphyxiation in a sex game gone wrong. In all those cases it was due to lack of support for a sleepwalking defence. There were other cases where the defendant pleaded guilty, but maintained that they were sleepwalking (drink driving cases).

7 In three cases the parasomnia was not specified; in one case the diagnosis was probably night terror; in one case there was not in fact any parasomnia claimed (*Jeal*); and in one case the defence was on the basis of sleepwalking or other cause of automatism.

8 In one case withdrawal from treatment for his parasomnia.

at Oxford Crown Court, initially claimed he had been sleepwalking but changed his defence to that of erotic asphyxiation after expert evidence did not support this. A Scottish man, Goldie, convicted of child abuse made an outrageous claim of sexsomnia in an email, but this was never credible enough to be argued in court (*Daily Record*, 2011). In other cases like that of *Thompson*, even though he dropped the sleepwalking claim, it cannot be assumed that this entails fabrication on his part (Dolan, 2012). In the lack of an explanation for the amnesic episode, it is a valid defence to mount where supported by medical evidence.

The most striking features of this analysis were that there was only acquittal on the ground of insanity, and the prominent role alcohol played. These are both important policy issues. The case law is not being applied on both counts, and so the opportunity to both impose social control measures and exclude questionable excuses is being lost. Addressing the two issues alone would prevent some of the more egregious injustices.

2 Legal aspects of automatism

Legal history

The automatism defence is essentially intertwined with the insanity defence. The insanity defence in England was introduced at the inception of the common law. In pre-Norman England the insane person's relatives (or friends) would pay compensation for his crimes, even homicide (this option was available to all under the principle of "buy off the spear or bear it") (Thorpe, 1840). By the 11th century certain wrongs could not be atoned for by compensation; they were "botless" and punishable by death and the forfeiture of property. This was the first emergence of a separate criminal law.

Prior to 1800, the defendant might as well argue temporary insanity as "automatism" (the term was not in use at that time), since the common law insanity defence results in a plain acquittal. The common law insanity defence still applies in summary trials, as the special verdict is only available in trial by indictment.

The few trials that are recorded where a state of unconsciousness was involved often did not result in exoneration of the individual. Although this predates the advent of psychology, the existence of sleepwalking and other parasomnic states was well-known. Homer describes an episode that sounds like a confusional arousal, where Elpenor falls from a roof, breaking his neck (although it could have been plain intoxication). A quote attributed to Socrates states:

> In all of us, even in good men, there is a lawless wild-beast nature, which peers out in sleep.

One of the best known fictional accounts of sleepwalking is that of Lady Macbeth. During her sleepwalking, she talks about the murder of Duncan (Act V, sc. i).

There were pronouncements from the church and jurists that the sleeping person lacked free will. It has been recognized since at least the Council of Vienne (1313) that a sleeper should not be held responsible for killing or injuring someone, and they reported instances of homicides by sleeping persons.[1] In the 15th century the phenomenon of "murderous sleepwalkers" was described.

1 The 15th Ecumenical Council of the Roman Catholic Church held 1311–12 in France.

The 16th-century canonist Covarrubias stated that the act of a sleeper was not a sin unless he deliberately arranged matters beforehand. The jurist Matthaeus in the 17th century considered that the sleepwalker deserved punishment if "he harboured enmity against that person", and the Scot McKenzie expressed a similar sentiment:

> Such as commit any crime whilst they sleep, are compared to Infants . . . and therefore they are not punisht, except they be known to have Enmity against the person killed; or that Fraud be otherways presumable: quo casu they be punisht extra ordinem. (1678).
>
> (Walker, 1968)

However, this principle was not followed in the cases recorded from this time. In 1600 the knight von Gutlinge, when awoken from sleep, stabbed his friend to death. He was found guilty and executed (Bonkalo, 1974). Colonel Culpeper in 1686 apparently shot a guardsman and his horse during a dream; he was found guilty of manslaughter whilst insane, and pardoned a few weeks later.[2]

During the latter half of the 18th century, evidence from physicians about insanity was allowed at trial. This permitted a more nuanced understanding of the effect of mental illness on criminal responsibility. The common law definition of insanity prior to *Hadfield* was the "wild beast" (in the sense of a dumb, untamed, animal, lacking rationality – often misunderstood as "wild" in the sense of raging) of De Bracton or the simpleton with the moral understanding of a child under the age of 14. These individuals when acquitted would be discharged to the care of relatives, the church or the state, as they were a continuing danger. Therefore, disposal of the defendant found not guilty on the ground of insanity had not been an issue.

The statutory special defence of insanity was created by the Criminal Lunatics Act 1800. This was an emergency measure to prevent the imminent release of Hadfield after his acquittal for the attempted assassination of King George III. The evolution of the insanity defence during the 19th century had a distinct political element, which arguably continues to be the case to this day (c.f. the changes in the insanity defence around the time of Hinckley, would-be assassin of Ronald Reagan (Mackay, 1988)). The sole disposal under the Criminal Lunatics Act was detention at His or Her Majesty's pleasure. This was required due to the acceptance of a more nuanced definition of insanity. Erskine had argued that an ingredient of insanity was delusion (*Hadfield*). This partial insanity was more likely to entail that the individual did not pose a continuing danger to society. Hadfield would not be subject to civil commitment as he was not insane at the time of trial.

It is no coincidence that many of the early insanity acquittals involved charges of treason. It meant the accused had a mandatory 15 days before trial (Bellingham, whose victim was the Prime Minister, was hanged the same day)

2 Robert MacNish in *The Philosophy of Sleep* relates a simplified version of the tale, changing the name to Sir Peter Lely who is acquitted.

and the right to counsel (O'Reilly-Fleming, 1992). It has been speculated that the insanity defence was a way of discrediting assassins. Moran argues persuasively that the Chartist Daniel McNaughtan,[3] who tried and failed to assassinate Robert Peel, far from being delusional, had a genuine and well-founded fear of Tory spies and was motivated by politics rather than psychosis. Prime Minister Gladstone stated that the removal of the threat of punishment for the insane was "an inducement . . . to morbid minds for the commission of crime by an apparent declaration of innocence in the teeth of the facts" (Eigen, 2011).

It was considered by many (and most influentially perhaps Queen Victoria) that the insane could still be deterred by the threat of punishment, and so the Trial of Lunatics Act 1883 replaced the special verdict of "not guilty by reason of insanity" with "guilty of the act but insane at the time" (reminiscent of the verdict in some US states of "guilty but mentally ill"). The previous wording was reinstated by the Criminal Procedure (Insanity) Act 1964, which still applies today.

It is also during the Victorian era that the concept of a dissociation between the mind and body emerges as a prominent theme. Eigen quotes John Hunter describing a patient who appeared to "want [a] connection between the mind and the body". The description sounds more like a dissociative episode. In 1827 one defendant stated that "My mind was overcome in a moment . . . and of my being at the time I did so misconduct myself in a way of total absence of thought, never contemplating such a crime." Another defendant stated "It was like a dream to me, when I saw the deed was done it struck me with terror instantly" (Eigen, 1995).

Eigen discusses how the Victorian jurors might have responded to the "missing defendant", who did not fit the lay understanding of insanity (Eigen, 2003). He describes the notion of crimes occurring whilst sleepwalking or under hypnotic suggestion as being committed by another self, in a parallel with Multiple Personality Disorder (MPD, also known as Dissociative Identity Disorder or DID). MPD/DID has created novel problems for the criminal justice system in the USA at least (discussed further in Chapter 5).

Examples of crimes committed in a state of automatism include the sleep-related cases of Esther Griggs and Simon Fraser mentioned below, but also the case of Elizabeth Carr who was found "not guilty on the grounds of unconsciousness" in 1876 after she cut off her daughter's hand during an episode of *vertige épileptique*, or "epileptic vertigo". She apparently mistook her daughter's arm for a loaf of bread during an episode that sounds like dissociation or a complex partial seizure (Eadie, 2002). Eigen argues that this narrative verdict introduced a new criminal defence (Eigen, 2004). This author agrees that this was the foundation for the defence now known as automatism.

3 Although this name has been given as M'Naghten in the eponymous rules for the insanity defence, the spelling used here is taken from Moran's monograph (1981) *Knowing Right from Wrong: The Insanity Defence of Daniel McNaughtan* as most likely to be the correct version.

The 19th century heralded the systematic study of the criminal mind by alienists, including Isaac Ray, Philippe Pinel, Henry Maudsley, John Conolly, Charles Bucknill, Forbes Winslow and Harrington Tuke. There was a deep interest in states of altered consciousness such as hypnosis and sleepwalking, with various conditions recognized (from Beard, 1881):

- Intellectual trance (absent-mindedness)
- Emotional trance
- Spontaneous trance
- Somnambulistic trance (somnambulism)
- Cataleptic trance (catalepsy)
- Ecstatic trance (ecstacy[sic])
- Alcoholic trance
- Epileptic trance, or epilepsy
- Trance sleep
- Trance coma
- Trance rigidity
- Trance lethargy
- Self-induced trance
- Mesmeric (artificial) trance.

Wharton's criteria for assessing the sleepwalking defence bear examination by modern experts. There are similarities with the criteria of Bonkalo and subsequent forensic sleep experts (Bonkalo, 1974). The difficulties in determining whether or not a particular episode was parasomnia mandates that circumstantial factors such as lack of motive, out-of-character behaviour and no attempts at concealment remain important.

- A general tendency to deep and heavy sleep must be shown, out of which the patient could only be awakened by violent and convulsive effort
- Before falling asleep, circumstances must be shown to produce disquiet which sleep itself does not entirely compose
- The act under examination must have occurred at the time when the defendant was usually accustomed to have been asleep
- The cause of the sudden awakening must be shown. It is true that this cannot always happen, as sometimes the start may have come from a violent dream.

(Weiss and del Busto, 2011)

In 1853 Sarah Minchin, a 17-year-old servant girl who had stabbed one of her master's children in the middle of the night, put forward a sleep-related defence but this did not succeed. It has been suggested she suffered sleep terrors as her mother confirmed she often screamed in the night. The possibility of somnambulism was raised after comparing her behaviour to a description of somnambulism in *Taylor's Medical Jurisprudence*. The doctor who testified to the court, Henry Bullock (a house surgeon rather than a forensic psychiatrist) was not convinced

(Ekirch and Shneerson, 2011). The case attracted no publicity and she was sentenced to three months in jail on the relatively minor count of unlawfully wounding (although she had been charged with attempted murder and grievous bodily harm) (Old Bailey, 1853).

Esther Griggs was tried in 1858 for throwing her baby to its death from a first-floor window after having a nightmare (or more likely night terror) that the house was on fire. The grand jury refused to indict her. These early cases were not recorded by law reporters but by journalists – a trend that continues to the current day as their salaciousness often outweighs their legal importance. The Griggs case was also reported in the second edition of Bucknill and Tuke's *Manual of Psychological Medicine* (1862). A famous case from 19th century Scotland involved Simon Fraser, a known sleepwalker who threw his 18-month-old son against a wall, killing him. Fraser was not formally acquitted according to Walker – the Court "deserted the diet simpliciter" (that is, the trial was abandoned; the jury returned a narrative verdict – "The jury find that the panel killed his child when he was unconscious of the nature of the act which he committed, by reason of a condition arising from somnambulism; and that the panel was not responsible"). The judge advised Fraser not to sleep in the same room as anyone else in an ad hoc arrangement. The case was reported in the medical literature with the warning that:

> [s]omnambulism is a condition so obscure and ill-defined, and might so easily be simulated and used as a cloak for crime, that considerations of public safety make it necessary to examine the patient's history very closely.
>
> (Yellowlees, 1878)

From 1800 to 1992, the disposal that automatically followed from the special verdict was detention at Her (or His) Majesty's pleasure i.e. indefinitely. Although this entails the possibility of release, many individuals stayed in secure hospitals for their entire life. McNaughtan died in Broadmoor of diabetes. Victorian asylums subjected patients to appalling conditions, and the only benefit for the individual was avoidance of capital punishment, which was the mandatory punishment for murder (subject to commutation by the monarch), until the Homicide Act 1957. Where capital punishment was not relevant, there was no reason for the defendant to opt for pleading insanity. The prosecution cannot ask for the insanity verdict to be considered (unless the defendant is arguing diminished responsibility).

The insanity defence was little used because of this inflexibility of disposal, particularly after the introduction of the partial defence of diminished responsibility with the Homicide Act 1957. The automatism defence was a welcome option for those defendants where the judiciary had no stomach for incarcerating someone whose condition could be cured by simple means. Lawton LJ argued in *Quick*:

> No mental hospital would admit a diabetic merely because he had a low blood sugar reaction; and common sense is affronted by the prospect of a diabetic being sent to such a hospital, when in most cases the disordered

> mental condition can be rectified quickly by pushing a lump of sugar or a teaspoonful of glucose into the patient's mouth.
>
> (p. 918)

However, it was some 32 years before the possibility of a hospital order for those suffering from a physical disorder was abolished, in section 24 of the Domestic Violence, Crime and Victims Act 2004.

There was concern about the defence, precisely because it led to a plain acquittal. The case law charts the addition of a number of qualifiers following the first use of the term in the bizarre case of *Harrison-Owen*. There was some initial uncertainty over what a disease of the mind is, Devlin J stating in *Kemp*:

> there is . . . no general medical opinion upon what category of diseases are properly to be called diseases of the mind.

Charlson attacked his son, hitting him over the head with a mallet and throwing him out of the window. This behaviour was attributed to a brain tumour. The defence did not raise the defence of insanity, and he was acquitted by the jury. His behaviour was quite complex, and out of keeping with the modern understanding of automatism:

> The accused called his ten-year-old son Peter into the back room telling him that there was a rat to be seen standing on a stone in the river. When the boy came to the window the accused picked up a wooden mallet from the floor and struck the boy twice on the head, breaking the skin of the scalp and causing blood to flow. The boy tried to defend himself from further attack by wrapping his head in a towel. The accused thereupon picked the boy up and threw him out of the window.

The episode shows deception and planning, both of which are inconsistent with automatism.

Kemp hit his wife over the head with a hammer. He suffered arteriosclerosis affecting the brain, and Devlin J directed the jury that this must be considered a "disease of the mind". The verdict of guilty but insane was returned (both cases were decided at the court of first instance). Both these cases involved arguments by the defence that physical diseases were not causes of legal insanity. Devlin J states in *Kemp*:

> In my judgment the words "from disease of the mind" are not to be construed as if they were put in for the purpose of distinguishing between diseases which have a mental origin and diseases which have a physical origin, a distinction which in 1843 was probably little considered. They were put in for the purpose of limiting the effect of the words "defect of reason." A defect of reason is by itself enough to make the act irrational and therefore normally to exclude responsibility in law. But the rule was not intended to apply to defects of reason caused simply by brutish stupidity without rational power.

In the important case of *Hill v. Baxter* it was established that there was an evidential burden which must be discharged by the defence before the issue of automatism could be put to the jury. If there was no such evidence then the judge should tell the jury to ignore the defence and related evidence. Medical evidence is nearly always required to get the automatism defence off the ground (an exception being the effect of sneezing, as demonstrated in *Woolley*). Once the evidential burden has been satisfied, the burden of proof in the automatism defence is on the prosecution. The prosecution must prove that there was a voluntary act that satisfied the *actus reus* requirement for the offence. This is still the position today.

In the case of *Bratty*, Lord Denning formulated a distinction between insane and non-insane automatisms which had considerable merit. He argued that:

> It seems to me that any mental disorder which has manifested itself in violence and is prone to recur is a disease of the mind. At any rate it is the sort of disease for which a person should be detained in hospital rather than be given an unqualified acquittal.

Quick saw the introduction of the currently accepted legal test for distinguishing between insanity and *automatism simpliciter*. It was held that:

> malfunctioning of the mind of transitory effect caused by the application to the body of some external factor such as violence, drugs, including anaesthetics, alcohol and hypnotic influences cannot fairly be said to be due to disease.
>
> (p. 922)

Lawton LJ also stated:

> No mental hospital would admit a diabetic merely because he had a low blood sugar reaction; and common sense is affronted by the prospect of a diabetic being sent to such a hospital, when in most cases the disordered mental condition can be rectified quickly by pushing a lump of sugar or a teaspoonful of glucose into the patient's mouth.

Despite these considerations of the issues of continuing danger and sensible disposal (see above), Lawton LJ specifically excluded the issue of recurrence and treatment from the assessment of legal insanity:

> If an accused is shown to have done a criminal act while suffering from a "defect of reason from disease of the mind," it matters not whether the condition of the mind is curable or incurable, transitory or permanent: see per Devlin J. in *Reg. v. Kemp* [1957] 1 Q.B. 399, 407. If the condition is transitory, the Secretary of State may have a difficult problem of disposal; but what happens to those found not guilty by reason of insanity is not a matter for the courts.
>
> (p. 918)

The same considerations would also not have prevented a patient with an insulin-secreting tumour or epilepsy being found not guilty by reason of insanity. A disorder in many systems of the body can constitute a disease of the mind for the purposes of the law. It has even been held that an abnormal heart rhythm is capable of being held as a disease of the mind (*MacBrayne*, reported only in the press (Lazzari, 2011)). It should be noted that although external factors are always a non-insane cause of automatism (unless they are so routine that the reaction to them is evidence of an internal disorder e.g. *Rabey*), not all internal disorders are diseases of the mind. An example would be where a muscle spasm is caused by a disorder of the muscle itself or the spinal cord, as happened in the case of *Pull* (see further in Chapter 4 (*The Guardian*, 1998)). The issue of whether or not a particular disorder was a disease of the brain or a disease of the mind has arisen in Canada (Can LII, 2014). It would be unlikely for this to be an issue in the British courts.

The theme that this author draws from the case law is the attempt at an easy distinction between the conditions where there is a need to impose social control measures to ensure the safety of the public, and those where there are no such concerns. The external factor doctrine does not draw a clear line in the sand, as most medical disorders are the product of a combination of a predisposition and an external precipitant. Furthermore, some external causes are likely to recur – ironically, insulin administration in the case of diabetes being a prime example. The results in more recent cases suggest a move to a more pragmatic and holistic assessment, but this is as yet unsupported by the legal precedents.

The position on prescribed drugs is also unclear. In the case of *Hardie*, the trial judge held that "voluntary self-administration of the drug was irrelevant as a defence since its effect could not negative *mens rea*", but the Appeal Court quashed his conviction stating that:

> under section 1(2) of the Act of 1971 a defendant's state of mind had to be considered only when he did the relevant act and the requirements of the subsection were established if the defendant when doing that act created an obvious risk that property would be destroyed and life endangered and gave no thought to the possibility of either risk; that, in considering his state of mind, the self-administration of a sedative or soporific drug, even in excess, did not automatically raise a conclusive presumption that its effects could not negative *mens rea* in the way that self-induced intoxication by alcohol or dangerous drugs could; that the trial judge had misdirected the jury that the effects of such a drug leading to a defendant's incapacity were irrelevant; and that, accordingly, the conviction had to be quashed since the jury should have been directed that if they concluded that by taking the drug a defendant could not appreciate the risks to property and persons from his actions, they should consider whether the taking of the drug was itself reckless.

However, the Appeal Court held in *McGhee* that a combination of temazepam and alcohol taken for the relief of tinnitus and causing disinhibition could not amount to automatism – Hughes LJ stated emphatically that "Disinhibition is exactly not automatism."

The fact that involuntary intoxication makes a choice harder is irrelevant – as Stephen Fitzjames (1883) put it, "If the impulse was resistible, the fact that it proceeded from disease is no excuse at all."

The trial judge directed the jury in Hardie that "an intoxicated intent was still an intent". It is not clear why diazepam could negative *mens rea* but temazepam (another benzodiazepine which has an identical effect) could not. It has been suggested that Hardie was decided *per incuriam*, as the effect of diazepam was misunderstood (Somers and Weller, 1991).

The Canadian approach addresses this question more directly. Since 1992 it has had the verdict of not criminally responsible due to mental disorder (NCRMD) under section 672.34 of the Canadian Criminal Code. This gives three options for disposal – an absolute discharge, a conditional discharge and detention in custody in a hospital. One of the most interesting innovations of the enabling Act was that detention should be capped at the maximum tariff for the offence in question, unless there was proof that the interest of public safety demanded otherwise. This would make the plea a more attractive proposition compared to indefinite hospitalization, although this measure would arguably make little difference in the UK because of the existing flexible powers of disposal. This was the most controversial part of the Act; it was not proclaimed and eventually repealed on the advice of the 14th report of the Standing Committee on Justice and Human Rights, 2002. This was largely due to concerns about the ability of the civil commitment system to protect the public. The current situation is that those who plead NCRMD are detained longer on average than if they had been sentenced to prison (Crocker et al., 2015).

This system can lead to paradoxical conclusions. In the case of *Luedecke* it was held that his condition, sexsomnia, was likely to pose a continuing danger so therefore the verdict of NCRMD was appropriate. However, at the civil commitment panel, the opposite conclusion was reached – it was considered that he required no continued monitoring or compulsory treatment. The two aspects of the NRCMD verdict that are particularly attractive are (1) that it is made clear that the causative condition does not have to be a mental health condition and (2) the move away from the stigmatizing label of insanity in these cases.

Legal principles

The basis of the legal defence of automatism is the requirement in the common law for a voluntary act. The decision in *Woolmington v. DPP* was that the prosecution has the burden of proof for all the elements of the offence (except where reverse burdens are required by statute). It was also confirmed in *Woolmington* that all the common law defences except insanity required only an evidential burden to be satisfied by the defence, but thereafter the burden was on the prosecution to disprove it beyond reasonable doubt. This exception is considered by some to be an historic anomaly (Jones, 1995).

As Windeyer J. commented in *R v. Ryan*:

> That an act is only punishable as a crime when it is the voluntary act of the accused is a statement satisfying in its simplicity. But what does it mean? What is a voluntary act? The answer is far from simple, partly because of the ambiguities of the word "voluntary" and its supposed synonyms, partly because of imprecise, but inveterate, distinctions which have long dominated men's ideas concerning the working of the human mind.

There have been numerous attempts to define automatism in the case law, which attest to the difficulties:

- "total destruction of voluntary control" (Lord Taylor CJ in *Attorney-General's Reference (No. 2 of 1992)*);
- "acting involuntarily in the sense that his actions are independent of his will, and therefore not subject to any conscious control" (Tompkins J in *R v. Campbell*);
- "an act which is done by the muscles without any control by the mind such as a spasm, a reflex action or a convulsion; or an act done by a person who is not conscious of what he is doing such as an act done whilst suffering from concussion or whilst sleepwalking" (Lord Denning in *Bratty v. Attorney General for Northern Ireland*);
- "the mind does not go with what is being done" (Viscount Kilmuir L.C. in *Bratty*);
- "all the deliberative functions of the mind must be absent" (North P. in *R v. Burr*).

All these descriptions vary to a degree – in particular the last two seem to describe something far more like unconsciousness than involuntariness. They all tend to suffer from the use of terms like "will" and "voluntary", which are not defined satisfactorily in the law. The courts assume that the juror knows what these terms means, and so leave the issue to the realm of folk psychology. This assumption seems dubious, given the difficulties lawyers have in defining what they mean. Yeo states:

> an accurate and comprehensive definition of involuntariness has thus far eluded both the courts and law reform bodies that have considered the issue.
>
> (Yeo, 2001)

As Windeyer J states in *Timbu Kolian v. R*:

> one of the difficulties comes from the need to relate will to acts, and to define precisely the distinction, commonly accepted by lawyers, between intention and volition. These words are used glibly; and often with little definition of the sense in which they are used.

The terms "voluntary", "will" and "act" are largely defined with respect to each other – a "willed act" is voluntary, an act requires "will", a "voluntary" act is willed. This is perhaps one area where the recommendations of the Law Commission would (if adopted) bring some much needed clarity, as the proposed new mental condition defence does not rely on this distinction (Law Commission, 2013). The requirements for voluntariness are problematic. The driving cases have required that there be a "total loss of voluntary control". Although this might seem to clearly define legal automatism, it is problematic because of the difficulties in defining "voluntary". These issues were perhaps most clearly demonstrated in the case of *R v. Ryan.*

The defendant was convicted of an armed robbery where he had shot and killed the garage attendant. He pleaded guilty to manslaughter, but in the state of New South Wales, there was a felony-murder rule which rendered any homicide in the course of a felony murder rather than manslaughter. This meant that any argument based on the lack of intent to kill was irrelevant. Ryan's contention was that when he had the sawn-off shotgun trained on the garage attendant, a sudden movement by the attendant made him pull the trigger reflexly. He argued that this was an involuntary act. In support of his version of events, when the police recreated the scenario, the officer holding the gun reflexly pulled the trigger when the officer playing the garage attendant moved. It was argued that his action was non-voluntary, rather than involuntary. Elliott compared his reaction to "the sudden movement of a tennis player retrieving a difficult shot; not accompanied by conscious planning, but certainly not involuntary."

Given all this, on what basis was Ryan's conviction upheld? The court held that by holding a gun on the garage attendant in this way, primed to react, Ryan's act was:

> a consequence probable and foreseeable of a conscious apprehension of danger, and in that sense a voluntary act.
>
> (Windeyer J)

Thus, Ryan was guilty on the basis of pointing a loaded gun at the garage attendant, rather than the fact that he pulled the trigger. Just as the tennis player retrieving the difficult shot is praiseworthy for his reflex action, likewise Ryan was blameworthy for his reflex action. Further, if Ryan had had a legal reason for holding a gun on his victim (for example, if he was detaining a criminal), then the shooting would have been excusable.

In the example given in obiter in *Kay v. Butterworth* of a person stung by a swarm of bees losing control would also arguably not be an involuntary reaction. Although the reactions would be instinctive, they would be potentially controllable. In a German case, it was held that someone swatting a fly whilst driving could not be said to be acting involuntarily (unlike a reflex action such as blinking) (Dubber and Hornle, 2014). Likewise, the acute effect of a concussion would not involve a total loss of voluntary control. This suggests that there are a number of overlapping justifications for the automatism defence, at least as it is applied in the courts. In some circumstances, the absence of the deliberative capacity is sufficient to prove automatism, whilst in other circumstances a total loss of control is required. The requirements for a total loss of voluntary control seem particularly harsh in driving cases. There are several cases where drivers have been clearly impaired, but because their loss of control was not complete, they were held responsible. An expert witness opined in *Clarke (Trevor Norman)* that because the driver did not swerve off the road immediately, he had not suffered a total loss of control.[4] It should be noted that total loss of voluntary control is not the same as total loss of control. However, the precise difference has not been fully elucidated in the courts.

It has been held in the past that an individual who was for example sleepwalking is not in voluntary control of their actions. Moore (1979) states that:

> Cases of sleepwalking, post-hypnotic acts, and similar acts are often sufficiently complicated that they appear to be intelligently directed actions. In such cases, one is loathe not to attribute these acts to some agency, but if not to X [the defendant], then to whom?

The Victorian answer to this dilemma was that the person has two souls, one being responsible for sleep behaviour (this distinction could be mapped onto McLean's triune model of the human brain). It has been argued by Bayne and others that agency is a marker for consciousness (Bayne, 2013). However, we can easily find counter-examples from the animal kingdom that dispute the attribution of moral agency. Although we may punish a dog for running off with a string of sausages, we do not consider the animal a criminal. Even though chimpanzees can be trained to perform complex motor tasks such as driving, they lack the deliberative functions to do so to socially acceptable standards – for example, they can be trained to stop at a red light, but they will drive off at a green light no matter whether it is safe or not (Calisher, 2008).

The question is not whether the sleepwalker has any level of consciousness at all, but whether this is the level and type of consciousness to which we would attribute criminal responsibility.

Schopp and Moore both examined the issues of voluntariness and intentionality, and came to similar conclusions (Schopp, 1991; Moore, 1993). Santoni de Sio analyses the similarities in their models for criminal responsibility, and concludes that they:

> seem to agree that the presence of a minimal belief-desire-behaviour combination is not in itself a sufficient condition for the presence of a voluntary action, i.e. the product of a person or an agent.
>
> (de Sio, 2006)

As Schopp puts it, the actor who is a practical reasoner:

4 Source solicitor's notes, with kind permission of Mr Clarke himself.

> selects an action-plan through a causal process that allows access to the comprehensive set of wants and beliefs. In contrast, the actor who selects an action-plan in a state of impaired consciousness acts without the benefit of the causal force that would ordinarily be exerted by certain wants and beliefs that constitute reasons for acting in a certain manner.

Moore (1993) expresses very similar thoughts:

> volitions must be responsive to all (or at least a fair sample) of what one desires, believes, and intends. And this is what being asleep, being unconscious, or being hypnotized prevents. These states seem to break the unity of consciousness that allows volitions to be formed that are responsive to all of one's desires, beliefs, and intentions, and not just responsive to a small subset.

By contrast, Ryle sees the concept of volition as "just an inevitable extension of the myth of the ghost in the machine" (Ryle, 1970). Relying on ascriptive language to define voluntary actions can cause confusion for non-lawyers – one expert witness recounts the judge saying of the defendant "he wasn't driving", and retorted "Well, he was behind the wheel!" Presumably the judge meant that the accused was not acting voluntarily, so was not driving in the sense that the consequences of the vehicle's speed and direction could not be attributed to the accused. Hart classifies four types of responsibility – causal, role, liability and capacity. The hypoglycaemic driver who crashes into a pedestrian has causal responsibility for their injury or death, but may or may not have role-, liability-, or capacity-responsibility depending on his actions (Hart, 1968). In one sense, he is responsible for the crash by being in the car, but in another sense, he may not be responsible if his incapacity was blameless.

It can be argued that the vital incapacity of medicolegal automatism is the inability to evaluate one's actions, rather than the inability to form the requisite intent. The sleepwalker can form the intention to eat or have sex, but this action is not truly voluntary. The concept of the practical reasoner displaces the intangible "will" or "volition" as the source of moral agency. The practical reasoner can weigh up choices and choose to comply with the law and/or the moral standards of his community. The person who has lost these capacities should not be held criminally responsible. This view is reflected in the Law Commission's proposed new mental condition defence of "not criminally responsible by reason of recognized medical condition" which focuses on the capacity for practical reasoning (Law Commission, 2013).

The US Model Penal Code (American Law Institute, 1985) provides a more specific definition of acts that are involuntary:

> A reflex, convulsion, movements during unconsciousness or sleep, conduct during hypnosis or due to hypnotic suggestion, and any movement that otherwise is not the product of the effort or determination of the actor, either conscious or habitual.
>
> (Article 2, Section 2.01(2))

Bars to the defence of automatism

The main bars to the defence of automatism are:

- Prior fault
- Voluntary intoxication
- A disease of the mind.

Prior fault

Prior fault can manifest in a number of ways. It may be culpability for bringing about the cause of incapacity. It may be culpability for adopting a course of action whilst knowingly in a dangerous state. It may be culpability for failing to take appropriate preventive action when loss of capacity was imminent or developing.

The example of diabetes mellitus will demonstrate all three of these fault elements. If a diabetic driver has mismanaged his condition so that the risk of hypoglycaemia is increased, then he may be held responsible for illegal acts during any episodes of hypoglycaemia. Professor Marks's experience of providing expert evidence in criminal trials across the world is that the defendant is found guilty on the basis of prior fault (personal communication, 2013). However, the failure to eat properly following the administration will not automatically disqualify the defendant from arguing automatism. In *Bailey* it was held that the defendant's failure to eat food after administration of insulin was not to be treated in the same way as voluntary intoxication with drink and drugs, on the grounds that:

> It is common knowledge that those who take alcohol to excess or certain sorts of drugs may become aggressive or do dangerous or unpredictable things, they may be able to foresee the risks of causing harm to others but nevertheless persist in their conduct. But the same cannot be said without more of a man who fails to take food after an insulin injection. If he does appreciate the risk that such a failure may lead to aggressive, unpredictable and uncontrollable conduct and he nevertheless deliberately runs the risk or otherwise disregards it, this will amount to recklessness. But we certainly do not think that it is common knowledge, even among diabetics, that such is a consequence of a failure to take food and there is no evidence that it was known to this appellant. Doubtless he knew that if he failed to take his insulin or proper food after it he might lose consciousness, but as such he would only be a danger to himself unless he put himself in charge of some machine such as a motor car, which required his continued conscious control.

Bailey was decided on a subjective standard, as the court held that:

> if the accused knows that his actions or inaction are likely to make him aggressive, unpredictable or uncontrolled with the result that he may cause

> some injury to others and he persists in the action or takes no remedial action when he knows it is required, it will be open to the jury to find that he was reckless.
>
> (p. 765)

This ruling also suggests that the standard depends on the offence, so carelessness or negligence with blood sugar management will be sufficient for prior fault in driving offences.

By contrast, where raised blood sugar due to diabetes was considered as one of the causes for a lack of capacity in *Hennessy*, this was considered to be an insane automatism. This case is complicated by the coexistence of stress, anxiety and depression. Lord Lane stated about the sum of the factors that:

> [t]hey constitute a state of mind which is prone to recur. They lack the feature of novelty or accident, which is the basis of the distinction drawn by Lord Diplock in *Reg. v. Sullivan.*

Another example would be the accused exposing himself to a known trigger for the condition that caused a lack of capacity. This could be drinking alcohol when this is known to precipitate sleepwalking, as per *Finegan v. Heywood*. It could be putting oneself in a highly risky situation with a history of sexual behaviour in sleep, as per the case of *Machin*. Here the defendant was charged with rape after he volunteered to escort an extremely intoxicated woman back to her chalet in Butlins. The woman was so drunk she was unable to stand. The defendant put her to bed, and then laid down to sleep next to her on the mattress. He subsequently had sex with her in the night. He had a long-standing history of sexual behaviour in sleep, confirmed by his partner. He was acquitted (Bentley, 2013). It is somewhat surprising that the jury did not find that he was at fault for putting this vulnerable woman at risk in this way.

Voluntary intoxication

The case law suggests that voluntary intoxication requires more than the voluntary consumption of intoxicating substances. In the case of *Hardie*, the defendant had taken some of his partner's diazepam tablets on her advice, whose tablets they were. He set fire to the flat in which they lived whilst under the influence of the drug, and was charged with arson, contrary to section 1(2) and (3) of the Criminal Damage Act 1971. This offence requires intention or recklessness, and so is an offence of basic intent. His conviction was quashed on the ground:

> that the jury should have been directed that if they concluded that by taking the drug a defendant could not appreciate the risks to property and persons from his actions, they should consider whether the taking of the drug was itself reckless.

It is assumed by the courts that everyone knows about the effects of alcohol, but the reasonable man would not necessarily know the effects of prescription drugs – therefore *Hardie* was not objectively reckless. Virgo argues that: "Intoxication is not deliberate if the intoxicant is taken solely for medicinal, sedative or soporific purposes" (Virgo, 1993). However, the cases of *McGhee* and *Kingston* contradict this position (see further in Chapter 5).

Where alcohol is suggested as a cause for sleepwalking, the law is not clear whether or not this trigger disqualifies the accused from arguing automatism. In the Scottish case of *Finegan v. Heywood*, the defendant drove a car whilst under the influence of alcohol. The sheriff held that this episode occurred whilst sleepwalking. His tendency to sleepwalk after consumption of alcohol was already known. He was convicted on the basis that his condition was self-induced, and this conviction was upheld on appeal. The ratio of the High Court is not entirely clear; it was argued both that all the effects of intoxication whether foreseen or not rendered the individual criminally responsible, and that self-induced incapacity was not an excuse (see further below).

A disease of the mind

Where the cause of incapacity is a disease of the mind, this must be insane automatism. The term "insane automatism" creates a certain amount of confusion in the literature and in practice. This author prefers to use the term automatism for non-insane automatism and insanity for insane automatism. These terms will be used throughout the rest of the monograph.

A disease of the mind has never been precisely and exhaustively defined, although a number of conditions have been excluded (such as personality disorders). Dickson J in the Canadian case of *Cooper* commented:

> Let me say by way of commencement that, to date, the phrase "disease of the mind" has proven intractable, and has eluded satisfactory definition by both medical and legal disciplines. It is not a term of art in either law or psychiatry. Indeed, Glanville Williams (*Textbook of Criminal Law* at p. 592) says that the phrase is no longer in medical use. "It is a mere working concept, a mere abstraction, like sin."

Although an external cause is not a disease of the mind, the opposite is not true. There are internal causes of automatism that are not due to a disease of the mind. A problem with the muscles or spinal cord that causes a muscle spasm would not be a disease of the mind. Multiple sclerosis was the cause of such a condition in *Pull*. The accused suffered such a spasm which caused a loss of control whilst driving, and he hit a number of pedestrians, killing one. If his insight had been intact, he would have been convicted on the basis of prior fault as he should have known that his disability would make it dangerous to drive. However, his multiple sclerosis had also affected his insight into his disability. Therefore, he was found not guilty by reason of insanity (*The Guardian*, 1998).

The English courts took the view that any internal cause might be liable to recur, and so poses a question of public safety. However, the opposite is not always true. A blow to the head is likely to be a one-off occurrence, but some other external causes (as defined in the case law) are quite likely to recur. The best example of this is hypoglycaemia produced by insulin administration, since most diabetics who take insulin need to take it for the rest of their life. This is ironic given that one of the motives behind distinguishing external causes was the desire not to detain diabetics in special hospitals.

The Canadian approach is to assess the condition in the round, as La Forest J states in *Parks* after citing Martin JA in *Rabey* with approval:

> The internal cause approach has been criticized as an unfounded development of the law, and for the odd results the external/internal dichotomy can produce; see Williams, Textbook of Criminal Law (2nd ed. 1983), at pp. 671–76; Stuart, Canadian Criminal Law (2nd ed. 1987), at pp. 92–94; Colvin, supra, at p. 291. These criticisms have particular validity if the internal cause theory is held out as the definitive answer to the disease of the mind inquiry. However, it is apparent from the cases that the theory is really meant to be used only as an analytical tool, and not as an all-encompassing methodology. As Watt J. commented in his reasons in support of his charge to the jury in this case, the dichotomy "constitutes a general, but not an unremitting or universal, classificatory scheme for 'disease of the mind'".

Equally, although there are several conditions that are not diseases of the brain that are nonetheless diseases of the mind, all diseases of the brain are potentially diseases of the mind. In the Canadian case of *SH* the Ontario Court of Appeal held that a disease of the brain causing incapacity constituted a disease of the mind.

Another distinction between automatism and insanity is chronicity. The acute physiological or psychological effects of trauma might be counted as automatism, but when the insult becomes chronic e.g. post-traumatic stress disorders, impairments due to brain injury this would considered as insanity. This distinction can be justified on policy grounds – where there are reasons to be concerned about continuing danger, then the special verdict is necessary to ensure public protection.

A further distinction between automatism and insanity is the severity of the insult. This mainly applies to "psychological blow" automatism, where an abnormal reaction to relatively routine events is considered insanity. This is on the basis that this reaction must therefore be due to an underlying abnormality of the mind. This principle was described in the Canadian case of *Rabey.* The defendant had been spurned in love, and attempted to strangle the object of his affections during what has held to be a dissociative episode. Martin JA found that "the ordinary stresses and disappointments of life which are the common lot of mankind" were not the type of events that could support the defence of sane automatism.

The severity of the insult can be contrasted with the traumatic episode that triggered the dissociation in *R v. T* (see further at Chapter 5). Here the defendant had been raped three days before she allegedly committed robbery with a knife. The case of *Rabey* was specifically distinguished. It was argued that:

> Rape is all too [prevalent] but we have not yet reached, and it is to be hoped we never shall reach, the stage when it has to be regarded as one of "the ordinary stresses of life." But, even it were so, *Rabey* is distinguishable because, as the judge in the present case found, "such an incident could have an appalling effect on any young woman, however well-balanced normally."

These cases have a bearing on the distinction between an external cause and an external trigger. It is apparent in sleepwalking cases that there can be a search by the defence for an external cause, in an attempt to distinguish the case from *Burgess* and secure a plain acquittal. Lord Lane commented:

> One can perhaps narrow the field of inquiry still further by eliminating what are sometimes called the "external factors" such as concussion caused by a blow on the head. There were no such factors here. Whatever the cause may have been, it was an "internal" cause. The possible disappointment or frustration caused by unrequited love is not to be equated with something such as concussion.

For example, it has been argued that where contact with another was the trigger for a violent confusional arousal, that this is an external cause. The fact that anybody is prone to a confusional arousal in the right circumstances is more relevant. It might be argued by counsel that the presence of a bed partner is an external cause for a sexsomnic episode. An external cause and an external trigger can be usefully distinguished on the basis of the exceptionality of the cause. The doctrine of automatism largely rests on the occurrence of an unusual event (although a bout of sneezing hardly qualifies). It can also be rationalized on the basis of considering automatism as an excuse. Therefore, it is not only the loss of control that forms the basis of the excuse, but also the reason for the loss of control. A similar principle applies to provocation or its replacement in England and Wales, the loss of control defence. Here there are particular causes that are disallowed, such as sexual jealousy. It is part of the normative function of the criminal law that certain causes of loss of control ought to be excluded.

There are clear policy issues that dictate the distinction between insanity and automatism. The criteria that operate in the courts are not clear. The two main issues are dangerousness and treatability. However, these issues have not been determinative in several precedents such as *Burgess* and *Sullivan*. There are also other issues at play, particularly judicial resistance to the consideration of the insanity defence.

Case law

The term automatism was first used in the case of *Harrison-Owen*, where it was suggested that the defendant carried out a burglary in a "state of automatism".

The flimsy attempt at a defence for a serial housebreaker was described as a "pack of absurdities". Automatism was described by Lawton LJ in *Quick* as a "quagmire . . . seldom entered nowadays save by those in desperate need of some kind of a defence."

This tendency continues to the current day; some of the accused would have no other defence, as it is clear that they committed the illegal act in question. In particular, some of the reported cases of sexsomnia appear to be intoxicated individuals with no other way to excuse their behaviour.

The comprehensive nature of the automatism defence and burden of proof on the prosecution quickly led to limitations on the defence. In the important case of *Hill v. Baxter*, it was established that there was an evidential burden which must be discharged by the defence before the issue of automatism could be put to the jury. If there was no such evidence then the judge should tell the jury to ignore the defence. This means that medical evidence is nearly always required to get the automatism defence off the ground. Once the evidential burden has been satisfied, the burden of proof in the automatism defence is on the prosecution. The prosecution must prove that there was a voluntary act that satisfied the *actus reus* requirement for the offence. This is still the position today.

The external factor doctrine also emerged in the case law in a policy-based attempt to limit plain acquittals to cases where there are only minimal public safety concerns whilst trying to prevent the plainly disproportionate disposal of indefinite detention being applied to those with physical illness. In *Quick* it was asserted that "disease of mind" only applied to an internal cause, and thus individuals suffering epilepsy (*Sullivan*) and sleepwalking (*Burgess*) could not rely on the automatism defence, but must instead rely on the insanity defence. As Lawton L.J. commented in *Quick*:

> No mental hospital would admit a diabetic merely because he had a low blood sugar reaction; and common sense is affronted by the prospect of a diabetic being sent to such a hospital, when in most cases the disordered mental condition can be rectified quickly by pushing a lump of sugar or a teaspoonful of glucose into the patient's mouth.

However, he acknowledged that this argument had its limitations, and felt that if the condition was a "disease of the mind", it should still be considered insanity – regardless of whether the treatment required for the condition was physical or psychiatric, and regardless of how transitory the condition was:

> If an accused is shown to have done a criminal act while suffering from a "defect of reason from disease of the mind," it matters not whether the condition of the mind is curable or incurable, transitory or permanent: see per Devlin J. in Reg. v. Kemp [1957] 1 Q.B. 399, 407. If the condition is transitory, the Secretary of State may have a difficult problem of disposal; but what happens to those found not guilty by reason of insanity is not a matter for the courts.
>
> (p. 918)

This comment demonstrates that his Lordship was explicitly rejecting continuing dangerousness as the deciding criterion between non-insane and insane automatism. Furthermore, he is contradicting his own inference that the sensible means of disposal should dictate the classification of a disorder. The crucial factor was the distinction between internal and external causes, because a

> malfunctioning of the mind of transitory effect caused by the application to the body of some external factor such as violence, drugs, including anaesthetics, alcohol and hypnotic influences cannot fairly be said to be due to disease.
>
> (p. 922)

This opinion presaged the decisions that epilepsy and sleepwalking are insane automatisms in *Sullivan* and *Burgess* respectively. Similarly, hyperglycaemia due to diabetes, and hypoglycaemia due to an insulinoma, would be insane automatisms.

There are a number of other ways of assessing the need for continuing treatment and monitoring to protect the public. In *Bratty* Lord Denning commented that:

> It seems to me that any mental disorder which has manifested itself in violence and is prone to recur is a disease of the mind. At any rate it is the sort of disease for which a person should be detained in hospital rather than be given an unqualified acquittal.

This was an excellent formulation in this author's opinion (bar the inclusion of "mental" rather than "medical"), but it was disavowed in *Quick* by Lawton LJ for the reasons given above.

There are particular objections to characterizing everyday events as "external causes". Take the example of a defendant sleeping with his usual bed partner, where their proximity triggers unwanted sexual activity. Characterizing this as an external cause is problematic, given the safety issues. Arguably a condition that is triggered so easily should be considered an "internal cause". Other causes that seem unexceptional include sleep deprivation, as per the case of Ecott (Salkeld, 2007). The search for an external cause, no matter how mundane or tenuous, can represent an attempt to divert the jury away from the special verdict.

Hughes LJ states in *Coley*:

> It is well known that the distinction drawn in *Quick* between external factors inducing a condition of the mind and internal factors which can properly be described as a disease can give rise to apparently strange results at the margin.

The cases of *Sullivan* and *Burgess* illustrate the fact that the requirement for specialist treatment for a mental health condition is not the sole determinant of insanity. The conditions discussed in *Sullivan* and *Burgess* were epilepsy and sleepwalking, respectively. However, the strength of these precedents is questionable, particularly in *Burgess*. Sullivan's condition is not entirely clear in the case report, as both petit mal and psychomotor epilepsy are mentioned. The proceedings of a symposium held on the case state that in fact Sullivan suffered complex partial seizures (temporal lobe epilepsy) (Fenwick and Fenwick, 1985). Despite this, the appellant contrasted his epilepsy with that of Bratty, where it was conceded that psychomotor epilepsy was a defect of reason (as opposed to an absence of reason). In the case of *Burgess*, Fenwick, as the expert witness instructed by the prosecution, considered that a dissociative episode was much more likely, and the behaviour described is far more consistent with this diagnosis. Burgess's actions according to his victim were related at trial:

> On the evening in question the appellant came up to her flat with the video tapes. They had one glass of Martini each. There is no suggestion of any intoxication. Having watched one video tape, she fell asleep on the sofa. The next thing she knew was that something hard had hit her on the head. This must have been about one to one and a half hours later, so it seems. She woke up, dazed, to find herself surrounded by broken glass and confronted by the appellant with the video recorder held up high, clearly intending to bring it down on her head, which he did. He was speaking loudly. He seemed vicious and angry – quite out of character. She fell to the floor, whereupon he put a hand round her throat. With great presence of mind, she managed to say "I love you Bar," whereupon he appeared to come to his senses and to show great anxiety for what he had done. He later telephoned for an ambulance. It seems that he must have unplugged the video recorder detaching the various leads and then carried it round to where Miss Curtis lay.

These actions demonstrate goal-directed behaviour, with no difficulty in bringing the defendant out of his state. The defendant describes repressed romantic feelings towards his victim, and feeling that he was "heading for some sort of breakdown". This is suggestive of a psychological cause, rather than parasomnia. In this author's opinion, these facts make it difficult to state definitively that the disposal in *Burgess* rested solely on the diagnosis of sleepwalking.

Strict liability offences

Automatism is a complete defence to all criminal offences, since the requirement for a guilty act is a constant (even for inchoate offences (Husak, 2006)). It has been confirmed that the insanity defence can be argued in the magistrates' courts, where the common law insanity defence still applies (rather than the special verdict) – *R v Horseferry Road Magistrates Court, ex parte K*. This means that the defendant will receive a plain acquittal. There is debate over whether or not the insanity defence is available for strict liability offences, due to conflicting case law (see further in Chapter 5). Reported cases involving driving offences where the presence of medicolegal automatism has been accepted have resulted in conviction (BBC News, 2014). In the Scottish case of *Finegan v. Heywood*, it was accepted that the offence of drink-driving occurred during an episode of sleepwalking. This was the basis for declining to issue a driving ban. However, it is not clear whether the ratio of the case is that blame rests on prior fault or voluntary intoxication.

In this case Finegan had consumed alcohol, which he knew sometimes caused him to sleepwalk. He drove someone else's car in a parasomnic state, and was charged with drink-driving and other offences. The American sleep expert Pressman (2007) has stated that the case was "treated as a case of voluntary intoxication only", and this interpretation is seemingly supported by the comments of the Lord Justice-General (Rodger), who stated:

> Approaching the matter in that way and having reviewed the relevant authorities, the court held at p 46: "In the law of Scotland a person who voluntarily and deliberately consumes known intoxicants, including drink or drugs, of whatever quantity, for their intoxicating effects, whether these effects are fully foreseen or not, cannot rely on the resulting intoxication as the foundation of a special defence of insanity at the time nor, indeed, can he plead diminished responsibility." Although their Lordships were not, of course, thinking of the situation where the voluntary consumption of alcohol for its intoxicating effect induced a transitory state of parasomnia, we consider that the same approach should be applied in such a case.

Another reading of the case is that the basis of rejecting automatism was prior fault – the behaviour was due to a "transitory state of parasomnia which was the result of, and induced by, deliberate and self induced intoxication" (para. 10). The immediate cause was recognized to be parasomnia, even if the trigger was alcohol. It would be superfluous for the court to declare that alcohol intoxication is no defence to drink-driving.

Certainly not all effects of alcohol are excluded from forming the basis of a mental condition defence. In the case of *Harris* (rolled-up appeal with *Coley*), it was held that the fact that indirectly alcohol consumption had triggered his condition did not preclude the use of insanity defence. The alcohol consumption had preceded the development of the direct cause of his incapacity, which was alcohol withdrawal, or delirium tremens (*R. v. Coley* [2013] EWCA Crim 223; (Mackay, 2013)). Similarly, a head injury that has resulted from alcoholic intoxication is not excluded, as per *Stripp*.

Operation of the automatism defence

As noted in Chapter 1, the defendant basing his defence on an episode of medicolegal automatism has three options. The differences between these options in English law are summarized in Table 1.1 (page XX). This demonstrates that the judge has a pivotal role in how the case is argued. It is for the judge and him alone to decide whether or not to direct the jury to consider the insanity verdict.

The prosecution cannot intervene (even though they do have the power to raise the issue when the defence is arguing diminished responsibility). Lack of *actus reus* or *mens rea* are both technically a failure to prove the required elements to make out the offence rather than defences per se. This entails that it is for the prosecution to prove that the defendant had the necessary fault elements, once the evidential burden has been reached in the case of automatism. In the case of lack of the *actus reus* (where the illegal act has been proven), total loss of voluntary control must be proved. Where the crime is not strict liability, it is more likely that lack of *mens rea* will be argued. There is a considerable advantage to the defence if they are not required to argue the insanity defence to the jury, where the burden of proof will be on them to prove that the defendant was impaired to the standard of the *McNaughtan Rules*. Defendants nearly always prefer to avoid the stigmatizing label of insanity.

It also demonstrates the potential for confusion. There is no specimen direction for those admittedly rare cases where both insane and non-insane automatism are possibilities for the jury to consider. The jury direction by HHJ Henriques in the case of *Lowe* was incorrect, stating that insane automatism required that "[Lowe's] ability to exercise voluntary control was totally destroyed". HHJ Lawrence made the same mistake in the case of *Roach*. It is the *McNaughtan Rules* in their entirety that apply in cases of insane automatism, or insanity as this author prefers.

There seems to be judicial resistance to consideration of the insanity defence. This is best illustrated by the case of Brian Thomas, where the judge heard evidence from two forensic sleep experts that the defendant had suffered from a sleep disorder at the time that he strangled his wife. The court heard from a forensic psychiatrist approved under Section 12 of the Mental Health Act 1983. She was not a sleep expert and simply gave evidence about whether or not Mr Thomas had a mental disorder that required hospital treatment. This is probably due to the restriction of Section 24 of the Domestic Violence, Crime and Victims Act, which precludes a hospital order where the condition is not a mental disorder under the Mental Health Act. A Home Office circular concerning Section 24 asserts that "physical disorders" are limited to supervision orders or absolute discharge. Mackay and Mitchell argue:

> Might this apply equally to findings of NGRI in respect of sleepwalking even where the charge is murder? This, however, is premised on accepting that such a condition is to be regarded in law as "a disease of the mind" within the *M'Naghten Rules* which is by no means clear cut.
>
> (Mackay and Mitchell, 2006)

However, the issue as regards the special verdict is purely whether or not the disorder is a disease of the mind. It was decided that there were no public safety issues, at which point the prosecution offered no further evidence. The jury were directed by the trial judge to acquit.

The special verdict has the advantage of enabling the imposition of social control measures, even where a physical disorder means that a hospital order is not allowed. It permits the imposition of a Sexual Harm Prevention Order (or prior to this, a Sexual Offence Prevention Order). An example was in the case of *Fallon* acquitted by reason of insanity, where the judge issued a Sexual Offence Prevention Order:

> banning from him from sleeping at friends' homes or any private home unless he has previously told house-holders he suffers from a sleep disorder and given details of his conviction [sic].
>
> (Allen, 2013)

When there is diversion from the criminal justice system on the basis of expert witness that avoids the special verdict, there is the risk that further victims will be created, as in the case of *Short (Joseph)* (only reported in the press). He was convicted of two sexual assaults, but only after a prosecution in Scotland was dropped on the basis of medical evidence (he was acquitted on another charge heard at Hull Crown Court). The medical expert claimed that Mr Short did not follow his advice on how to avoid a repetition (Mega, 2016a, 2016b). It is not known whether he was convicted on the basis that the jury did not believe the episodes were sexsomnic, or on the basis of prior fault because he continued to put his bed partners at risk. The risk of recurrence appears to be peculiar to sexsomnia among the parasomnias, with repetition of serious harmful behaviour with sleepwalking being almost unheard of (Rumbold, 2015, p. 281), so the special verdict has less justification on safety grounds in other parasomnia cases. The consideration of the special verdict also answers the criticism of the police officer in *Jeal*:

> I would like to see some sort of reverse burden of proof where the defendant has to come up with evidence to prove they have a history of sleepwalking, doctors' reports, and witnesses. Otherwise anyone can simply say "I was asleep". (DC Richard Rock, Hampshire Police).
>
> (Jamieson, 2008)

The jury will have to find that the incapacity caused by sleepwalking was proven on the balance of probabilities.

Reform of the automatism defence

The Law Commission examined the law on insanity and automatism as part of the tenth programme of consultations. A scoping paper was published in July 2012 after it became apparent that the issues required further definition with legal practitioners. A discussion paper was subsequently published in 2013 (Law Commission, 2013). They acknowledge the same difficulties as my interview data demonstrate:

- the law lags behind psychiatric understanding, and this partly explains why, in practice, the defence is underused and medical professionals do not apply the correct legal test;
- the label of "insane" is outdated as a description of those with mental illness, and simply wrong as regards those who have learning disabilities or learning difficulties, or those with epilepsy;
- the case law on insane and non-insane automatism is incoherent and produces results that run counter to common-sense.

The Law Commission proposes a new test for capacity. The accused must be able:

- rationally to form a judgment about the relevant conduct or circumstances;
- to understand the wrongfulness of what he or she is charged with having done; or
- to control his or her physical acts in relation to the relevant conduct or circumstances.

Further, once the evidential burden had been satisfied, the burden of proof would be on the prosecution to prove that the accused had the requisite capacities beyond reasonable doubt. The new special verdict for the defendant acquitted on the basis of the proposed statutory defence would be "not criminally responsible by reason of recognized medical condition". Thus, both psychiatric and medical conditions will be assessed by the same functional test. The defence of automatism would be retained, but for very limited circumstances; the "spasms, convulsions, and reflex acts" mentioned by Mackay (1995), when not caused by a chronic condition, and other rare occurrences like a head injury or a swarm of bees attacking.

There is an argument that more modest reform would be more likely to become law. Simply changing the definition of automatism from "total loss of control" to "effective loss of control", as per the Law Commission's Draft Criminal Code, would eliminate some of the problematic decisions with diabetic drivers. This could be achieved through the common law. Instructions to the judiciary about the greater use of the special verdict in cases of parasomnia would mean that weak medical evidence would be less likely to secure an acquittal. The main difficulty with the special verdict is the term "insanity", which would require statutory change.

There are valid objections to the expansion of the remit of the special verdict. One objection is increased cost – the risk of recurrence of harmful behaviour is extremely low, so supervision and treatment are not cost-effective from a harm prevention perspective. Another objection concerns the potential for state abuse of powers for social control, which echoes the concerns of the Law Commission above. A final objection relates to the impact of the special verdict. Despite being nominally an acquittal, being found not guilty by reason of insanity has the same effect as a conviction as regards the Sex Offenders' Register and it is discoverable on an enhanced criminal records check.

Comparative criminal law

All common law jurisdictions appear to have the automatism defence. Civil law jurisdictions will usually have an equivalent defence, typically called unconsciousness. However, their criminal codes may not explicitly require a voluntary act – this is not the case in Germany, for example. In the case at the Higher Regional Court (OLG) Hamm 5 Ss 331/74, NJW 1965, 657 (July 16, 1974), a driver was charged with negligent infliction of bodily harm under §23o of the Criminal Code. The driver was fending off a fly whilst driving around a bend, and so veered over the carriageway, hitting another vehicle. However, part of the reasoning behind this decision was that this reaction was not automatic or even semi-automatic (Dubber and Hornle, 2014). The same would be true of the reaction to the swarm of bees mentioned in *Kay v. Butterworth* (see also the Australian case of *Ryan*).

The dividing line between insanity and automatism/unconsciousness varies from jurisdiction to jurisdiction. The case of the would-be assassin of Ronald Reagan, Hinckley, led to many States dramatically limiting or "abolishing" the insanity defence (although the process of reform pre-dates his trial) (Mackay, 1988). In one challenge to the abolition of the insanity defence, the US Supreme Court denied certiorari, effectively ruling that it was not unconstitutional (Stimpson, 1994). It should be noted however that all States have some provision for evidence about lack of capacity due to mental health issues to be admitted, even if this is purely on the grounds of denying the relevant *mens rea*. In this author's opinion a bar on the admission of mental health evidence for arguing lack of culpability more broadly than simple lack of *mens rea* ought to be deemed unconstitutional, being contrary to due process. Morse shares that view but considers it unlikely that the US Supreme Court would strike down state insanity abolition measures (Morse, 1985).

Canada has since 1992 had the verdict of not criminally responsible due to mental disorder (NCRMD) under section 672.34 of the Canadian Criminal Code. This gives three options for disposal – an absolute discharge, a conditional discharge, and detention in custody in a hospital. One of the most interesting innovations of the enabling Act was that detention should be capped at the maximum tariff for the offence in question, unless there was proof that the interest of public safety demanded otherwise. This would make the plea a more attractive proposition compared to indefinite hospitalization, although this measure would arguably make little difference in the UK because of the existing flexible powers of disposal. This was the most controversial part of the Act; it was not proclaimed and eventually repealed on the advice of the 14th report of the Standing Committee on Justice and Human Rights, 2002. This was largely due to concerns about the ability of the civil commitment system to protect the public. In *Winko v. British Columbia (Forensic Psychiatric Institute)*, the Canadian Supreme Court found that it was required to be shown that the individual was a significant risk to the public, but a recent Bill which has received its second reading (C-54, "Not Criminally Responsible Reform Act") proposes more emphasis on public safety. The current situation is that those who plead NCRMD are detained longer on average than if they had been sentenced to prison (Crocker et al., 2015).

In South Africa, the common law defence of non-pathological criminal incapacity is available to defendants who argue that extreme emotional stress or provocation of a temporary nature made them unable to control their actions (Joubert and van Staden, 2016). This is similar in effect and scope to "psychological blow automatism", or the old exemption for *crime passionnel* under Section 324 of the 1810 Penal Code in France. In many jurisdictions, such a loss of control may be a partial defence, and then only in cases of homicide.

The main driving force for preferring a plain acquittal over an insanity defence is the presence of a quasi-punitive regime. Given the conditions for those found not guilty by reason of insanity in some US states, prominent US forensic sleep experts have been keen to emphasize that this verdict is not appropriate for parasomniacs (Rumbold, 2015). They emphasize the extreme rarity of recurrence. In jurisdictions like the UK where a hospital order is not permissible for physical disorders, this argument is weaker. However, there are issues of stigma around the label of insanity.

3 Medical aspects of automatism

Medicolegal automatism

Automatism has different meanings in medicine (stereotyped non-purposeful behaviour occurring during psychomotor seizures) and psychology than it does in law. Strictly speaking, in medicine an automatism is a stereotyped repetitive and non-purposeful behaviour occurring during psychomotor seizures. Typically, this is lip smacking, finger rubbing, chewing or swallowing. These behaviours are unlikely to cause any difficulties for the criminal justice system.

Medicolegal automatism is rather different. Fenwick's definition seems the most comprehensive and useful for medicolegal purposes:

> An automatism is an involuntary piece of behaviour over which an individual has no control. The behaviour is usually inappropriate to the circumstances, and may be out of character for the individual. It can be complex, co-ordinated and apparently purposeful and directed, though lacking in judgment. Afterwards the individual may have no recollection or only a partial and confused memory for his actions. In organic automatisms there must be some disturbance of brain function sufficient to give rise to the above features.
>
> (Fenwick, 1987)

The human brain comprises three levels of functionality according to the triune brain model of McLean (Ploog, 2003). There is the reptilian complex or reptile brain – this is responsible for aggression, territoriality and sexuality. These behaviours tend to be quite stereotyped. There is the limbic system – this becomes prominent in mammals and is responsible for drives, emotions, memory and social behaviour. There are also functions of the limbic system related to appetites, such as eating and sex. Finally, there is the neocortex – this becomes prominent in primates, and is responsible for executive functions (planning, logical thought, decision-making). There are problems with this model, but it does usefully illustrate the modular nature of the brain. However, all the systems interact and interconnect.

The main conditions that cause medicolegal automatism are those where the capacity for motor action are relatively preserved, but the executive capacities that regulate these actions are impaired – the actions that make human beings moral agents, and therefore liable for criminal punishment. Sleepwalking is a paradigmatic example of such a disorder. The sleepwalker has impaired awareness of his surroundings, although the ability to navigate his environment is relatively intact. He will not recognize familiar faces, and will react violently to being opposed.

One of the chief features of sleepwalking appears to be that the frontal lobe (neocortex) is not active, but the limbic system is. This is a typical functional impairment that is compatible with medicolegal automatism – the executive centres are impaired, but the central pattern generators or some other source of motor activity are still functioning (Tassinari et al., 2006). Central pattern generators are located in various parts of the brain, and are responsible for various activity such as walking, chewing and more complicated actions involved with flight or fight. The stereotyped behaviours of medical automatism arise from the central pattern generators. The central pattern generators may also be the source of the typical behaviour observed during parasomnias. This would explain the complex motor behaviour triggered by an emotional response but freed from the constraints of the executive centres (and so lack planning and intention). In a nutshell, the capacity for particular motor actions is decoupled from the capacity for moral reasoning, and so it follows that criminal responsibility should not be inferred

The frontal lobe's importance in conforming behaviour to social and moral standards was demonstrated in the famous case of Phineas Gage. This 19th century US railroad worker was tamping down dynamite during blasting work for a railway tunnel, when due to his omission of the sand plug, the dynamite detonated prematurely and drove the tamping iron through his skull. The iron entered his left eye socket and exited through the top of his skull, passing through the frontal lobe. There is a lot of mythology surrounding Gage, and many of the wilder accounts contradict the first-hand witnesses of Gage's behaviour (Kean, 2014). Nonetheless, it is accepted that lesions of the frontal lobe can lead to dramatic personality and behavioural change.

Although there are different patterns of activation and deactivation of parts of the brain during sleepwalking episodes, it is generally considered that sleepwalking is a single clinical entity. If this is the case, then the studies of brain function suggest that sleepwalking has a similar effect to Gage's injuries, albeit temporarily. Hypoglycaemia has also been demonstrated to have a selective effect on brain function (Rosenthal et al., 2001; Warren and Frier, 2005).

According to Bonkalo the characteristics that distinguish those report violent behaviours in sleep are:

- Male sex (47/50)
- Age 27–48
- A strong childhood and/or family history of sleepwalking
- Nocturnal enuresis
- Nightmares
- Agitation on awakening.

(Bonkalo, 1974)

Another more systematic way to look at automatism was suggested by Coles, who classified automatisms into five main categories as per Table 3.1.

Type 1a automatism involves processes like digestion and breathing that could not constitute illegal or criminal acts. Type 1b and Type 2a behaviours could result in harm in particular circumstances. Tics for example could result in injury to persons or damage to property. In some limited circumstances, it might be deemed that the person had a duty to suppress the reflex (where this is possible). For example, a person with Tourette's syndrome is able to suppress tics for a finite period of time. This may result in the courts ruling that the person has not suffered a total loss of voluntary control.

Type 1 and 2 automatisms are generally unlikely to cause any difficulty for the courts, as these actions would be easily recognized as involuntary. Type 1 activity would include tonic-clonic seizures. This author is not aware of any prosecutions related to tonic-clonic seizures, except where seizures have occurred at the wheel and the driver should not have been driving.

Type 3 behaviour is not generally considered legal automatism (but might come under insane automatism due to an hysterical dissociative state ["psychological blow automatism"] or the partial defence of provocation/ loss of control).

Types 4 and 5 are the most likely to involve complex behaviour AND be caused by conditions that would be recognized as automatism or insanity. Type 4a behaviour could come from a sudden awakening from sleep, or "confusional arousal". Type 4b is classical sleepwalking behaviour. Type 5a and 5c behaviours are generally due to psychoses (drug-induced or otherwise), although parasomniacs also respond to confused perceptions of reality. Type 5b is the classic

Table 3.1 Automatic behaviour: Behaviour where the conscious mind does not go with what is being done

(1) Absence of volition without conscious awareness for example, autonomic and central nervous system activity which would include:

- (a) physiological processes
- (b) neurological reflexes

(2) Absence of volition with clear conscious awareness

- (a) neurological reflexes

(3) Volitional behaviour with constricted conscious awareness

- (a) irrational behaviour while highly emotional

(4) Volitional behaviour with diminished conscious awareness

- (a) inadequate responses to partially perceived stimuli
- (b) habits and well learned skills

(5) Volitional behaviour with distorted conscious awareness

- (a) responses to confused perception of reality
- (b) responses to the content of dreams
- (c) responses to hallucinations

Table kind courtesy of E. Michael Coles (Coles, 2000)

automatism due to sleep terror, rapid eye movement sleep behaviour disorder (RBD) or even sleepwalking.

There are some general principles applied in the assessment of episodes believed to be automatistic. The perpetrator should have no motive. For example, there should be no history of personal animosity. There should be no evidence of planning or of a cover-up. These are not always straightforward factors to assess. Most importantly, it is for the jury to determine these issues (which are the facts of the case), and not the expert witnesses (see Appendix D).

Conditions that cause medicolegal automatism may be labelled as insanity, which is a legal term of art. The law is quite clear that the term insanity is not confined to psychiatric conditions. If the condition is a disease of the mind, then the judge may direct the jury to consider the special verdict. The conditions that cause medicolegal automatism will usually be assessed and treated by doctors outside the subspecialty of forensic psychiatry. They will have less experience of the criminal courts' requirements, particularly in the assessment of criminal capacity. Where the issue of insanity arises, even where the condition is a physical one, the opinion of a psychiatrist approved under section 12 of the Mental Health Act 1983 is required. This situation arose in the trial of Brian Thomas, where a forensic psychiatrist gave an opinion in addition to the two forensic sleep experts (de Bruxelles, 2009).

Medicolegal assessment

The defendant who has a possible automatism defence might not necessarily volunteer the correct information. One example is a forensic psychiatrist asked to examine an accused, who revealed a hitherto unsuspected history of sleepwalking. In any case where there is a claim of reduced consciousness or amnesia, this possibility needs to be entertained. The lawyer who suspects that his client may have the basis for a defence of automatism needs to consider the following factors:

- Was there a loss of consciousness? If there was a sudden loss of consciousness, was there any warning?
- Was there any amnesia for the events concerned?
  - This may be complete or partial amnesia.
- Is the act denied?
  - There may be disbelief that the accused has committed the act due to amnesia for the events. Emphatic denial is not consistent with automatism. When there is complete amnesia, there may be an attempt to fill in details called confabulation. This is not a deliberate attempt to deceive, but rather an attempt to be helpful.
- Were there any attempts to conceal the crime?
- Were there any abnormal movements?
- Was there any behaviour that was odd or confused?

- Was there any evidence that consciousness was impaired?
- Was the behaviour out of character?
- Did the behaviour occur during sleep, arise out of sleep, or just after awakening, or occur during the hours when the person would normally be asleep?
    - This might seem a self-evident requirement for a defence based on sleepwalking, but one expert witness reported being asked about possible sleepwalking when the solicitor's client had attacked someone in the middle of the day whilst awake.

(Rumbold, 2015)

If none of these questions can be answered in the affirmative, it is extremely unlikely that the behaviour would be explained by medicolegal automatism. There would appear to be no impairment of cognitive function that excuse the accused's behaviour.

- The final and most important question is: was the behaviour goal-orientated?
    - The evidence for this would be seeking out the victim, or any evidence of planning. Was there any speech accompanying the acts (not including mumblings)? The presence of these features is strongly against automatism, because they include that the executive centre of the brain is still functioning. Finally, a question that must be considered in all cases – could the defendant be malingering?

The answers to these questions may guide the selection of a suitable expert witness. Sudden loss of consciousness may suggest a cardiovascular cause for the episode. An abnormal heart rhythm would cause a collapse at the wheel, for example. Abnormal movements or odd behaviour may suggest a neurological cause. Epileptic seizures do not always involve jerking movements of the limbs.

The legal test for insanity, the *McNaughtan Rules*, is well described, but there is no definitive guidance on what capacities must be lost in order to qualify for the defence of automatism.

Pre-existing medical conditions are important. Where there have been any examples of similar episodes occurring previously, corroboration of this is important. The expert witness cannot simply take the accused's word for the occurrence of any episodes, as this may amount to "oath-helping", or compurgation. Any drugs taken, prescribed or otherwise, will be important. Any eye-witness accounts are crucial. If the lawyer believes that there is a viable basis for medicolegal automatism, a suitable medical expert is generally essential. Investigation of the defendant's condition may have already occurred, in which the appropriate specialty may be obvious and the expert witness's role will be to testify about the possible effect of a particular condition on criminal responsibility.

There is a major drawback to the special verdict in England and Wales. The defendant is found "not guilty by reason of insanity". The label of insanity has a marked stigma associated with it and indubitably makes a major impact on the willingness of defendants to plead insanity, despite the change in the options available for disposal. This label also affects the attitudes of expert witnesses, especially non-psychiatrists, towards the special verdict. The issue of insanity is for the jury to decide, if it is put to them. This depends on either the defendant pleading insanity, or the judge deciding that the special verdict should be considered by the jury.

Where the behaviour would satisfy the *McNaughtan Rules* but not provide a defence of lack of *mens rea* or lack of *actus reus*, there may be an advantage in pleading insanity. Otherwise, the burden and standard of proof all favour not pleading insanity.

The prosecution has no say in whether or not the insanity defence is considered by the jury (unless the defendant is arguing diminished responsibility). The special verdict will allow the imposition of control measures, particularly where there is a risk of recurrence of harmful behaviour. This would apply in cases of sexsomnia in particular.

Risk assessment

The courts may consider the question of risk – when the judge is considering how to direct the jury or deciding on disposal. The medical and legal literature on forensic sleep disorders is relatively sparse, partly due to the apparent rarity of serious harm to others during parasomnias. Cartwright estimated in 2000 that there were 68 cases where sleepwalking was invoked as a defence to murder reported in the forensic literature (Cartwright, 2000), whilst Ebrahim counted approximately 100 in 2009 (Ebrahim and Shapiro, 2010). The occurrence of potentially harmful behaviour during sleep on the other hand is relatively common. The risk of recurrence of serious harmful behaviour due to sleepwalking is extremely low, and there have been very few cases recorded. It is not known exactly why this is the case. There has only been one instance of a second trial (and third and fourth) of an individual for serious crimes where sleepwalking was argued in defence (the case of *Joseph Short* reported in Mega, 2016c), so it is not certain what legal approach would be taken (in one instance where a sleepwalker committed a second violent act, he pleaded guilty (Rumbold, 2015)).

One explanation is that, as Schenck puts it, the more extreme acts that lead to involvement of the criminal justice system arise from a "perfect storm" of circumstances which would be very unlikely to recur. However, Schenck and Mahowald do not consider that this is always the case, and recommend the medicolegal concept of "parasomnia with continuing danger as a non-insane automatism" (Schenck and Mahowald, 1995). This is a reflection of the politico-legal milieu of the USA where indefinite hospitalization is the common disposal under the insanity defence. Another explanation for the lack of recurrence is that sufferers receive and adhere to an effective treatment regime. Treatment is generally very effective at reducing sleepwalking and other parasomnias. Clonazepam is the first line drug but other treatments have been used including non-pharmacological modalities – hypnotherapy and cognitive behavioural therapy work by enabling sufferers to cope with stress better (a common trigger). Violence may be recurrent with the other parasomnias, and violence towards the bed partner is a particular issue with RBD.

The exact prevalence of violence during sleepwalking is difficult to ascertain because violence probably makes it far more likely for sleepwalkers to seek referral. Another difficulty is that the studies of violence do not necessarily distinguish between self-injury, injury to others and damage to property. Ohayon et al. in a study of the UK population by telephone interviews found that 2.1 per cent of adults reported currently experiencing violent or injurious behaviour during sleep. This survey used a validated computerized diagnostic tool, but nonetheless this is probably an overestimate of violence related to parasomnia given the estimated prevalence. However, of the 106 subjects reporting violent behaviour in sleep (VBS), only 15 (0.3 per cent of the population) had actually hurt themselves or their bed partner. The incidence of VBS in males was 2.6 per cent and in females 1.7 per cent. These figures are likely to include confusional arousals and violence not truly related to sleep, as there was no assessment by a sleep specialist (Ohayon et al., 1997).

Moldofsky et al. found that 59 per cent of consecutive patients with sleep terrors and sleepwalking reported harmful behaviours (but only nine of the 26 were harmful to other people [14 per cent of the total] (Moldofsky et al., 1995). Guilleminault (1995) found in a retrospective review that 70 per cent of patients were "violent" (but only 41 per cent of their patients were violent to others, rather than only injuring themselves) (Guilleminault, Moscovitch and Leger, 1995). A case-control study found that among 95 confirmed sleepwalkers there was a history of violent and dangerous sleep-related behaviour in 57.9 per cent (n=55). In 31.2 per cent (n=30) of the sample the harm was directed to self, and in 45.8 per cent (n=44) it was directed at the bed partner. It also found that violent behaviour causing moderate to severe injury to the patient had occurred in 10.6 per cent (n=ten, eight males). Violent behaviour towards the bed partner requiring medical care had occurred in 6.4 per cent (n=five, four males) (Lopez et al., 2013). The most consistent risk factor for violence is sex, being 1.6–2.8 times more common in males with arousal disorders (Siclari et al., 2010).

4 Specific causes of automatism

Many different medical conditions and external causes can cause the syndrome of medicolegal automatism. Whether or not these conditions will be deemed automatism or insanity depends on a number of factors, as the discussion in Chapter 2 indicates. It would be impossible to discuss all the conditions that might theoretically cause automatism, but the conditions that are likely to be used for a possible automatism defence are described.

They are divided into seven categories:

- Sleep disorders
- Hypoglycaemia
- Neurological
- Cardiovascular
- Psychiatric
- Malingering/amnesia
- Miscellaneous.

The following, non-exhaustive, lists detail conditions that have been argued as constituting automatism.

The following medical causes of non-insane automatism have been successfully argued in court or mentioned in obiter:

- Sleepwalking and other parasomnias (confusional arousals, night terrors, sexsomnia and rapid eye moment sleep behaviour disorder): *Thomas*, *Parks* plus several others
- Hypoglycaemia due to insulin and/or oral hypoglycaemics: *Quick*
- Pneumonia: *Beaumont*
- Head injury (obiter by Humphreys J in *Kay v. Butterworth*)
- Swarm of bees (obiter by Humphreys J in *Kay v. Butterworth*)
- Unpredicted reaction to benzodiazepines: *Hardie*
- Combination of zolpidem and alcohol: *Buck*[1]

1 Peter Buck was cleared of assault and other charges after an "air rage" incident he claimed was due to the combination of zolpidem and alcohol (Vasagar, 2002).

- PTSD/acute adjustment reaction: *R v. T*
- Sneezing: *Woolley*
- Involuntary intoxication with LSD and temazepam: *Ross*
- Cerebral tumour: *Charlson* (but bad law now).

In the following cases, it was judged that the automatism was insane.

- Sleepwalking: *Burgess*
- Epilepsy (temporal lobe, frontal lobe and postictally): *Bratty*, *Sullivan*
- Hyperglycaemia due to diabetes: *Hennessy*
- Dissociative episode due to emotional stress: *Rabey*
- Combination of antidepressants and sleeping tablets in doses higher than those prescribed: *Ball*
- Arteriosclerosis: *Kemp*
- Multiple sclerosis: *Pull*
- Presumed cardiac arrhythmia (*MacBrayne* cited in Lazzarri, 2011).

In the following cases, automatism was argued but not successfully:

- Citalopram medication: *Smallshire*
- Dysexecutive syndrome as a sequela of head injury: *Wood*
- Sleepwalking known to be induced by consumption of alcohol: *Finegan v. Heywood* (also *Pooley* cited in *Bucks Herald*, 2007)
- Hypoglycaemia of sudden onset when the tendency to this was known: *Marison*
- Epileptic seizure where the likelihood of this was known: *Sims*
- Unknown cause: *Costantini*
- PTSD: *Narbrough*
- Involuntary intoxication with sedatives or amphetamines: *Kingston*, *Mulrainey*
- Prescription of triazolam: *Carrington*
- Driving without awareness: Attorney-General's Reference (No. 2 of 1992)
- Mistakenly pressing the accelerator instead of the brake: *Attorney-General's Reference (No. 4 of 2000)*
- Hypoglycaemic episode of gradual onset whilst driving: *Broome v. Perkins*, *Watmore v. Jenkins*.

Sleep disorders

The two main types of sleep disorders likely to cause medicolegal automatism are parasomnias and sleep apnoea/hypopnoea syndromes. They cause lack of capacity in completely different ways. Parasomnias are states related to sleep. During parasomnic episodes, the person is a state somewhere between sleep and wakefulness (with the exception of rapid eye movement sleep behaviour disorder) as per Figure 4.1.

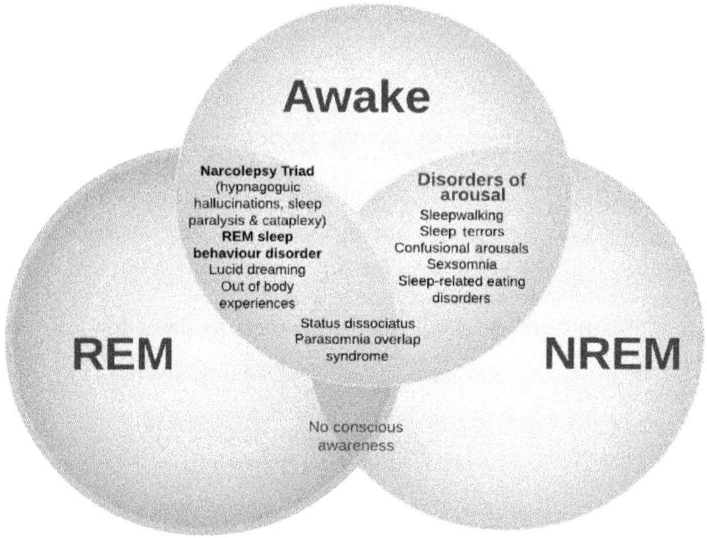

Figure 4.1 Venn diagram of intersections between wakefulness, non-REM sleep and REM sleep

(after Mahowald, Bornemann and Schenck, 2009)

Sleep apnoea/hypopnoea syndromes disturb sleep due to cessation or reduction of breathing during sleep (hypopnoea is reduction in breathing, apnoea is absence of breathing). This results in excessive sleepiness during the day, with the tendency to fall asleep suddenly. The situation where this is most likely to be relevant to the criminal law is at the wheel of a motor vehicle. Sleep apnoea can also predispose to parasomnias, by producing sudden arousals from deep sleep.

The parasomnias that are most likely to be relevant to the criminal law are:

- Sleepwalking/sexsomnia (also known as somnambulism)
- Sleep terrors (also known as night terrors)
- Confusional arousals
- Rapid eye movement sleep behaviour disorder (RBD)
- Sleep-related dissociative behaviour.

Disorders of arousal include sleepwalking, sexsomnia, sleep terrors and confusional arousals. They occur during NREM sleep. They usually occur during the first third of the night, when the greatest amount of NREM sleep occurs. Most NREM parasomnia occur in individuals under 40 years of age, as the quantity of deep sleep decreases with age.

Sleepwalking, sexsomnia and sleep terrors occur out of phase three of non-rapid eye movement sleep. This means that they will typically occur within the first third of the night and not within the first 20 minutes of sleep. All the parasomnias are known to be familial to a greater or lesser degree, with the exception of RBD (although several of the conditions causing RBD can be inherited). Pedigrees of severe parasomniacs often show a high proportion of different parasomnias among relatives – the greater the number of close relatives with parasomnia, the worse the parasomnia is likely to be. The pattern of sleep disorders amongst family members of some of the most dramatic sleepwalkers have been reviewed in the literature (Cartwright, 2000). A relevant history for sleepwalking must include other sleep disorders: night terrors, nocturnal enuresis (bed-wetting), night terrors, sleep talking and bruxism (grinding the teeth and clenching the jaw). The parasomnia with the strongest genetic component is sleep terrors. Up to 90 per cent of sufferers have a family history of sleep terrors or sleepwalking.

Sleepwalking is the commonest parasomnic condition, estimated at between 1 and 4 per cent of the adult population. The prevalence in childhood is up to 10 to 30 per cent. Ohayon et al.'s study (1997) of the UK adult population found a prevalence of 2.0 per cent. It follows that most childhood sleepwalkers do not become adult sleepwalkers. Conversely, it is uncommon for someone to be an adult sleepwalker if they were not a sleepwalker as a child or adolescent, although one study puts the figure as high as 16.9 per cent (Lopez et al., 2013). Brain injury (traumatic and non-traumatic) can cause adult onset sleepwalking. Drugs may also induce sleepwalking: propranolol, lithium, valproic acid, paroxetine, amitriptyline, venlafaxine, bupropion, zolpidem and zopiclone (Lopez et al., 2013), sodium gamma oxybutyrate, and quetiapine and other atypical antipsychotics (Dagan and Katz, no date). However, in most cases these are simply reports of possible adverse effects, with no confirmation of their parasomnic nature. Given that many of these reactions have been in people with a psychiatric disorder, alternative explanations such as sleep-related dissociative episodes are possible or even probable. In the case of propranolol, nightmares are a known side-effect and might be confused for RBD. Several of the reports cite sleep eating, which is not always parasomnic and is correlated with psychological and psychiatric disorders to a much greater extent than parasomnias (Vetrugno et al., 2006; Howell, Schenck and Crow, 2009).

The exact nature of sleepwalking is still poorly understood, although it has long been conceptualized as a disorder where the brain is somewhere between full wakefulness and sleep. Sleep studies show that sleepwalking arises from deep sleep. The subsequent EEG findings are variable. The exact pathophysiology of sleepwalking is uncertain, but functional neuroimaging in one patient showed that activity in the frontal lobe was suppressed, and activity in the limbic system increased (Bassetti et al., 2000). Intracerebral EEG recordings, again in a single patient, showed that during confusional arousals there was activation of the motor and cingulate areas, whilst delta wave activity characteristic of slow wave sleep persisted in the prefrontal cortex (Terzaghi et al., 2009). Certainly, the violent and sexual behaviour exhibited is consistent with the limbic system. The violent behaviour is usually only a reaction to opposition – so the advice is that rather than confront a sleepwalker, one should gently guide them back to bed. The defensive rage exhibited has been studied in animal models, and contrasts with the other main form of aggression, predatory attack. Defensive rage is reactive, affective and impulsive. Predatory attack is pre-meditated and goal-orientated. It is not generally accepted that sleepwalking-related violence is caused by a switch from sleepwalking to sleep terror as Levy and Cartwright suggest (Levy cites Cartwright's account of violence at the end of a sleepwalking episode associated with sudden interruption – this description is more suggestive of confusional arousal, which is well recognized to arise out of sleepwalking (Cartwright, 2004; Levy and Bayne, 2004)). Involvement of the fusiform gyrus is suggested by the problem with recognition of faces seen in sleepwalking, most vividly demonstrated by Kenneth Parks where he described attacking a woman without being aware that it was his mother-in-law (see further in Case histories). Ekirch and Shneerson (2011) also report this phenomenon.

Some experts believe that the longer episodes represent a merging of sleepwalking into a secondary dissociative episode. Sleepwalking could be considered a variety of dissociative disorder, albeit not psychogenic in nature. Podolsky states:

> Somnambulistic activity is closely related to a form of behaviour known as a fugue. In a true fugue the individual suddenly leaves his previous activity and does something which has no apparent relation to what he has just been doing, and for which he has complete amnesia. In somnambulism there is an identical dissociation except that it begins during sleep.
>
> (Podolsky, 1961)

A single case of a patient with a very complex dissociative disorder undergoing positron emission tomography (PET) scanning showed bilateral, temporal frontal lobes and right caudate lighting up in association with the manifest behaviour (Magnin et al., 2014). A single patient with fugue state displayed waking EEG rhythm at the point in time when the patient stated that they had been asleep and experienced their fugue behaviour (Mortati, 2012).

By contrast, the single arousal disorder documented with intracerebral EEG monitoring showed a pattern of wakefulness in the motor and cingulate gyrus arising out of Stage 2 Non-REM sleep (N2) with simultaneous intermittent bursts of delta sleep (slow wave sleep (SWS)) in the fronto-parietal lobes (Terzaghi et al., 2009). This is considered to explain the lack of awareness and insight typically observed during simple arousal disorders. The single patient SPECT study demonstrated active limbic activity and suppressed frontal activity (Bassetti et al., 2000), fitting with the picture on fMRI seen by van der Kruijs et al. of increased connectivity between the insula and motor systems, but reduced connectivity between the executive centres and the motor system (van der Kruijs et al., 2012). These studies of brain function have only looked at single patients, so it is impossible to draw any firm conclusions about the general population of sleepwalkers from them. It cannot be assumed that sleepwalking has only one phenotype, and there is some evidence to the contrary – some patients exhibit much more complex behaviours than the majority.

There have been widespread media reports in the USA of acts committed under the influence of Ambien (zolpidem, also marketed as Stilnoct). The so-called "Ambien defence" has received great scrutiny, especially given the prominent warnings in the patient information leaflets (c.f. *Hardie*). "Z-drugs" (zolpidem, zopiclone) induce amnesia and confused and/or disinhibited behaviour, and these impairments will not automatically excuse the accused from any illegal acts (see *Kingston*). Vincent and others have questioned whether the "Stilnox defence" (Stilnox is a brand of zolpidem) is really automatism or simply amnesia (Vincent, 2013). Such episodes must be carefully distinguished from genuine parasomnia. The "Ambien defence" is probably the inspiration for the movie "Side Effects". Alcohol and other agents acting on gamma-aminobutyric acid (GABA) receptors (including benzodiazepines and Z-drugs) affect memory more than motor skills, and therefore seem a more plausible explanation than parasomnia for some of the more complex behaviours (see below). Those with behaviour triggered by Z-drugs will usually lack a family history of parasomnias.

Sleepwalking involves the person walking and performing simple acts in a state of reduced consciousness and decreased awareness of surroundings. The range of activities reported during sleepwalking is extensive, ranging from simple wandering to driving a car. There are even reports of emailing, although this may have been a drug-induced episode rather than true sleepwalking. Episodes typically last less than ten minutes. The eyes will be open. The person will be able to navigate around obstacles. Amnesia for events during the episode will often be complete, but fragmentary recollections are common. The person will be difficult to rouse from the sleepwalking episode. They may become violent if they are opposed or obstructed.

The typical sleepwalker just sits up, or walks around looking for something and goes back to bed without incident. More complex behaviour has been described, including driving, cooking and eating food, texting and emailing. However, the texts and emails do not have the same content as texts and emails sent by an awake person. For example, one patient sent an email saying:

> "I don't get it. please esplain LUCY!!
>
> cOME TOMORROW AND SORT THIS HELLHOLE Out!!!!!
>
> Dinner & drinks, 4;00pm shars house. Wine and caviar to bring only. everything else a guess?
>
> MANANA XXOO D"

The evidence that these more complex episodes are sleepwalking is not robust, and at least some of them are more likely to be sleep-related dissociation.

There is some debate about sleep-related driving and sleep-related eating; sleep driving in particular is associated with Z-drugs rather than sleepwalking, although Mahowald and Schenck's long distance driver was not taking any medication (Schenck and Mahowald, 1995). Sleep-related eating disorder (SRED)

Table 4.1 Triggering factors

Trigger	*% reported*
Stressful events	52.04% (n=51)
Strong positive emotions	41.84% (n=41)
Sleep deprivation	26.53% (n=26)
Alcohol	12.24% (n=12)
Intense physical activity	5.10% (n=5)

(Lopez et al., 2013)

and nocturnal eating syndrome (NES) are seen as distinct entities; SRED is considered parasomnic and NES is not (Vetrugno et al., 2006).

The triggering factors recorded by sleepwalking patients in one case-control study are listed below in Table 4.1

Sexsomnia is considered either as a distinct parasomnia, a variant of sleepwalking, or behaviour caused either by sleepwalking or confusional arousal. Other terms that are used include "sexual behaviour during sleep", "abnormal sexual behaviour in/during sleep", "atypical sexual behaviour during sleep" (ASBS, Guilleminault et al., 2002), "somnambulistic sexual behaviour", "sleep-related abnormal sexual behaviour" or "sleep sex". These may be used as synonyms for sexsomnia or simply a description of the behaviour regardless of cause (see below). In this author's opinion, sexsomnia is a variant of sleepwalking. The term "sexsomnia" was coined by Shapiro in 2003 (Shapiro, Trajanovic and Fedoroff, 2003), although sexual behaviour during sleep was first described in 1955 by Langelüddeke (Langelüddeke, 1955). Some specialists consider it to be a separate disorder.

The complexity of behaviour is dramatically greater than the typical sleepwalking behaviour. Sexsomnia is usually triggered by the presence of a bed partner, hence the recommendation that sleep studies be conducted in the presence of the bed partner (Shapiro, Trajanovic and Fedoroff, 2003). This is not the usual practice in UK sleep centres. The exact proportion of sleepwalkers with sexsomnia is not known, but it is estimated at approximately 10 per cent (personal communication).

Sleep sex has a number of causes:

- Non-REM parasomnia, sleepwalking and confusional arousal
- Sleep disordered breathing
- RBD
- Sleep epilepsy
- Sleep-related dissociative disorders
- Medication
- Malingering.

(Buchanan, 2011)

Clinical estimates are often low, because patients are reticent about volunteering such symptoms and physicians may not ask directly about them. Guilleminault et al. found that 4 per cent of sleepwalkers exhibit ASBS (Guilleminault et al., 2002), but a more recent study found 8 per cent of those referred with sleep disorders reported ASBS (how many of these were sleepwalkers is not known) (Chung et al., 2010). Unpublished data suggest one in ten sleepwalkers exhibit ASBS.[2] A Norwegian telephone survey found that 2.7 per cent of the adult general population reported sexual acts during sleep at least once in the last three months (Bjorvatn, Grønli and Pallesen, 2010). There is a figure of 1 per cent of the US population cited in the literature (Xu, 2009), but its origin seems to be an estimate given in an interview with "David Saul Rosenberg" (probably a misnomer of David Saul Rosenfeld) (Pasick, no date). Nielsen's study found that 16.8 per cent of undergraduates reported they often had dreams associated with sexual arousal; only 21.7 per cent said that they never had such dreams (Nielsen, Svob and Kuiken, 2009). His work suggests that state dissociation is much more common than previously appreciated. This may have important implications for the defendant accused of sexual offences committed during sleep – however the participants were asked about sexual arousal, rather than any interaction with bed partners. Further research is required to see what forms of behaviour are associated with these dreams and whether they cause interpersonal difficulties and the potential for criminal charges. It has been suggested that the typical sexsomniac will desist when the partner refuses their advances, but not in the forensic cases.

Sleep sex can be categorized according to the related harm:

1 Annoying to bed partner but not harmful. For example, sexual moaning and sexually related sounds.
2 Annoying to bed partner and at times harmful to index case. Examples of this category include violent masturbation with bruising and soreness of the genital area.
3 Harmful to bed partner or others, where sex was forcibly imposed on the bed partners.

(Guilleminault et al., 2002)

This classification may not be particularly sensitive to sexual behaviour during sleep with potential medicolegal consequences. Here the important issue is whether or not the sexsomniac desists when his (or her) bed partner does not assent to sexual activity.

There is no consensus on several features of sleepwalking episodes: the degree of complexity, the maximum duration, the ability of the sleepwalker to navigate their surroundings, or whether or not there can be "islands of lucidity" where the defendant is more conscious for a while before lapsing into a

2 Personal communication from Renata Riha and Ian Morrison.

less responsive state (Rumbold, 2015). The diagnosis of sleepwalking and sexsomnia remains clinical. The sleep study is unlikely to demonstrate parasomnic episodes, although there are techniques that will increase the likelihood of this (sleep deprivation to increase the proportion of deep sleep and acoustic stimuli to trigger arousals, although their use in expert testimony has been challenged) (Mahowald, Bornemann and Schenck, 2007; Pilon, Montplaisir and Zadra, 2008). Sleepwalkers often have abnormal sleep studies, but the specificity of the findings is questioned. Stephen Reitz was found to have a violent sleep terror during his sleep study, but nonetheless he was convicted (see Case Histories). Mahowald states:

> [You] can prove someone is a sleepwalker . . . But that is only Part 1 of a two-part question. The second question is whether he was sleepwalking on the night of the murder. Only God can answer that.
>
> (Stryker, 1999)

For these reasons, some forensic sleep experts consider that the PSG is unnecessary for expert testimony. One forensic sleep expert has stated "sleep studies are of absolutely no value whatsoever after the fact – period" adding:

> sleep studies end up as in the Falater case just being a smokescreen. It just confuses everybody. And you get people arguing over things that are totally irrelevant, and the jury, how can they be expected to sort through all of this testimony about sleep studies, when in fact the sleep studies should not be allowed in the courtroom because they're irrelevant.
>
> (Rumbold, 2015)

Many sleep experts disagree with this position, arguing that sleep studies may provide valuable corroboration of a sleep disorder. There is much debate over the significance of certain non-specific findings however. Where sleep disordered breathing triggers parasomnias, effective management will generally greatly reduce or eliminate parasomnic episodes. Whether sleep-disordered breathing leading to parasomnia is an insane cause of automatism or not is an open question. By contrast, video-PSG is essential to diagnose RBD (because of the other possibilities for dream-enacting behaviour), which is commonly associated with violence against the bed partner. However, they rarely get out of bed, so their harmful acts are less likely to reach the attention of the criminal justice system except when serious harm results. Some experts insist on "blinded" assessment of forensic sleep studies, but most do not. There have been no studies to assess the impact of "blinding" on the reporting of sleep studies.

There is no agreement in the literature on diagnostic features of sleepwalking on the video-PSG, apart from an actual sleepwalking episode. This is unlikely to occur during testing and as such may indicate malingering – apparent "sleepwalking" episodes are not always definitive proof because movement artefacts affect the EEG signal. If there is clear EEG evidence of the behaviour arising during sleep or from a state arising from deep sleep (N3), malingering can be excluded. There are a number of features on polysomnography which are suggestive of sleepwalking:

- a higher proportion of SWS, especially when very fragmented
- increased arousal index (arousals per hour)
- increased relative power of low delta activity
- hypersynchronous delta activity
- increased cyclic alternation pattern.

(Banerjee and Nisbet, no date)

Some forensic sleep experts believe that spectral analysis of EEGs is a reliable method for diagnosing sleepwalking. The method involves computerized analysis of EEG frequencies during slow wave sleep, as opposed to visual scoring of epochs. This shows greater numbers of micro-arousals, wake after sleep onset, and a decrease in slow wave activity during the first sleep cycle, in sleepwalkers. It is not universally agreed that it is suitable for forensic diagnosis, even when blinded assessment is used. Cartwright and Guilleminault report the use of spectral analysis in expert testimony, and they demonstrated that the specific markers persist after the index event (Cartwright and Guilleminault, 2013).

The thorniest issue in relation to forensic parasomnias is the contribution of alcohol. Many forensic sleep experts believe that a proportion of sleepwalkers will have episodes triggered by alcohol (with some sleepwalkers finding fewer episodes with alcohol consumption, and others with no change either way). This association is not accepted by all forensic sleep experts, most notably Pressman, Mahowald, Schenck and Cramer Bornemann (although one of the older publications of Mahowald and Schenck designates alcohol-induced parasomnia as an example of a "parasomnia with state-dependent continuing danger as a non-insane automatism"; the presence of continuing danger *might* suggest the more appropriate disposal would be the insanity defence (Schenck and Mahowald, 1998)). There are clear issues in distinguishing the effects of alcohol intoxication from sleepwalking/sexsomnia. However, this is not a reason in law to disallow the possibility of a defence based on parasomnia where alcohol has been consumed.

Sleep terrors (also called night terrors) are characterized by the sufferer sitting up in bed, and emitting a blood-curdling scream. Episodes can also occur during daytime naps, so "sleep terrors" is the preferred term to "night terrors". They occur most commonly between the ages of five and seven, affecting up to 6 per cent of children. They affect less than 1 per cent of adults, and then are much more likely to be associated with psychopathology. A sleep terror can then result in a confusional arousal. Sleep terrors can result in directed and purposeful violence relating to the content of the night terror. The cases of *Fraser* and *Thomas* were probably sleep terror-related.

Confusional arousals occur during or just after awakening from NREM sleep. It can occur in anyone, and can result in a violent reaction to forcible rousing of the subject. This phenomenon is recognized by soldiers:

> A common belief among young soldiers living in the barracks, propagated by the "barracks lawyer", is that a soldier could not be court martialled for striking someone attempting to wake him if the conduct occurs during the first few seconds of waking. While simplistic, this belief contains a kernel of truth.
>
> (Davidson and Walters, 1993)

Confusional arousals typically last 30 seconds to a minute, although some last up to five minutes. They are more likely to occur from deep sleep and are much more common in children. This is the main parasomnia that is recognized as a non-insane automatism, as there needs to be no predisposition and it always requires an external trigger. Sleep-disordered breathing may result in frequent confusional arousals, and can also trigger sleepwalking. The circumstances of the death of Reeva Steenkamp's death at the hands of Oscar Pistorius raised the possibility of a confusional arousal[3] (Burke, 2016). This was raised with the defence team, who responded that they would not be running this defence as Pistorius did not claim to have been confused when he shot the person he believed to be an intruder. The possibility of a confusional arousal would arguably render having a firearm under one's pillow inadvisable, as illustrated by the case of *Ricksgers.* Cartwright believes that the shooting by Ricksgers was due to a confusional arousal induced by obstructive sleep apnoea. He shot his wife with a revolver he kept under his pillow (see Case Histories for further details (Nofzinger and Wettstein, 1995)).

Rapid eye movement sleep behaviour disorder (RBD) was first described as a distinct clinical entity in 1986 (Schenck et al., 1986). It consists of REM sleep without atonia (RSWA) with abnormal dreams which are then acted out. This discovery had been predicted by a condition induced in cats by surgical lesions of the brainstem near to the locus coeruleus. It usually occurs in males over 50 years of age, and often precedes the diagnosis of a neurodegenerative disorder (e.g. Parkinson's disease, dementia with Lewy bodies or multiple system atrophy) by several years. It can be induced by drugs such as propranolol, tricyclic antidepressants, selective serotonin re-uptake inhibitors, venlafaxine and caffeine. RBD can also be induced by stress, and there are reports of an association with post-traumatic stress disorder (Husain, Miller and Carwile, 2001). The discontinuation of REM suppressant agents such as alcohol, amphetamines, cocaine and imipramine can induce RBD, possibly via a rebound increase in REM sleep. Narcolepsy is often associated with RBD, where the prerequisite RWSA is present in 50 per cent according to one study (Dauvilliers et al., 2007). It is also common in narcolepsy to go straight into REM sleep, which can also happen after extreme REM deprivation. One estimate of the incidence of RBD from Ohayon's study of sleep violence is 0.5 per cent (Ohayon, Caulet and Priest, 1997). Despite the high frequency of harmful behaviour, the average diagnostic delay in one study was 8.7 years (White et al., 2012).

3 Personal communication from Dr Nisbet.

Episodes of RBD involve complex and varied motor behaviour, often related to dream enactment. This is enabled by one feature of RBD, REM sleep without atonia ("Atonia" means loss of muscle power). This atonia normally makes dream enactment impossible. Dream enactment behaviour alone is enough to diagnose "probable RBD", but video-PSG is required to make a definite diagnosis. Dream enactment occurs in normal individuals (Nielsen, Svob and Kuiken, 2009), and dream-like mentation can also occur with sleepwalking and sleep terrors – see Savarin's account in Appendix E, plus the case of Brian Thomas. Obstructive sleep apnoea hypopnoea syndrome (OSAHS) can resemble RBD – this may be because arousals from REM can result in acting out a dream during a confusional arousal. Another feature of RBD is that the dream content is altered, with much more confrontation, aggression and violence (Schenck, Hurwitz and Mahowald, 1993). The victim typically dreams he is the victim of aggression. This has been disputed; however, the patients studied were on a treatment (clonazepam) which may alter dream content (D'Agostini et al., no date). Schenck describes the typical sufferers of RBD as particularly "calm and pleasant" individuals (Schenck, 2005), but a recent study showed no particular personality types were associated with idiopathic RBD (Sasai, Inoue and Matsuura, 2012). It may be that the spouses or bed partners of people with long-standing RBD only stay with them if these violent sleep behaviours are out of character and their waking characteristics make up for the night-time problems. Alternatively, it has been suggested this apparent calmness is in fact the apathy of the neurodegenerative disorders associated with RBD . Usually the eyes are closed during an episode, and the patient rarely stands up or walks around – therefore the victim of any violence is almost always the bed partner. They are also much more easily awoken, which reduces the harm they inflict.

Schenck analysed Savarin's account of a somnambulist monk after Schulz and Curtin categorized it as an example of RBD, and details the features that point to sleepwalking:

1 The monk was a known sleepwalker, who opened doors and had his eyes open
2 The monk was acting purposively based on his dream and knew where to go
3 The episode happened shortly after falling asleep, far more typical for a NREM parasomnia.

(cited in Schenck, 2005)

This demonstrates that even an expert can be misled by the history (see further at Appendix E). Similarly, Brian Thomas's episode suggested RBD as a possibility. In fact video-PSG and his medical history suggest he suffered a sleep terror (or alternatively parasomnia overlap syndrome). Pressman, Mahowald and Schenck (2005) published a useful article on the issue of distinguishing sleep terrors from RBD.

Sleep-related dissociative disorder is a condition of psychogenic dissociation (sleepwalking is arguably a dissociative condition, but with a definite physical basis for the propensity). Sleep-related dissociative disorders are associated with mental health problems, particularly due to childhood physical or sexual abuse and/or post-traumatic stress disorder. There are several case reports of patients with dissociative disorders or psychogenic events presenting as apparent parasomnias. Sleepwalking itself has been considered a dissociative state in the past (Hartman et al., 2001), although this is not the current paradigm. The case series of Schenck et al. found eight patients with a dissociative order from 150 consecutive patients (Schenck et al., 1989). These patients experienced dissociative episodes both night and day, apart from one patient who would act like a jungle cat at night. Hartmann's series of patients referred to a quaternary care centre for parasomnias found that two out of 22 patients had dissociative elements, one of whom was diagnosed with multiple personality disorder (Hartman et al., 2001). Molaie and Deutsch (1997) report a paediatric case of violent psychogenic episodes, where wakefulness during the episodes was confirmed by video-EEG monitoring. Agargun et al. (2001) reported that in a series of 29 patients with dissociative disorder there were eight patients with nocturnal dissociative episodes. They found that in two patients with multiple personalities, sleep facilitated the transition from one personality to another. If the initial trauma is associated with bed or sleep e.g. sexual abuse, this association would explain the triggering. This mechanism could explain the change from being right-handed to left-handed with patient RG, a phenomenon observed alters in dissociative identity disorder (although the psychiatrist who reviewed him considered that there was no evidence for day-time dissociative episodes). Plante and Winkelman comment in their review of parasomnias that:

> since these disorders are behavioral in nature, often co-occur with psychiatric illness, may present as psychiatric complaints, and can be induced by psychotropic medications, parasomnias are best conceptualized from an interdisciplinary perspective, and their optimal management requires that psychiatric considerations be understood by all clinicians who treat them, regardless of discipline of origin.
>
> (Plante and Winkelman, 2008)

Although the consensus is that the tendency to sleepwalking is not associated with psychopathology, dissociative disorders are strongly related to a history of previous abuse and/or PTSD (Schenck et al. 1989). Further, mental health issues have the capacity to trigger sleepwalking in susceptible individuals (Selby, Morrison and Riha, 2012). Some studies have found an increase in psychological disorders among current sleepwalkers (Labelle et al., 2013). Stress is a well-recognized precipitant of sleepwalking episodes (Lopez et al., 2013), and stress management and other psychological therapies are recognized as having a role in the treatment of sleepwalking. The association between stress and alcohol consumption is posited as one confounding factor in the apparent association between alcohol and sleepwalking seen in an observational study (Lopez et al. 2013).

All the parasomnias are known to be familial to a greater or lesser degree, with the exception of RBD (although several of the conditions causing RBD can be inherited) (Kales et al., 1980). Pedigrees of severe parasomniacs often show a high proportion of different parasomnias among relatives – the greater the number of close relatives with parasomnia, the worse the parasomnia is likely to be. The sleep pedigrees of some of the most dramatic examples of sleepwalkers have been reviewed in the literature.

The sleep disorder pedigree for Scott Falater, who stabbed his wife 44 times and then drowned her in the pool shows 17 relatives with sleep disorders (sleepwalking=5, sleep talking=10, nocturnal enuresis=4, sleep terrors=1). Another infamous sleepwalker is Kenneth Parks, a Canadian "gentle giant" who drove 23 km to his in-laws house and killed his mother-in-law and seriously injured his father-in-law. Like Scott Falater, he had a strong family history of sleep disorders. Twenty members of his family suffered parasomnias or related phenomena: (sleepwalking=5, sleep talking=7, nocturnal enuresis=5, and sleep terrors=3; there is no full Parks family pedigree for sleep disorders in the literature. Three had been known to leave the house while sleepwalking (Broughton et al., 1994; Cartwright, 2004). These two cases illustrate that a relevant history for sleepwalking must include other sleep disorders: night terrors, nocturnal enuresis (bed-wetting), night terrors, sleep talking and bruxism (grinding the teeth and clenching the jaw). There are further details of these cases in Case Histories.

A further difficulty is that the use of zolpidem, zopiclone or other psychotropic drugs may cause amnesic nocturnal wandering, popularized in the USA as the "Ambien" defence. However, Pressman and others have demonstrated that these cases can be distinguished from genuine parasomnia, particularly when sleep driving is involved (Pressman, 2011b, 2011c Vincent, 2013). In particular, the case report of nocturnal emailing is more consistent with a simple effect of zolpidem than a drug-induced parasomnia (Siddiqui, Osuna and Chokroverty, 2009). Nocturnal dissociative episodes appear to be much more commonly associated with violence than sleepwalking or other NREM parasomnias.

Malingering must be considered in any case where a parasomnic episode is being alleged. All the forensic sleep experts with a substantial workload spoke of cases they refused to take, because there were insufficient facts to support putative parasomnia. On the other hand, there were few cases where they felt there was definite subversion – only one expert reported a case where he felt the defendant had been "put up to it" by his lawyer (Rumbold, 2015). There have been cases where a parasomnia was claimed but later an alternative story was presented, such as Sean Freaney, who was convicted of murder at Oxford Crown Court (*Oxford Mail*, 2011). He initially claimed he had been sleepwalking but changed his defence to that of erotic asphyxiation after expert evidence did not support his claims. By contrast, in the case of Zack Thompson, even though he dropped the sleepwalking claim, it cannot be assumed that this entails fabrication on his part (Dolan, 2012). An individual who is amnesic for the criminal act in question will be genuinely seeking an explanation for that loss of memory.

Sleep apnoea/hypopnoea syndromes are conditions where the individual has episodes where breathing reduces or stops during sleep. The most common cause is obstructive sleep apnoea/hypopnoea syndrome (OSAHS). These conditions cause excessive daytime somnolence (EDS), which has the potential for causing the individual to fall asleep during driving, thereby resulting in a loss of control.

In *Kay v. Butterworth* it was established that even when the accused was asleep at the time of the offence, he could be held liable through prior fault in continuing to drive after he had "felt the onset of drowsiness". This assumes that the driver has warning that he might fall asleep at the wheel, an assumption that continues to be held for policy reasons as much as anything. Horne (2011) reports that 16–20 per cent of incidents on major roads are sleep-related. Long, straight roads are particularly likely to induce sleep in the sleep-deprived driver.

One study reported that almost 10 per cent of HGV drivers had symptoms of suspected undiagnosed OSAHS. HGV drivers were found to have an increased prevalence of risk factors of OSAHS for a number of reasons. Additionally, professional drivers are unable to avoid driving when tired, they spend more time at the wheel, and they are often overweight. The study also found that even when successfully treated, OSAHS sufferers were especially sensitive to sleep deprivation.

A sleep-related incident should be considered where:

- There is no other explanation e.g. mechanical defects, alcohol, bad weather, speeding or tail-gating
- The point of impact could be seen for at least seven seconds prior to the incident (pointing to at least a micro-sleep)
- Additional pointers are a dull road (hence the association with motorway travel) and the incident occurring between 0200–0600 and 1400–1600 hours.

Drivers often will not remember being sleepy or falling asleep, so a denial of either state should not rule out a sleep-related incident, no matter how genuine it is. Evidence of measures to fight sleep is more reliable (cold air via vents or window, music turned up).

Despite the excessive daytime sleepiness (EDS) that occurs with obstructive sleep apnoea/hypopnoea syndrome (OSAHS), there have been a number of acquittals for driving offences where the accused claimed to be unaware of his condition. In *Thomas* (unreported, Maidstone Crown Court in 2011), the prosecution offered no evidence on a charge of causing death by dangerous driving when it was found he had undiagnosed sleep apnoea (Purton, 2011). Certainly, where the individual is aware of OSAHS, then he will be found liable on the basis of prior fault. There have been no precedents set on whether or not OSAHS is an insane cause of automatism. It is an internal cause, but it is probably not a disease of the mind. The excessive sleepiness is caused by an obstruction of the upper airways. It might be argued that the effect on the brain of sleep deprivation is a disease of the mind. Alternatively, the disease of the mind is the effect of OSAHS on the ability of the person to perceive how sleepy they are (which is the defect that causes the accident). Certainly, the DVLA would require evidence of effective treatment before the person's driving licence was reinstated following a OSAHS-induced incident.

There has been no ruling on whether falling asleep at the wheel with no warning in a sleep-deprived individual would still constitute prior fault or not, on the grounds of driving in a dangerous condition (sleep deprivation). A recent study found that even in healthy sleep-deprived volunteers, there is not always warning prior to falling asleep. In contrast, Professor Jim Horne found that:

> people who fall asleep at the wheel are aware that they are doing so at the time, but that for plausible reasons, they will subsequently not recall being sleepy, even though at the time they would have done things to keep themselves awake (e.g. allowing cold air onto the face or turning up the radio).
>
> (Horne, 2011)

This is a view supported by the majority of the literature (Lisper, Laurell and Loon, 1986; Reyner and Horne, 1998; Horne and Baulk, 2004; Otmani et al., 2005). It seems unlikely that in cases of moderate to severe sleep apnoea, the accused would not be aware there was something wrong, even if they did not recognize the severity of their condition. Therefore, on policy grounds it is more appropriate that most of these individuals be found guilty of what is a strict liability offence.

Truck drivers are particularly vulnerable to sleep-apnoea accidents because they drive more often for long distance and long hours on the type of roads where falling asleep is a higher risk (see below). Where driving is the individual's vocation, this compounds matters for two reasons: (1) they are unable to avoid driving when they are aware of impairment due to lack of sleep; and (2) they are more likely to avoid consulting healthcare professionals about EDS, as they fear losing their livelihood.

Even though 21 hours sleep deprivation causes psychomotor impairment equivalent to being over the drink drive limit (Dawson and Reid, 1997), there are no specific offences in the UK relating to driving whilst sleep deprived. New Jersey has a law on "drowsy driving", known as "Maggie's Law". Driving whilst fatigued (defined as 24 hours sleep deprivation or more) is an offence. Any deaths resulting from such a state may be classified as vehicular homicide. There has been no ruling in the UK on whether falling asleep at the wheel with no warning in a sleep-deprived individual would still constitute prior fault or not, on the grounds of driving in a dangerous condition (sleep deprivation).

A sleep-related incident should be considered where:

- There is no other explanation e.g. mechanical defects, alcohol, bad weather, speeding or tail-gating.
- The point of impact could be seen for at least 7 s prior to the incident (pointing to at least a micro-sleep).

(Horne and Reyner, 1995)

Additional pointers are a dull road (hence the association with motorway travel) and the incident occurring between 0200–0600 and 1400–1600 hours. Drivers often will not remember being sleepy or falling asleep, so a denial of either state should not rule out a sleep-related incident.

The assessment of OSAHS requires a PSG plus either multiple sleep latency tests or, more appropriately, maintenance of wakefulness tests. The latter is considered more directly relevant to driving as it is conducted in conditions close to driving. In severe sleep apnoea the apnoea/hypopnoea index (AHI – the total number of episodes of apnoea and hypopnoea divided by the number of hours of sleep) should be greater than 30/hour.[4] The usefulness of the AHI is disputed (Stradling and Davies, 2004) and there are several other measures e.g. the Respiratory Disturbance Index (RDI – average number per sleep hour of apnoeas, hypopnoeas and respiratory effort-related arousals), Oxygen Desaturation Index (ODI – the average number of significant oxygen desaturations per hour of sleep) and arousal index (number of EEG arousals per hour). Sleepiness is usually assessed by the Epworth Sleepiness Scale, those scoring over 12 having EDS (normal average score is five) (Johns, 1991). The test that is most applicable to driving is the maintenance of wakefulness test. This test will be relevant to other causes of hypersomnia such as narcolepsy.

The investigation of parasomnias and OSAHS requires overnight polysomnography (sleep study). This may be for one or two nights, depending on resources and protocols. The justification for a two-night study is that this reduces the effect on the quality and quantity of sleep of sleeping in an unfamiliar place. The investigation of OSAHS may also require maintenance of wakefulness or multiple sleep latency tests to assess the tendency of the individual to fall asleep. The former better reflects the ability to keep awake, which is the important capacity for the criminal law.

Sleep studies may demonstrate confusional arousals and other parasomnias, particularly if the testing involves prior sleep deprivation and acoustic stimuli to provoke an episode. Although there are some markers associated with parasomnias, their significance is not universally accepted. It is uncommon for the individual to have a sleepwalking episode during a sleep study, and an episode during the sleep study may raise the suspicion of malingering (Ebrahim and Fenwick, 2008). The diagnosis of sleepwalking remains primarily clinical. The main source of information will be bed partners, flatmates, relatives and friends who have witnessed episodes. The individual will have complete or near complete amnesia for the episodes, although they may relate episodes of waking up in strange places. Forensic sleepwalking episodes require a credible history from an eyewitness of a previous sleepwalking episode. It is quite common that sleepwalkers have not sought medical help prior to a forensic sleep episode, even where there have been violent episodes for example.

4 Figures courtesy of Dr Chris Idzikowski.

Hypoglycaemia

Hypoglycaemia is the condition of low blood sugar. The threshold for the DVLA (less than 4 mmol/l) is not the threshold used in medical practice (less than 2.2 mmol/l|) (DVLA, 2004). Glucose is particularly vital for the brain, as most other tissues in the body can use alternative substances such as free fatty acids as fuel. Hypoglycaemia will affect the performance of complex actions (such as driving) and cause impaired consciousness when severe. The cognitive impairment is normally preceded by warning signs of pallor, sweating, tremor, hunger and anxiety that are related to adrenaline release. These will give the person with hypoglycaemia the opportunity to consume something sugary to raise their blood sugar.

The most common cause of this condition in most countries is treatment for diabetes. There are a number of other possible causes including:

- Liver problems
- Insulin-producing tumours
- Alcohol-related.

The liver usually maintains a stable blood glucose by the production of glucose from amino acids and stored glycogen. An insulin-producing tumour (an insulinoma) was responsible for the condition of Tarleton in the civil case of *Mansfield v. Weetabix*. Here a truck driver ran into the claimant's house, partially demolishing it. He was (posthumously) absolved of blame, despite an episode of erratic driving earlier that day when he was stopped by the police. Alcohol can product hypoglycaemia, particularly in children. As the symptoms of hypoglycaemia can resemble alcoholic intoxication, this may lead to the arrest of people with diabetes or worse. One man was tasered when he developed hypoglycaemia on a bus, shortly after the 7 July 2005 suicide bombings in London (Brooke, 2007).

As already noted in Chapter 2, the legal regime prior to 1992 made the insanity verdict unpalatable for minor offences. The solution for diabetics was the designation of those causes of medicolegal automatism not due to a disease of the mind as non-insane automatism. This means all external causes, and some internal causes that are not diseases of the mind. Therefore Tarleton's insulinoma or the effects of diabetes itself (which would cause hyperglycaemia) are causes of insane automatism.

The key issues with hypoglycaemia cases, particularly when driving, are prior fault and total loss of control. World-renowned expert witness on hypoglycaemia Professor Marks comments that most of the criminal trials hinge on the issue of prior fault (personal communication, 2013). The DVLA's instructions for diabetic drivers recommend that blood glucose be checked less than two hours before driving, and every two hours whilst driving. The DVLA defines hypoglycaemia for diabetics on hypoglycaemia treatment as blood glucose less than 4 mmol/l. The diabetic driver will not automatically be at fault for not following this advice to the letter. The Court of Appeal in *Gilbert* heard evidence that testing blood glucose prior to driving was a "council of perfection" and declined to find fault with the driver on that occasion. There are two main grounds on which diabetic drivers are convicted for motoring offences committed when hypoglycaemic.

Most often, it is because they are at fault in some way for the episode of hypoglycaemia. They have mismanaged their diabetes, and this negligence satisfies the *mens rea* requirement for the offence. The other ground is the lack of a total loss of voluntary control. In several cases, either the onset of warning symptoms or the gradual onset of impairment with deepening hypoglycaemia has been deemed to represent an opportunity for the driver to recognize the impairment and pull over. People with diabetes *usually* have the adrenaline-related warning symptoms listed above prior to the onset of cognitive impairment. However, hypoglycaemia unawareness is relatively common, affecting up to 40 per cent of type 1 diabetics within ten years of diagnosis. The person with diabetes will often be made aware of this condition, as relatives, friends or colleagues will notice strange behaviour. Those that live alone may be completely oblivious to hypoglycaemic unawareness.

One such case was that of Trevor Norman Clarke. Mr Clarke had been driving along a very familiar route, when he suffered a hypoglycaemic episode. The effect of that was to cause him to drive erratically for just over two miles. Bystanders noted that the driver looked "paranoid", "fidgety" and "out of it". He was seen to accelerate and then brake for no reason, to put his windscreen wipers on when there was no need, and to stop at a green light. Throughout this time he was swerving and weaving about the road. The defendant narrowly avoided a collision with another car only by the corrective action of the other driver. Throughout this bizarre driving the defendant appeared to be oblivious to other drivers sounding their horns. Eventually the defendant's car left the road and went on to a footpath where two boys were walking. The younger boy, who was just four years old, was struck by the car and gravely injured. He died two weeks later in hospital. The elder boy, the deceased's 14-year-old stepbrother, was also injured.

The defendant was found guilty of causing death by dangerous driving. He was sentenced to three years in prison, which was reduced to one year on appeal. The experts on diabetes and hypoglycaemia instructed by the defence were unanimous in their belief that Mr Clarke would have had no warning of the developing hypoglycaemia (Rumbold and Wasik, 2011). Cases such as *Broome v. Perkins* and *Watmore v. Jenkins* found guilt partly on the basis that there was a window of opportunity for the defendant to pull over, when the warning symptoms developed. The courts need to acknowledge that the medical science shows that this can no longer be assumed to be the case. The existence of hypoglycaemic unawareness was the basis of prior fault in the case of *Marison*. A driver that is aware that he suffers hypoglycaemia unawareness is taking a risk by driving at all.

The other ground, also seen in the case of Trevor Norman Clarke, is whether or not there was a total loss of control. In the case of *Jean Gilbert*, the 45-year-old defendant had been diagnosed with diabetes as a young child. She had no convictions or endorsements on her driving licence. Her car was seen by witnesses to be weaving from side to side before the accident in which a passenger in another vehicle was killed and the defendant herself was severely injured. The judge, having heard evidence from two experts ruled that the jury be directed to acquit the defendant on the charge of causing death by dangerous driving. The Court of Appeal upheld the judge's ruling that "there was no evidence to support a finding of fault on her part sufficient to engage criminal liability". This was despite the fact that the defendant had suffered three hypoglycaemic attacks at work which had come on without warning, and so, unlike Mr Clarke, she could not be said to be unaware of hypoglycaemic unawareness. There was also a lack of evidence as to whether she had tested herself before setting out on her journey, although always testing before driving was described by experts in this case as a "counsel of perfection". Hypoglycaemic unawareness, or at least sudden onset of hypoglycaemia, had been noted previously by the defendant. However, because there were no witnesses to the driving prior to the incident, it was assumed that the episode was of sudden onset.

By contrast, the bad driving by Mr Clarke was observed to extend over two miles and included one minor route correction. It was asserted by the prosecution that for at least part of this period, Mr Clarke had enough control and insight to pull over, realizing his driving had become dangerous. Again, the experts on diabetes and hypoglycaemia instructed by the defence were unanimous in their belief that this was not the case. So the lack of any witnesses to a gradual deterioration of control during a hypoglycaemic episode therefore is as the law stands a distinct advantage for the defendant.

A final note on diabetes: although hyperglycaemia is mentioned in the case of *Hennessy*. The evidence for hyperglycaemia causing incapacity in this case is dubious. The expert evidence was not strongly in favour of the possibility that his hyperglycaemia would cause confusion. Where hyperglycaemia is severe and accompanied by other physiological disturbances such as acidosis and dehydration, confusion will occur but these individuals will be in a state of near-collapse at best. This would be considered as an insane automatism.

Hypoglycaemia can occur in any diabetic treated with hypoglycaemic agents, whether insulin or drugs such as sulphonylureas that increase insulin secretion. If the blood sugar is not tested soon after the incident, it will often rise even without treatment (due to adrenaline release). A rapid change in mental state after administration of glucose or sugar would indicate hypoglycaemia. Hypoglycaemia is said not to occur with agents that only affect insulin sensitivity, such as metformin, or newer agents that affect the renal threshold for example.

The presence of hypoglycaemia unawareness is assessed by a period of continuous glucose measurement via a subcutaneous glucose sensor that measures the glucose level of interstitial fluid (which has a relatively consistent relationship with blood glucose). If biochemical hypoglycaemia is documented that coincides with observed symptoms of hypoglycaemia but without the warning signs, this is indicative of hypoglycaemia unawareness. The patient will usually only be unaware of hypoglycaemic unawareness if they live alone. This condition can be managed either by relaxation of glycaemic control or by islet cell or whole pancreas transplantation.

Neurological/neuropsychiatric

A number of neurological disorders could result in a loss of control, through loss of motor coordination or abnormal muscular tone. These include epilepsy, Tourette's syndrome and cataplexy. There are other conditions which may cause medicolegal automatism for other reasons. Stroke is discussed under "cardiovascular" below.

Epilepsy

Although generalized seizures could result in flailing limbs hitting someone, there are no reported criminal cases where such a clearly unintentional act has been prosecuted. Seizures occurring at the wheel could result in a collision, and those who continue to drive despite having uncontrolled epilepsy will be found criminally liable for any incidents resulting from these. An example is the case of *Sims*, who had presumed epilepsy and had been warned not to drive. His refusal to adhere to this advice was an exacerbating factor in sentencing. One study noted that of eight driving incidents reported in the press as due to epilepsy, five drivers were not previously known to have epilepsy (Parsons, no date). This may well not be a representative cross-section, since cases where the diagnosis of epilepsy was in doubt would be more newsworthy.

Non-adherence to treatment should be considered. Inadequate anti-epileptic treatment can also be due to the accused deliberately concealing the severity of their condition (*Akinyeme*). Tiredness and alcohol consumption are not factors considered contributory to epileptic seizures (*Cox v. Rawlinson*).

Psychomotor seizures can result in bizarre behaviours, which are rather more difficult to distinguish from voluntary behaviour. The author recalls being almost bowled over in a hospital corridor by a patient having a temporal lobe seizure. Psychomotor epilepsy is the only form of epilepsy that can be treated in a special hospital. This means that sufferers who receive the special verdict can receive a hospital order, unlike the other forms of epilepsy which would fall under section 24 of the Domestic Violence, Crime and Victims Act 2004, and expanded on in Home Office circular 24 / 2005 (The Domestic Violence, Crime and Victims Act 2004: provisions for unfitness to plead and insanity), which has the effect of excluding physical disorders from the disposal of a hospital order.

Postictal[5] confusion could also result in medicolegal automatism. An aggressive reaction to people often trying to help may result in physical violence. There are no recorded cases of postictal confusion resulting in a prosecution, which probably reflects the clear confusion and close temporal relationship to an epileptic fit. Individuals with frequent seizures of various types report contact with the police when their behaviour is reported by members of the public (for example, wandering into a restricted area whilst postictal). Whilst this does not proceed to any further action, it does cause them considerable disruption and distress.

5 Postictal means in the immediate aftermath of a seizure.

Tourette's syndrome is a disorder characterized by involuntary movements known as tics. Uncontrollable swearing is only present in a minority of cases (approximately 10 per cent). It may be possible for the sufferer to suppress the tics temporarily. There are no known cases of prosecutions resulting from Tourette's syndrome. Cataplexy is the sudden loss of sudden muscle tone, often associated with narcolepsy. This could result in a sudden loss of control. Cataplexy is often precipitated by strong emotions; it can be elicited in the clinic by tickling. A sudden attack of dystonia could cause a sudden loss of control whilst driving. The same would apply to other movement disorders, which would therefore generally be incompatible with holding a driving licence.

Lesions of the frontal cortex can result in disinhibition. One example is the man with a right orbitofrontal tumour that caused the emergence of aberrant sexual behaviour including paedophilia. His behaviour was apparently incorrigible, but the development of neurological signs led to the diagnosis of the tumour. The change in his behaviour was clearly correlated to the tumour, as its recurrence corresponded with a recurrence of the tumour (Burns and Swerdlow, 2003). Other conditions that can cause hypersexuality include Kleine-Levin syndrome, Klüver-Bucy syndrome, and treatment of Parkinson's disease with dopaminergic agents.

The legal position on hypersexuality of any cause is that it is very unlikely to meet any of the legal standards for a mental condition defence. A possible defence for those afflicted by a condition that fundamentally affects their ability to constrain the behaviour has been proposed by Horder (Horder, 1993). An involuntary loss of capacity can be accommodated within the current legal framework relatively easily. Hale in *Pleas of the Crown* (1736) distinguished "phrenzy" induced by involuntary intoxication from voluntary intoxication; he also recognized the disorder of dementia affectata, or "induced witlessness", mental states induced by drink or drugs . This was not an excuse to a crime unless induced by a negligent physician or caused by "the contrivance of his enemies" (c.f. *R v. Kingston*), or where heavy drinking had caused "an habitual or fixed phrenzy" (possibly the chronic neurological sequelae of chronic alcohol abuse such as alcoholic encephalopathy and Wernicke's encephalopathy). Sullivan proposed a similar defence of "destabilisation" (Sullivan, 1996). This is discussed more fully in Chapter 5.

Cardiovascular

Where there is a problem with the circulatory system such that the blood supply to the brain is reduced, this may cause medicolegal automatism. This could be due to a sudden drop in blood pressure affecting the whole brain, which leads to syncope. There are a large number of causes of syncope (see below re *Beaumont*, diagnosed with pneumonia). The classic faint, known as vasovagal syncope, could be a cause of automatism. A coach driver Peter Huggett described an episode that could have been vasovagal syncope. A putative heart rhythm abnormality was accepted as a cause of insane automatism in *MacBrayne* (unreported (Lazzari, 2011)). Where the cause is internal, it is possible that it could be deemed an insane automatism. Where the cause is an acute illness, this seems a largely theoretical consideration.

A reduction in blood supply could also be due to a blockage of the arteries to the brain, causing a transient ischaemic attack or a full-blown stroke. In the civil case of *Roberts v. Ramsbottom*, it was held that although the defendant had suffered a stroke whilst at the wheel, he had retained sufficient control to still be liable for the damage caused by his vehicle.

A head injury is mentioned in obiter in *Kay v. Butterworth* as a potential cause of automatism. The long-term sequelae of head injuries will fall squarely within the realm of a disease of the mind, even though their ultimate cause is an external one. There have been no cases in the UK that have hinged on a fine distinction between the acute and chronic effects of a head injury. It is likely that this would rest on the facts of each case. The likelihood of the effects of the lesion persisting and the person representing a continuing danger to the public would be the most important factors, if the position of the judge in the case of Brian Thomas indicates the current practice of the courts.

Psychiatric

This category might seem an anomaly. Most psychiatric disorders where they form the basis of a mental condition defence are causes of insanity. Moreover, they do not typically result in medicolegal automatism. However, as the case of *R v. T* demonstrates, a dissociative episode following trauma could constitute automatism. The defendant in this case had been raped three days prior to the robbery. During the robbery, she was heard saying "I'm ill, I'm ill". This case was distinguished from cases such as *Broome* and *Isitt* by the contention she acted as if she were "within a dream". She was convicted by the jury. Two similar Australian cases are *Falconer* and *Radford*. The two cases differ dramatically in the circumstances. In *Falconer*, the defendant was a victim of sexual and physical abuse from her husband, as were her children. On the day that she killed her husband, whom she was separated from, he assaulted her again and taunted her that she would not be believed by the courts. It was ruled on appeal that evidence supporting automatism should be admitted.

By contrast, Radford went to the house of his ex-wife's friend, whom he blamed for the break-up of their marriage. He suffered PTSD from his service in Vietnam. He took a rifle with him, with which he shot Nancy Grugan. He described feeling like he was an observer, as if his "whole body was just a head about two feet above the shoulder – the right shoulder of the soldier". In *Isitt*, the defendant fled the scene after a road accident, evading a police roadblock then running into the woods. He claimed afterwards to have no memory of these events. This putative dissociative episode was deemed incompatible with automatism. His actions were purposeful. It is difficult to see a meaningful difference between the behaviours objectively, and the distinction is more likely down to the very different causes and circumstances.

In *Rabey*, the triggering event was considered part of "the ordinary stresses and disappointments of life which are the common lot of mankind". Such psychological vulnerability was considered to be a disease of the mind. Lord Lane came to a similar conclusion in *Burgess*:

> the possible disappointment or frustration caused by unrequited love was not to be equated with something such as concussion.

The reaction of a normal person to overwhelming events as in *R v. T* has been described as "psychological blow automatism". By contrast, established PTSD is a disease of the mind. There is indubitably a duty to public safety, regardless of the fact that the same causes produce both the acute reaction and the chronic condition. Where the line is drawn between psychological blow automatism and chronic PTSD is not known. Given the uncertainty surrounding how an individual will cope with the kind of traumatic events that might cause psychological blow automatism, there is a case for the special verdict regardless.

Sleep-related dissociative disorders may be difficult to distinguish from parasomnias. Typically, there will be dissociative episodes during the daytime also. The behaviour is more complex, and there will usually be a history of trauma. An example related to this author is a patient who ran after some children waving a baseball bat during an episode. She had dissociative episodes during the day when observed as an inpatient in a mental health facility. The associated mental health issues make the special verdict appropriate.

The impairment of higher cognitive functions falling short of satisfying the *McNaughtan Rules* will not be considered as automatism, although the impairment of executive functions is certainly *capable* of constituting diminished responsibility. The inability to control impulses or make rational decisions has never been successfully argued as automatism, although some jurists argue that there is a good legal theoretical basis to such an argument. There are however no cases of tics or tonic-clonic seizures being the basis of criminal prosecutions, which may be indicative of the refusal of prosecutors to try individuals on the basis of such actions. The distinction between a disease of the mind and a disease of brain was explored in the Canadian case of *SH*, which determined that the disorder was a disease of the mind based on several considerations: the likelihood of recurrence, and the commonplace nature of the triggers in this case. It was ruled that the risk of violent recurrence was not the sole consideration, and that the trial judge should have also taken into account the fact that medication was required to reduce the risk of recurrence.

Malingering/amnesia

The expert witness must always bear in mind the possibility of malingering whenever a mental condition defence is being argued. A disorder whose first manifestation is the episode that has brought the accused to the attention of the criminal justice system must be treated with the deepest suspicion. Corroboration of previous episodes from others is invaluable.

The decision to argue the defence of automatism is often partially based on the assertion that the accused cannot remember the events in question. This means that he cannot realistically dispute the victim's account, although it is of course still for them to prove this. If the victim is unable to recount the events due to severe injury or death, this makes it very difficult to infer the mental state of the accused. In driving cases, the amnesia might be due to a micro-sleep. There are many possible explanations for amnesic episodes, including transient global amnesia, epilepsy and alcoholic blackouts. Alcoholic blackouts are a far more plausible explanation for many sexual assaults where sexsomnia has been claimed (White, Jamieson-Drake and Swartzwelder, 2002; Jnr, 2004).

Alcoholic blackout is an important differential diagnosis for sleepwalking. Alcohol and Z-drugs have an almost identical effect on the brain as sleepwalking, except alcohol affects the cerebellum more (leading to slurred speech and unsteadiness), and both alcohol and Z-drugs affect memory more than motor skills. Some sleep experts believe it is impossible to reliably distinguish clinically alcohol intoxication from sleepwalking or sexsomnia (presumably in the lack of the cerebellar signs mentioned above) (Pressman et al., 2007, 2013). It would also be a reasonable position to take that alcohol-induced sleepwalking ought not to be an excuse, being a consequence of alcoholic intoxication as per *Finegan v. Heywood* (albeit a rare consequence).

All the sleep experts I spoke to started from an assumption that the accused was not sleepwalking until persuaded otherwise. All the experts with a substantial workload spoke of cases they refused to take, because there were insufficient facts to support putative parasomnia. This includes the previously mentioned enquiry where the client had a history of sleepwalking, but the incident occurred in broad daylight and was in no way connected to sleep. Some American expert witnesses related an increasing tendency for verbal enquiries in order to avoid disclosing any adverse opinions. On the other hand, there were few cases where it was felt there was definite subversion – only one expert reported a case where he felt the defendant had been "put up to it" by his lawyer. There have been cases where a parasomnia was claimed but later an alternative story was presented (see Freaney, Chapter 1).

Outside of criminal proceedings, Mahowald et al. report an individual who attended for assessment whom they suspected was malingering. The man reported increasingly violent episodes directed at his wife, apparently arising during sleep, including chasing her with a hammer. After exhaustive testing, no sleep disorder was diagnosed. It was suspected he was trying to have his violent behaviour legitimized in case he was ever charged with a violent offence, including murder (Mahowald, Schenck and Bornemann, 2005). One sleep expert described a patient whose wife alleged episodes of sleepwalking and sexsomnia that could never be substantiated on testing and circumstantial evidence suggested the accounts were untrue. This is effectively "gas-lighting" (Rumbold, 2015).

Miscellaneous

Pneumonia was the cause of a temporary impairment in the case of *Beaumont*, who lost control of her car. The episode sounds like syncope. Any severe acute illness might produce temporary impairment of the ability to drive. They would be unlikely to produce a total loss of control

A swarm of bees attack is mentioned in obiter in *Kay v. Butterworth*. An attack of sneezing was accepted as an excuse in the case of *Woolley* (this case demonstrating the rare exceptions to the requirement for medical evidence to support the automatism defence).

Unpredicted reactions to psychotropic medications have been the basis of a successful automatism defence. This rests on the particular facts of the case, as usually intoxication inducing incapacity does not excuse. This is the case even when the substance was taken involuntarily, as in the cases of *Kingston*, *Mulrainey*, *Carrington* and *Smallshire*. In the case of *McGhee* (rolled-up appeal with *Coley*), the Appeal Court held that a combination of temazepam and alcohol taken for the relief of tinnitus and causing disinhibition could not amount to automatism – Hughes LJ stated emphatically that "Disinhibition is exactly not automatism."

Although voluntary alcoholic intoxication is not an excuse, certain conditions associated with alcohol consumption may provide an excuse. Alcohol is considered to be a trigger for sleepwalking in some individuals with the tendency to sleepwalk. It is not entirely clear whether or not alcohol-induced sleepwalking is an excuse or not (see above). Delirium tremens was considered in the case of *Harris* (rolled-up appeal with *Coley*) to be distinct from intoxication; although alcohol withdrawal could be traced back to alcohol consumption at a previous date, the psychosis was not due to alcohol intoxication per se.

There have been widespread media reports in the USA of acts committed under the influence of Ambien (zolpidem, also marketed as Stilnoct). The so-called "Ambien defence" has received great scrutiny, especially given the prominent warnings in the patient information leaflets (c.f. *Hardie*). "Z-drugs" (zolpidem, zopiclone) induce amnesia and confused and/or disinhibited behaviour, and these impairments will not automatically excuse the accused from any illegal acts (see *Kingston*). Such episodes must be carefully distinguished from genuine parasomnia. The "Ambien defence" is probably the inspiration for the recent cinematic release *Side Effects* (2013). Alcohol and other agents acting on gamma-aminobutyric acid (GABA) receptors (including benzodiazepines and Z-drugs) affect memory more than motor skills, and therefore seem a more plausible explanation than parasomnia for some of the more complex behaviours. Those with behaviour triggered by Z-drugs will usually lack a family history of parasomnias.

Side-effects to other medicines can cause harmful behaviours. Dopaminergic medications used for the treatment of Parkinson's disease can cause compulsive behaviours. These include compulsive betting, sexual gratification, eating, shopping, and "punding" (continually sorting and handling objects).

Hypnotism is often included in possible causes of automatism mentioned in obiter and for example the Model Penal Code. It is mentioned in *Quick*:

> A malfunctioning of the mind of transitory effect caused by the application to the body of some external factor such as violence, drugs, including anaesthetics, alcohol and hypnotic influences cannot fairly be said to be due to disease.

There are no recorded cases where hypnosis has been the basis of a successful defence to a criminal charge.

5 Criminal law theory

This chapter will discuss some of the wider issues surrounding medicolegal automatism. In particular, the legal and moral principles behind the exemption from criminal responsibility for acts committed during medicolegal automatism need to be examined, and whether or not there are coherent and consistent principles underpinning the law in this area. Firstly, we need to examine the jurisprudence behind the automatism defence.

Justification of the automatism defence

When the English case law is examined, it is difficult to formulate a unifying doctrine for the automatism/insanity distinction. It seems that none of the following factors alone are determinative:

- External cause
- Exceptional nature of causative factor
- Risk of recurrence
- Continuing danger
- Physical illness versus psychiatric illness.

The Canadian approach acknowledges explicitly that the assessment of whether or not social control measures are required involves a holistic assessment. The English courts have made no such declaration, although decisions at the court of first instance indicate that such assessments are being made e.g. the case of Brian Thomas (de Bruxelles, 2009).

Automatism simpliciter and the insanity defence share several justifications for their status as excuses in criminal law (Hart, 1968). If we look at the justifications for criminal punishment, it can be seen that several of these cannot be applied to the defendant who was in a state of medicolegal automatism without any disqualifying conditions such as prior fault or involuntary intoxication. Individual deterrence cannot be justified, as he cannot be deterred. Where all of the executive functions of the brains have been disabled, the person is no longer able to weigh up his options and choose to avoid punishment for violations of the law.

The works of legal philosophers Hart and Schopp are instructive on the legal concept of automatism. Hart in *Punishment and Responsibility* (1968) lays out his positivist justifications for punishment. Crucially, he sees the punishment of people who cannot be deterred as generally unjustified. When the person cannot avoid breaking the law, punishment cannot be justified under positivist jurisprudence. Hart's justification for mental condition defences rests on this lack of capacity to be deterred. The "policeman at the elbow test" arguably fails for the religiously or politically motivated fanatic, but it might be argued they still have the capacity to be deterred. A practical reasoner can assess the law and his own circumstances, and come to a rational decision whether or not to break the law. He considers it the way to maximize freedom – for Hart, the law has no necessary moral content and so individuals may rationally decide to break the law. The threat of punishment is a relevant factor to deter law-breaking. For those who are not practical reasoners, the threat of punishment will not deter them, and so Hart reasons that there is no justification for punishing them (there is the general effect of deterrence on others, but again Hart considers this unjustifiable where the person is not a practical reasoner).

This leads into the question of the nature of the automatism defence.

Classification of the automatism defence

Schopp in *Automatism, Insanity and the Psychology of Criminal Responsibility* (1991) examined the nature of automatism excuse and concluded that it could be categorized as either as a variant of insanity, a failure-of-proof or a status defence (pp. 72–73). He deconstructs the automatism defence to try to define exactly what it is about automatism which excuses the individual. As per earlier discussions, the person arguing automatism typically is not unconscious, nor are they acting entirely involuntarily in the neurological sense. Further, given the current understanding that the brain is modular, we should not be looking at global assessments of consciousness. Formulations like "effective loss of control", whilst more appropriate than the absolute and inflexible standard of "total loss of control", are rather difficult to define and apply in practice. Schopp turns to Goldman's action theory approach to classify acts (for the purpose of the criminal law) as rather more than Austin's "willed body movement" or Holmes's "willed muscular contraction" (which would restrict legal automatisms to the narrow realm of "spasms, convulsions, and reflex acts", which Mackay rejects.

Schopp deconstructs the automatism defence to try to define exactly what it is about automatism which excuses the individual. Goldman distinguishes act-types from act-tokens. An act-type may be a willed muscular contraction, or series of them. An act-token is an example of an act-type by a particular actor at a particular type. Act-tokens may be basic, or part of an action plan or act-tree which links act-tokens by level-generations. The different levels are linked by the intentions and beliefs of the actor. Thus, the act-tokens of pointing a gun at someone and pulling the trigger may be either a tragic accident or murder, depending on the intentions and beliefs of the actor. In the case of *Lamb*, the accused was playing with a gun, again believing the firing pin would fall on an empty chamber. In this case, it could be said that Lamb did not fire the gun, because when he pulled the trigger he neither intended to fire the gun nor believed he would fire the gun. Similarly, Ryan argued that he did not intend to shoot the garage attendant. However, he intentionally held a loaded gun in the knowledge that this created the danger of shooting the garage attendant. The Goldman action theory accommodates the unintended consequences of actions, reflecting the generally accepted division of *mens rea* into intent, knowledge, recklessness and negligence (as per the Section 2.01 US Model Penal Code).

These distinctions are those encapsulated by the requirement for many crimes of the requisite *mens rea*. Strict liability laws are typically instituted because of difficulties in proving *mens rea* to the requisite standard (e.g. drug and firearm possession offences), or overriding public safety or public health concerns (e.g. driving and environmental offences, selling of unfit food). There are concerns about prosecutions for failure to "do the impossible" (meaning in these cases the physically impossible (Smart, 1987)). However, for many offences classified as strict liability, there is still a required fault element. It is "hidden" within the conduct element. Thus, possession requires some knowledge, constructive or actual, of possession of the item. The requirement for voluntary action is another example of a hidden fault element. Where the offence attracts custodial sentences as opposed to fines for the company, the argument for strict liability is weaker. There is some debate over whether or not the insanity defence applies to crimes of strict liability. There are also concerns about punishment for something that was impossible for the person in question, because of their particular incapacity. Hart argued that it was only right to hold someone criminally responsible for negligence if the following questions could be answered affirmatively:

1 Did the accused fail to take those precautions which any reasonable person with normal capacities would in the circumstances have taken?
2 Could the accused, given his mental and physical capacities, have taken those precautions?

This principle would potentially excuse the diabetic driver, or the person with Tourette's syndrome tics for example. The same principle applies to crimes of omission – where the accused is unable to fulfil their duties through no fault of their own, they should not be held liable. Thus parents and carers can be found guilty for injuries and illness due to wilful neglect (*R v. Stone and Dobinson*), but not for failing to provide the appropriate level of care despite their best efforts (*R v. Sheppard*, *R v. Hopkins*).

Where the crime is not a crime of strict liability, it is not the illegal act by itself that is punished – it is the illegal act committed for the designated, blameworthy reasons. Can these same principles be applied to crimes of strict liability? It is certainly difficult to consider the action plan relevant to certain motoring offences, where the issue is the loss of control – the motorist driving fast around a corner does not usually intend to cause an accident. It could be argued that the intentional creation of a risk can be considered part of the action plan. Similarly, although harsh, it is possible to see the judicial reasoning behind holding the bus driver responsible in *Attorney-General's Reference (No. 4 of 2000)*. In this case, a bus driver mistakenly pressed the accelerator instead of the brake. Tragically the bus shot forward and travelled across a pedestrian island where it struck a number of pedestrians, two of whom died from their injuries. He did not do this intentionally; however, his action in pressing that particular pedal was intentional and deliberate, and therefore not an automatism. His actions were accidental, but not involuntary. His intention in pressing that pedal was irrelevant, because the aim of the law is to protect the public by ensuring that drivers take all necessary precautions. However, the driver's action plan was to stop the bus, and he had no intention of creating any risk, unlike the stereotypical boy racer who deliberately takes a corner at excessive speed. The difference between this case and *Lamb* (see above) appears to rest largely on the ages of the defendant, by which the reasonableness of their incorrect beliefs was judged (age being the only relevant factor in an objective test of recklessness). There is also the issue of the degree of fault required.

The required *mens rea* for some offences of general intent is minimal. This potentially has implications for sexsomniacs. Another very similar distinction is between de re and de dicto, which can be broadly considered as distinguishing general intent from specific intent. Moore explains thus:

> Sometimes the question of intentionality arises, not with respect to the consequences of our actions . . . but with respect to circumstances. Suppose I shoot and kill Bill, as I intended; if Bill is a police officer, did I intend to kill a police officer? Does the answer change if I knew Bill was a police officer? Or must I be motivated by that fact, as I would be if I were in a cop-killing contest, for example? Ordinary language here is also indeterminate, even with respect to noun/verb usages of "intend". In one sense (often called the "de re" sense) of intend, if Bill is a cop and I intended to kill him, I intended to kill a cop; in another sense (often called the "de dicto" sense), even believing that Bill is a cop is not enough – I have to represent the state of affairs I intend to bring about as the killing of a cop.
>
> Most crimes having some form of intentions as *mens rea* are general intent crimes, such as rape, arson, and murder; specific intent crimes tend to be inchoate crimes (where the evil the law ultimately seeks to prevent need not have occurred).
>
> (Moore, 2013)

General and specific intent is being used here in a slightly different sense to that employed in English criminal law, where murder is considered a crime of specific intent. The list of basic and specific intent crimes is based more on policy than principle – although one distinction is between crimes with a *mens rea* satisfied by proof of negligence and recklessness (basic intent) and crimes with a minimum *mens rea* of knowledge or intent. Lord Diplock in *Caldwell* quoted with approval Lord

Elwyn-Jones LC in *Majewski* who stated that "self-induced intoxication is no defence to a crime in which recklessness is enough to constitute the necessary mens rea."

The Law Commission stated in 1995 "It is apparent . . . that there is no general agreement on the test which should be applied in order to distinguish offences of basic and of specific intent." (Law Commission, 1995)

Coles and Jang (1996) argue that intoxication cannot affect a person's intent. The main effect of alcoholic intoxication is disinhibition, which does not affect intent in the eyes of the law (although it can nonetheless prevent the formation of a specific intent).

Many legal philosophers and jurists have made similar comments about the qualities of a moral agent in law. Morse states:

> For the law, then, a person is a practical reasoner. The legal view is not that all people always reason and behave consistently rationally according to some preordained, normative notion of rationality. It is simply that people are creatures who are capable of acting for and consistently with their reasons of action and who are generally capable of minimal rationality according to mostly conventional, socially constructed standards of rationality.
>
> (Morse, 2004)

As previously stated, Hart considered that it was only right to hold someone criminally responsible for negligence if the accused had both the mental and physical capacity to take the precautions a reasonable person would take. That would seem to include the capacity for practical reasoning.

However, this is not the law as it stands. It seems wrong that someone should not be held criminally responsible for failing to consider the risks inherent in driving a particular way – however, if for some reason they were unable to appreciate or properly consider the risks because of hypoglycaemia or some similar condition, it is reasonable to excuse them if this condition was not self-inflicted. The emphasis above on the capability for rationality addresses the problematic lacuna of those who fail to use their practical reasoning and/or omissions. The essential ingredient for criminal responsibility with certain crimes is the capacity for practical reasoning. An omission is culpable where any reasonable person would both know the duty owed and was able to fulfil it. On these grounds we can distinguish the negligent or reckless driver from the driver with diabetes who suffers a hypoglycaemic episode. This to an extent involves merging the character theory of excuse with the choice theory of excuse, as Crosby (2010) points out.

The act requirement

It is generally required in criminal law that the *actus reus* and *mens rea* coincide. It is particularly evident in the automatism case law and elsewhere that the courts have had to engage in mental gymnastics to maintain that fiction. The traditional division of the elements of a crime in common law between *actus reus* and *mens rea* draws on Aristotle's *Rhetoric* and is later supported by Descartes.

The requirement for a guilty act serves the function of ensuring that people are not punished simply for their wrongful thoughts and desires, popularly described as "thoughtcrime" (from George Orwell's novel *1984*). Similarly, acts that are more than merely preparatory are required to make out criminal attempts, so as to distinguish those who are seriously attempting a criminal act from those who are not so committed to such action.

Robinson considers that the *actus reus* requirement includes four distinct doctrines:

- the act requirement;
- substitutes for an act: omission to perform a legal duty or possession of contraband;
- the voluntariness requirement;
- objective elements of offensive definitions: conduct, circumstance and result.

(Robinson, 1993)

He comments on the "thick" concept of *actus reus* that:

> The act requirement and the voluntariness requirement, frequently treated as one actus reus requirement, are related but distinct doctrines. Several writers assure that the two are treated as one by defining an "act" as a "willed movement".

One example of this is Holmes, who stated that an action "is a willed muscular contraction, nothing more" (Holmes, 1881). This definition covers the actions of the tennis player retrieving a difficult shot (as per Ryan, see Chapter 2) or the person swatting a fly (Dubber and Hornle, 2014). These actions are intended, even if they are largely instinctive. A better alternative to *actus reus* is arguably the "external element" (or "conduct element"), which would be synonymous with the illegal act. This would mean that the aspect of willing or voluntariness would fall under the "fault element".

Connection between *mens rea* and *actus reus*

The traditional analysis is that *mens rea* and *actus reus* have to coincide in time to make out the offence. As a basic proposition this holds good in very many cases. An exception to this is when the person is so intoxicated that they cannot form the *mens rea* for a crime of specific intent; nonetheless their intoxication forms the basis of the *mens rea* for a crime of basic intent. Another exception is *Callagher*, where the *mens rea* was formed before the *actus reus*. In the case of driving offences when the issue is the *actus reus*, driving is seen as a continuing act. Even when the accused is no longer "driving" (due to a state of automatism), the previous period of dangerous driving for example has a sufficiently proximal causal connection with the fatal accident that results. By contrast, in the cases of *Thabo Meli v. The Queen* and *MPC v. Fagan*, the criminal acts were viewed as a whole to maintain the connection between *mens rea* and *actus reus*. In *Thabo Meli*, the act that killed the victim was the disposal of the "body" over a cliff. The intent to kill did not coincide with the act of killing per se. In *Fagan*, a man was charged with assault after stopping his car on a policeman's foot by accident and then refusing to move it. The maintenance of the car's position was part of a continuing act.

This analysis is difficult to apply in all cases. The issue of prior fault is often used to deny the defence of automatism to diabetics suffering a hypoglycaemic episode whilst driving. Here the requisite *mens rea* is continuing to drive when warning symptoms occur, and the *actus reus* is the continuing act of driving. In the case of someone driving with knowledge of a dangerous condition such as uncontrolled epilepsy or hypoglycaemic unawareness, the *mens rea* is recklessness in getting behind the wheel and the actus reus is again the continuing act of driving. Where the accused has self-induced incapacity in other situations, this analysis breaks down. A diabetic who assaults someone whilst hypoglycaemic or a sleepwalker who commits a crime may have the requisite *mens rea* if their incapacity is self-induced, but what is the *actus reus*? There is no continuing act, and so the *mens rea* and *actus reus* do not coincide in any way. The defence of automatism is ruled out by prior fault, but the offence still needs to be made out. This is not to argue that there is no criminal responsibility in these cases, simply that they do not fit the current model of legal analysis. This author agrees with Arenson's assertion that it may be better to argue these cases on the principle of legal causation (Arenson, 2013). Robinson simply argues that the *actus reus/mens rea* distinction is incoherent (Robinson, 1993).

Theoretical issues in automatism

Involuntariness versus unconsciousness

A large amount of the confusion surrounding the defence of automatism arises from the conflation between involuntariness and unconsciousness. As we have seen, involuntariness is a denial of the *actus reus*, and is applicable to any crime including those of strict liability. Unconsciousness is a denial of the *mens rea*. A lack of *mens rea* is easier to establish in most circumstances that go to trial than a lack of the *actus reus*, especially if the bar is set at the high standard of a total loss of voluntary control. Doghramji, Bertoglia and Watson assert that:

> In cases where a violent act is committed during sleepwalking, it is often the *actus reus* requirement that first comes under fire, as the presence of an *actus reus* element implies that the defendant's actions were voluntary.
>
> (Doghramji, Bertoglia and Watson, 2013)

This is certainly not the way English cases would be argued, and it is possible the authors are confusing voluntary (and therefore intentional) action with possessing the necessary intent (c.f. the case of the bus driver confusing the accelerator and brake pedals). The negation of the *mens rea* is often the basis of the defence, rather than being merely theoretical. If this is established, there is no need to demonstrate that the defendant did not act voluntarily. Not all common law jurisdictions are settled on automatism being a denial of the *actus reus* however, so their argument may hold true for other jurisdictions.

Lord Denning acknowledges the two concepts that have been subsumed into automatism in his comment in *Bratty*:

> an act which is done by the muscles without any control by the mind such as a spasm, a reflex action or a convulsion; or an act done by a person who is not conscious of what he is doing such as an act done whilst suffering from concussion or whilst sleepwalking.

The former part of the definition refers to involuntariness, the latter to limited or impaired consciousness. Whichever is being argued, if the cause of the condition is a disease of the mind and the defendant is found to be insane, then the special verdict is applicable. If the defendant is not found to be insane, then the defence is either automatism (lack of *actus reus*) or lack of *mens rea*. If it is posited that a total lack of control is required to negative *mens rea*, this is a clear error of law.

It is assumed in law that the unconscious person cannot act voluntarily. Are there any grounds in neuroscience to dispute this? It is recognized that the person can perceive information without being consciously aware of it. The phenomenon of "blindsight" also known as "cortical blindness") illustrates this potential. When the cortical visual centres have been damaged, the person will be unaware of seeing anything. However, if they are asked to point to where a certain object is, they can do so. This peculiar phenomenon only occurs secondarily to a brain injury, but recent research on the "sixth sense" suggests that we may identify differences without consciously being able to identify them. These observations may have limited if any relevance to the area of criminal responsibility. The neuroscientific concept of voluntariness will not necessarily correspond to the legal concept.

Similarly, the ideomotor effect could potentially pose a problem. This explanation for the unconscious movement of the planchette when using the Ouija board posits that the person is acting on unconscious desires, also known as the Carpenter effect. Faraday, Chevreul, James and Hyman have demonstrated that many supposedly supernatural phenomena are due to this effect (Faraday, 1853; Chevreul, 1854; James, 1890; Hyman, 1999). There is no evidence to suggest the ideomotor effect is relevant to parasomnia or other. In any case, the effect of unconscious desires on criminal responsibility is doubtful. In the case of *King v. Cogdon*, unreported but discussed by Morris and Eigen, the defendant was considered by the various mental health experts to harbour "subconscious emotional hostility" (Morris, 1951; Eigen, 2003). Nonetheless, because the state arose out of sleep she was not held not responsible under the principle of "*In somno voluntas non erat libera*" (A sleeping person has no free will). However, if she had been judged to have been in a dissociative state (which is a reasonable possibility, given her history of neurosis), she might have been found culpable. Horder contrasts this repressed desire with the purportedly subconscious fetish that motivated the defendant in *Court*. When asked about his reason for spanking a young girl, he responded "I don't know; buttock fetish". Giving expression to this desire was evidence of bad character (Horder, 1993).

The current doctrinal basis for the defence of automatism in England and Wales is settled as a denial of *actus reus* on the grounds of the lack of a voluntary act. The illegal act alone does not constitute the *actus reus*, and hence automatism is a defence to even strict liability crimes. Another, and this author would argue better, way to categorize the effect of automatism is to consider that even strict liability crimes have an implicit mental element, such that the person without the ability to avoid committing them, due to lack of control over their limbs for example, has a defence. Hawthorne in his analysis of strict liability crimes argues that the requirement of *mens rea* can and should be presumed even when the statute is silent about the necessary *mens rea*, and by this device it is possible to accommodate a minimal fault *mens rea* for many strict liability crimes (Hawthorne, 2011). This approach was advocated by the House of Lords in *Sweet v. Parsley*, although the case is not always applied. The current cases of automatism could then be categorized as purely a denial of *mens rea* and the *actus reus* would simply be the illegal act. The distinction between denial of *actus reus* and *mens rea* arguably results in a great deal of confusion in the criminal courts, which Yeo argues is down to the confusion between involuntariness and unconsciousness (Yeo, 2001). Both these causes of incapacity would be subsumed into automatism.

Both Hart and Williams suggested that as a bare minimum for criminal liability, the individual should have been able to avoid the act or omission in question. Williams suggests the relevant question is: "Whether the offender could have acted otherwise if he had willed?" (Williams, 1982)

The Hart formulation is more expansive, arguably covering a subjective test for negligence where mental capacity is impaired.

McSherry categorizes criminal offences as comprising a guilty act plus a guilty minus a relevant defence (see further details in Tables 1.1 and 1.2, Chapter 1) (McSherry, 2003). This reflects the recognition that not all defences involve a negation of either *actus reus* or *mens rea*. McSherry's involuntary conduct and unintentional conduct correspond with Yeo's involuntariness and unconsciousness. In this schema, internal or external cause is irrelevant. Insanity is a status excuse, necessary only when the *actus reus* and *mens rea* requirements are met.

Involuntariness versus irresistible impulse

Yeo makes a useful contrast between involuntariness and unconsciousness, but his analysis includes disinhibition and irresistible impulse as forms of automatism (Yeo, 2001). This is not the current law in the UK, although disorders causing difficulties with impulse control may satisfy the partial defence of diminished responsibility. Many jurisdictions do have a volitional limb to their insanity defence, but not English law. An irresistible impulse alone that is the result of an abnormality of mind is not sufficient, as *Byrne* demonstrates. The Law Commission's proposed tests for capacity suggest an expansion of the special verdict to include a volitional limb, namely the ability:

> to control his or her physical acts in relation to the relevant conduct or circumstances.
>
> (Law Commission, 2013)

It appears from Chapter 4 of the discussion document that this is not just referring to the difficulties of motor control that would occur from Tourette's syndrome or during an epileptic seizure or a hypoglycaemic episode. It also would cover the inability to refrain from an act, although the effects of a personality disorder would be excluded from the new defence. It might cover the situation of a defendant with hypersexuality from Kleine-Levin syndrome, Klüver-Bucy syndrome, or dopamine agonist treatment, for example. However, there is no case law on this.

The objections to the volitional defence arise from policy and epistemological concerns. The fact that an impulse was not resisted does not inform us whether or not the impulse could have been resisted. Should greater weight be given to excusing someone who never resists a particular impulse or someone who nearly always resists a particular impulse? These investigations are considerably easier in cases related to a diagnosed neurological disorder such as Tourette's syndrome, where all the evidence is that it is impossible to resist the tic over time.

There have been arguments that instinctive reactions due to for example post-traumatic stress disorder should be counted as involuntary actions. Given the clear public safety issues, it's arguable that classification of this as automatism would be highly undesirable. The deeply entrenched reaction of a soldier certainly could be argued to constitute an irresistible impulse. These instincts, unlike those of *Ryan* in the Australian felony-homicide case (see above and Chapter 2), were developed and honed for morally legitimate purposes.

Denial of *mens rea* with a "disease of mind"

As discussed previously, apart from strict liability offences generally it is sufficient to establish a lack of *mens rea*. Professor Martin Wasik related to me a High Court judge's ruling on a moot held at Keele University on the issue of manslaughter caused by a violent reaction during a confusional arousal. The judge commented that these cases were resolved on the basis of a lack of *mens rea* rather than trying to negotiate the "quagmire" of automatism. It is undeniable that the conditions that cause automatism will enable the accused to argue lack of *mens rea*. This would be true in many cases where there is a disease of the mind. Nonetheless, it is problematic that these individuals could receive a plain acquittal if they satisfy the criteria for legal insanity, because as Jones put it:

> The courts strive to keep the defence of insanity, with its distinctive burden of proof, separate from questions of *mens rea* and voluntariness . . . what underpins this approach is a concern with social protection. Potentially dangerous individuals could be unconditionally acquitted if it were possible to use evidence suggestive of insanity as the foundation for an argument of lack of *mens rea* or voluntariness falling short of insanity.
>
> (Jones, 1995)

Lord Hutton concurs with this opinion in *Antoine* when he comments on the case of *Attorney-General's Reference (No. 3 of 1998)* stating that:

> a man who had committed very violent acts at a time when he was insane and did not realise that his acts were wrong was set at liberty.

Jones further states:

> courts do not permit evidence suggestive of insanity to be used in considering an argument of lack of *mens rea* independently of the insanity defence. There would otherwise also exist "the possibility of using a bad case of insanity to make a good case of reasonable doubt".
>
> (p. 488)

The data on the sleepwalking defence suggest that this is exactly what is happening – bad cases of insanity are making good cases of reasonable doubt. The main caution for the defence counsel arguing either lack of *mens rea* or lack of *actus reus* due to a mental condition is the ability of the judge to direct the jury to consider the special verdict, whether non-insane automatism is argued or simply lack of *mens rea*, where he believes the *McNaughtan Rules* are satisfied (*R v. Thomas*). Similarly, when the defence is arguing diminished responsibility, the judge or the prosecution may raise the issue of insanity (s6 of the Criminal Procedure (Insanity) Act 1964, in which case the prosecution would have the burden of proving insanity as per *Bastian*).

In the recent case of *R v. Seun Oye* it was confirmed that where a delusion due to a disease of the mind caused a defendant to have a subjective but erroneous belief that he was being attacked to which he responded with excessive force, he was not entitled to a plain acquittal. The Appeal Court commented that:

> An insane person cannot set the standards of reasonableness as to the degree of force used by reference to his own insanity. In truth it makes as little sense to talk of the reasonable lunatic as it did, in the context of cases on provocation, to talk of the reasonable glue-sniffer.

They followed the case of *Canns* where a patient with paranoid schizophrenia had killed a nurse under the delusion the nurse had attacked him. His belief in the necessity for self-defence (and the degree of violence) may have been sincerely held, but it was mistaken – and the reason for the mistake was his mental disorder. It is unclear from these two cases whether or not a genuinely held belief in self-defence due to a delusion would lead to a plain acquittal or not. Can the *McNaughtan Rules* be applied to a subjective belief in the need for self-defence?

Slobogin argues that:

> mental disorder should be relevant to criminal culpability only if it supports an excusing condition that, under the subjective approach to criminal liability increasingly accepted today, would be available to a person who is not mentally ill.
>
> (Slobogin, 2006)

He is explicitly rejecting a status defence of insanity, arguing that an alternative framework can accommodate all the justifications for excusing the mentally ill without a specific separate defence. The main practical difficulty in applying such a defence are that the lay jury will not be able to apply their own theories of mind to an accused whose mind may be functioning in an entirely different way. Thus, for this version of the insanity defence to work, it would require testimony by forensic psychiatrists and it would therefore probably be little different from the current insanity defence in practice. In the states of the USA where the insanity defence has been abolished but defendants can argue lack of *mens rea* due to their psychiatric condition, there is concern. There is some academic debate about the nature, classification and justifications for the insanity defence. It has been argued that it is an excuse, a status defence or a *sui generis* (Schopp, 1991). The Law Commission debates the merits of these arguments in the recent discussion paper (Law Commission, 2013).

There are counter-examples against the position that mental conditions should not allow the defendant to plead lack of *mens rea*. An extreme example is given by Prowse, JA who states:

> If a defence of insanity failed, evidence of brain injury that affected the accused's eyesight would be relevant on the issue of whether the accused had the requisite intent or believed that he was shooting a moose.

In *Clarke* in 1972 it was accepted that the absent-mindedness caused by depression caused to her to walk off without paying, thereby denying the *mens rea* for theft. Is it possible to discern a legal principle on which to distinguish *Clarke* from *Canns*, rather than simple policy considerations? Does it make a difference whether the requisite *mens rea* is objective or subjective in nature? In *Stephenson*, a tramp suffering with schizophrenia set light to a straw stack to keep himself warm; the fire grew out of control causing considerable damage to property. If Stephenson's schizophrenia affected his insight into the risk from the fire he set, should he have received a plain acquittal or the special verdict? The court stated:

> the jury had not been left to decide whether the appellant's schizophrenia might have prevented the idea of danger entering his mind at all, and the conviction was unsafe and would be quashed.

This implies that he should have received a plain acquittal, with no mention of the special verdict at all (this case was decided pre-*Caldwell*, so the test was subjective recklessness).

The accepted rationale for distinguishing the cases is the simple fact that the mental disorder did not satisfy the *McNaughtan Rules* but merely affected their assessment of the facts. *Clarke* wasn't arguing insanity, and the Appeal Court stated the evidence

> fell very far short of showing either that she suffered from a defect of reason or that the consequences of that defect in reason, if any, were that she was unable to know the nature and quality of the act she was doing. The *M'Naghten Rules* relate to accused persons who by reason of a disease of the mind are deprived of the power of reasoning. They do not apply and never have applied to a momentary failure by someone to concentrate.

However, this leaves us with the problem of how judges decide not to leave the insanity defence to the jury, in cases where the condition involved would clearly satisfy the *McNaughtan Rules*. The case of *Attorney-General's Reference (No. 3 of 1998)* states that once insanity has been established, the Crown only has to prove the *actus reus*. Lack of *mens rea* will not result in an acquittal. This suggests that if insanity is established, lack of *mens rea* is not available as a separate defence. If the accused's mental state does not satisfy the *McNaughtan Rules*, then they are entitled to an acquittal on the grounds of lack of *mens rea* (like *Clarke*).

In the case of *Thomas*, the appellant's conviction was quashed because:

> the jury may well have supposed that the appellant would only have been incapable of forming the necessary specific intentions if she had been legally insane . . . In our judgment, that first matter was a material irregularity which justifies the quashing of the appellant's conviction.

So as the law stands a defendant who doesn't satisfy the *McNaughtan Rules* can argue lack of *mens rea* on the basis of a mental disorder (or at least supported by evidence of a mental disorder), and there is no way to impose treatment, supervision or monitoring. The Law Commission also takes this view in their 2013 discussion document:

> 1: That if a person is non-culpable because of mental disorder, then that should be the true ground for the verdict, not the presence or absence of mens rea
>
> We consider that the analysis which depends purely on whether the elements of an offence (the *actus reus* and *mens rea*) are satisfied can lead to unwelcome results, as described below, and also that it fails to reflect what a mental disorder defence is about. Our analysis of the foundations of an insanity defence led us to conclude that it is essentially a denial of criminal responsibility due to a person's lack of capacity. That effectively amounts

> to a plea: “I, the defendant, deny responsibility for what it is I have done. I do so on the basis of my medical condition at the time, irrespective of whether I could be said to have had any particular *mens rea* at the time”. If the accused’s medical condition explains why he or she either did or did not have the relevant *mens rea* for the offence, then the defence should apply. Similarly, if his or her medical condition was such that he or she did not have the capacity to avoid performing the proscribed conduct, then it does not matter whether the offence required any particular *mens rea* or not.

Their conclusion is that

> there should be a defence which allows for a special verdict where the case is not proved against the accused because of his or her mental disorder as well as where it is proved because of the mental disorder.
>
> (Law Commission, 2013)

The expanded test for capacity would apply to more defendants pleading a lack of *mens rea* due to a medical condition (whether a mental disorder or not), and so a greater number of potentially dangerous people would be monitored and treated. This would have cost implications. There might also be implications for stigmatization of more people who pose only a minor risk. Further, the Law Commission’s proposals do not seem to prevent bypassing of social control mechanisms.

De facto categorization on the basis of continuing dangerousness

It seems to be implicit in some of the cases where lack of *mens rea* alone as the basis of the defence that a judgment has been made about lack of continuing danger to the public. May Clarke was no danger, but Stephenson potentially was. There are cases where it seems likely that the *McNaughtan Rules* would be satisfied, and there seems to be no compulsion to try to prove insanity where the defendant is arguing a lack of *mens rea* due to a mental disorder. This appears to come under prosecutorial discretion. Roch LJ in *Thomas* quoted Watkins LJ in *R v. Dickie*:

> We have come to the conclusion that we are unable to say there are no circumstances in which a judge may of his own volition raise an issue of insanity and leave it to a jury, provided that if he chooses to do so there is relevant evidence which goes to all the factors involved in the M’Naghten test. We envisage, however, that circumstances in which a judge will do that will be exceptional and very rare.

Roch LJ adds:

> There may be cases, for example, cases of homicide, where an accused has raised a defence of, say, diminished responsibility where a judge would be entitled, of his own volition to raise the issue of insanity with the jury. However, it would have to be a rare and exceptional case. This was not such a case in our judgment.

This pragmatic approach was made more explicit in the case of Brian Thomas. The two experts instructed by prosecution and defence agreed that Mr Thomas was suffering from a sleep disorder. They also agreed that Mr Thomas required further psychiatric treatment, more for his own well-being than public safety (he was suicidal following the incident), and so the insanity verdict was appropriate.[1] The prosecution therefore did not pursue a guilty verdict, but required a special verdict for any necessary social control measures. The opinion of a psychiatrist approved under Section 12(2) of the Mental Health Act 1983 was required; this was given by Dr Jacob, who stated there would be no benefit from making a hospital order. The prosecution offered no further evidence, and the trial judge then instructed the jury to acquit. This decision was pragmatic and probably fair, but arguably legally incorrect – especially given the flexibility of disposal which would permit outpatient supervision or even an absolute discharge.

Automatism and strict liability

Non-insane automatism is a complete defence, applicable even to strict liability crimes. Whether or not insane automatism is a defence when there is no *mens rea* is debated. The decision in *DPP v. Harper* suggests that the insanity defence is not applicable where the crime requires no *mens rea*. Recently, a district judge stated that sleepwalking was no defence to drink driving (BBC News, 2014) (also see *Finegan v. Heywood*). However, Herring comments:

> it made no reference to an earlier decision, *Hennessy*, which had stated that insanity was a defence to a strict liability offence. Secondly, the reasoning used in *DPP v. Harper* was suspect. It was claimed that insanity is a denial of *mens rea*; however, if that was all insanity was there would be no need to have a special defence of insanity because any defendant who was legally insane would simply be able to claim they lacked the *mens rea* of the offence.
>
> (Herring, 2006)

Many legal commentators agree with this analysis (including this author). The problems of a lack of *mens rea* approach have been highlighted in US reforms of the insanity defence (Mackay, 1988). Some commentators state that strict liability crimes require no fault on the part of the accused, but the requirement for voluntary action suggests otherwise. The position is surely clear – strict liability

1 This is legally incorrect, as any commitment for his own safety ought to be civil commitment.

offences require no proof of *mens rea* but they do involve conduct and hence require commission of the relevant *actus reus.*

Smart discusses a number of examples of the lack of criminal responsibility for failing to do the impossible, even where the offence is strict liability, e.g. failing to stop and report an accident where the driver was oblivious to the accident (Smart, 1987). *Actus rei* include some mental elements – there is no sharp distinction between *actus reus* and *mens rea*. As well as the requirement for voluntariness, there are other subjective elements typically included under *actus rei* e.g. some knowledge in instances of possession, and the above example of failing to report an accident. Furthermore, acting often involves references to beliefs. Returning to the example of *Lamb*, it can be argued that the defendant did not shoot his victim, even though he pointed the gun at him and pulled the trigger. As Holmes (1881) put it "Even a dog knows the difference between being kicked and being stumbled over."

Robinson argues about the *actus reus/mens rea* distinction that:

> this most basic organizing distinction is not coherent. Rather than being useful to criminal law theory, it is harmful because it creates ambiguity in discourse and hides important doctrinal differences of which criminal law should take account. I suggest we abandon this distinction in favour of other conceptualizations.
>
> (Robinson, 1993)

Even in the problematic case of *Larsonneur*, there was arguably a required mental element. Larsonneur had been deported from the Irish Free State in the custody of the police back to England, where she was convicted for being found in the UK despite being refused leave to land. Most commentators argue that she should not have been convicted for a situation over which she had no control. However, Lanham argues that Larsonneur was at fault for going to the Irish Free State, from where it was inevitable she would be deported back to England. She set into motion the chain of events (Lanham, no date). Of course, there was not the usual close nexus between the *mens rea* and *actus reus*, but it can be argued that there was a fault element.

The same principle applies to crimes of omission – where the accused is unable to fulfil their duties through no fault of their own, they should not be held liable. Thus, parents and carers can be found guilty for injuries and illness due to wilful neglect (*R v. Stone and Dobinson*), but not for failing to provide the appropriate level of care despite their best efforts (*R v. Sheppard*, *R v. Hopkins*).

Criminal responsibility

Amnesia

The issue of amnesia, whilst problematic for the defendant, has been dealt with clearly by the courts in *Podola*. There it was held that amnesia alone was not a sufficient ground for unfitness to plead, because the defendant could still direct his defence, even if he had to be informed of his actions by his defence counsel. That decision was based largely on policy issues, because of the difficulties in determining whether amnesia is genuine or not. There is also the issue that it is irrelevant to criminal culpability, if not criminal liability. An individual with dementia, for example, may not remember certain acts, but at the time clearly had moral ownership of them. Someone who has consumed large amounts of alcohol may similarly fail to remember his actions (White, 2003).

The issue with amnesia is not so much about culpability, but whether the defendant should be liable for criminal punishment. Amnesia causes problems for the communicative model of criminal punishment. It could be argued that someone with no memory for illegal acts cannot have their wrongdoing effectively communicated to them. Duff argues that amnesia renders the accused unfit to plead, as he is unable to answer for his actions (Duff, 1986). Punishment of those who cannot recall their actions is permissible even under the communicative account of criminal justice, since they can be informed of their actions. For example, a defendant with sexsomnia accused of rape can be confronted with DNA evidence and will then able to take some ownership of his "act". The person with dementia mentioned above would be a different matter – even if he were able to direct his own defence, if the communicative function of the law was impossible (although the two functions are unlikely to be independent) then arguably he should not be held criminally liable. It would be inhumane and morally wrong to punish someone who continued to be perplexed by his predicament.

Ownership and psychological continuity

As noted, there have been parallels drawn between parasomnias and multiple personality disorder (MPD), which is also known as dissociative identity disorder (DID). In both conditions, there are issues about the ownership of the crime, as well as legal personality. In MPD/DID, there is a host personality, with one or more separate identities known as "alters" that control behaviour at different times. It is believed this condition may arise as a protective mechanism against past trauma. It must be noted at this point that the status of MPD/DID is contested, and considered by many forensic mental health professionals to be either part of borderline personality disorder or a product of therapy, especially those trying to "recover" memories (also linked with the iatrogenic condition "false memory syndrome"). Saks describes the three distinct approaches which have been taken in the United States towards defendants with putative MPD/DID:

> The first view found in the courts is that a multiple is not guilty by reason of insanity ("NGRI") if the alter that is in control at the time of the act meets the insanity test of the particular jurisdiction. Thus, experts are directed to look at the mental state of that alter. If the alter, for instance, were psychotic and did not know what she was doing, the multiple would be criminally insane. Or if the alter were a child who did not know what she

> was doing—which is not always the case since child alters are not actually children—the multiple would also be insane. Otherwise, the multiple would be guilty of the crime.
>
> The second view of courts is that a multiple is insane if any alter meets the insanity test. This view is less well grounded in the courts because the decisions that take this position also contain language suggestive of the first position. For example, in *State v. Rodrigues*, the court reviews the expert's testimony about each of the three alters' knowledge at some length.
>
> The third view of the courts is found in a Tenth Circuit case, *United States v. Denny-Shaffer*. This view suggests that a multiple is criminally insane if the host personality did not plan or participate in the offense. In essence, Denny-Shaffer takes the position that the "defendant" is the host personality. This view is quite plausible but, as I shall argue, does not go quite far enough.

He goes on to propose a fourth test, that

> a person suffering from MPD should not be held responsible for a crime unless all of her alters knew about and acquiesced in the crime.
>
> (Saks, 2001)

If it was held that the sleepwalker's actions were due to a repressed desire, it could be argued that this is very similar to a second, hidden personality, which only acts during a parasomnia. On any of the tests mentioned by Saks, the sleepwalker would not be held liable. The English courts have not heard any arguments that MPD/DID might exempt the defendant from criminal responsibility other than by satisfying the *McNaughtan Rules* in the usual way. The court agreed with the expert witness in one such case that "A depersonalised intent is nevertheless an intent" (Rix and Clarkson, 1994; Rix, 2011).

However, Williams considered that dissociation could support an acquittal, but that the evidence should be tested by "skilled and deeply sceptical cross-examination" (Williams, no date). The difference between dissociative states and fugue amnesia must be emphasized here, as there is some confusion and conflation in the literature. Simple amnesia for the reasons above does not have the same connotation of lack of ownership, but some authors use the term fugue for dissociative states where depersonalization occurs. An example of the latter from Australia is the case of *Radford*, where the defendant stated he felt like an observer, as if his "whole body was just a head about two feet above the shoulder – the right shoulder of the soldier". This account is somewhat reminiscent of "out of body" experiences. Other dissociative experiences are less dramatic e.g. *Burgess* who had fragmentary amnesia for the attack on his friend.

The issue of lack of psychological continuity is not a new one – it is common in folk psychology to speak of someone "not being himself" or that certain behaviour is "not like him", to mean that the person's behaviour is uncharacteristic of him. When someone's behaviour is dramatically transformed by a brain tumour or a medical treatment, often there is an intuitive reaction to excuse their actions as not indicative of intrinsically bad moral character. For example, there has been a case reported of a man who became suddenly interested in child pornography. A brain tumour was diagnosed, and this behaviour ceased when the tumour was resected. When the behaviour recurred, brain scans showed that the tumour had recurred also. People with brain tumours often have questions about identity and ownership of their acts – when the late Labour politician Mo Mowlam learned that she may have had her brain tumour for many years, she asked "[So] good old Mo, larger than life Mo . . . it could all be because of the tumour? [But] which part's the real me?" (Cooke, 2010) A similar issue arises with persons who have had neurosurgery, particularly deep brain stimulator (DBS) implants. These devices modify brain activity in a select part of the brain by means of electrical impulses. Are these devices *causing* particular behaviours? Should they be counted as an internal or external cause? Would it be logical to treat them differently from drug treatments or not?

It has been argued that even if the court does not accept that there is objective psychological discontinuity, the subjective psychological discontinuity experienced by the defendant entails that the communicative function of the criminal law is impaired (they do not have "ownership" of their acts) and so the person with DID should not be held criminally liable. Do these issues apply to the sleepwalker? The very limited studies of the brain during parasomnia suggest that (at least for some) the executive functions are disabled, and limbic system-driven behaviour becomes unrestrained. This could be likened to the fictional Dr Jekyll/Mr Hyde dichotomy. A proportion of people suffering sexsomnia exhibit different sexual behaviour during episodes compared to their waking selves – they may be rougher, gentler, or even assume a different sexual orientation. The partner of one man acquitted of rape on the grounds of sexsomnia described his behaviour:

> It's like he's hypnotised and someone's got the remote control on. He's disgusted with himself. He just can't help it.
>
> (Bentley, 2013)

Whether or not hypnosis/post-hypnotic suggestion could amount to legal automatism is a moot question. I could find no British judgment where this issue has arisen, but some US jurisdictions recognize the possibility. As noted above, Moore included post-hypnotic acts within the class of actions without agency. If the caricature of the hypnotized individual as someone whose will had been completely subsumed was true, this would undoubtedly qualify as automatism (although there would be considerable evidential difficulty and policy concerns about accepting such a defence). There are two main schools of thought about hypnosis – "state" and "non-state". The state school believe that hypnosis involves a special state of altered consciousness. The "non-state" school of hypnotists believe that the hypnotized person is simply suggestible. There is little support from either school for the notion that a hypnotized individual has no control over their actions at all.

In short, in the British courts, ownership of one's acts generally has little relevance to criminal responsibility. The exception may be psychotic episodes where the accused has been commanded by a divine figure to do something.

Intention and automatism

The difficulty for laypeople (and of course juries) with the idea of the automaton is that very often there seems to be an agent; that is, there is an apparent author of the acts. As Moore puts it:

> Cases of sleepwalking, post-hypnotic acts, and similar acts are often sufficiently complicated that they appear to be intelligently directed actions. In such cases, one is loathe not to attribute these acts to some agency, but if not to X [the defendant], then to whom?
>
> (Moore, 1979)

Bird, Newson and Dembny observe that the person committing the illegal act, whether whilst sleepwalking or in some other state, is rarely the stereotypical shuffling automaton:

> Complete lack of consciousness and control rarely accompanies a potentially criminal act; hence, difficult judgments need to be made about the degree of loss of consciousness and attention at the specific time.
>
> (Bird, Newson and Dembny, 2009)

A defendant with a total loss of control could not walk, let alone perform the more complicated motor acts necessary for many criminal acts. In this respect, the work of Schopp is most helpful. In his monograph, he analyses those capacities which distinguish automatism from moral agency (Schopp, 1991). For Schopp, sleepwalking is automatism because although the sleepwalker has some vague awareness, he does not will his actions. The executive functions of the brain are paralysed and he cannot be truly described as a moral agent. Children and animals can make purposive actions directed towards goals, but we do not attribute criminal responsibility to them (neither would we categorize them as automatons).

Also, we can draw on cognitive neuroscience, which describes actions as arising from either from the higher centres (responsible for executive functions) or elsewhere (limbic system, motor cortex, epilepsy in the frontal or temporal lobes). Thus, actions during complex partial seizures may appear to be purposive, although they are stereotyped. A personal experience of the author involved being almost bowled over by a patient in a hospital corridor – the patient was having a temporal lobe epileptic seizure.

In English law it is now settled that automatism is a denial of the *actus reus* rather than the *mens rea* (this is not true for all common law jurisdictions). For crimes where a particular intent is required, this distinction makes little practical difference in court. Intention has several distinct meanings, which are drawn out by Anscombe. She describes "intention-in-acting", "acting intentionally" and "intention for the future". "Intention-in-acting" may describe the *mens rea*, the reason for an action (although many crimes require only recklessness, knowledge or negligence) (Anscombe, 1957). In crimes of strict liability, all that is required is "acting intentionally" (or voluntary action). This is illustrated by the case of *Attorney-General's Reference (No. 4 of 2000)*. Here a bus driver who was unfamiliar with the controls of the particular bus he was driving pressed the accelerator pedal instead of the brake pedal. Tragically the bus shot forward and travelled across a pedestrian island where it struck a number of pedestrians, two of whom died from their injuries. He did not do this intentionally; however, his action in pressing that particular pedal was intentional and deliberate, and therefore not an automatism. His actions were accidental, but not involuntary. His intention in pressing that pedal was irrelevant, because the aim of the law is to protect the public by ensuring that drivers take all necessary precautions. Clearly there is not the same level of recklessness and disregard for safety as a driver speeding around a blind corner on the wrong side of the road, but nonetheless there was a failure of the necessary care and attention. To take another example, in the film *Lethal Weapon 3* (1992) Murtagh is practising a roundhouse kick at Riggs's urging and kicks over the water cooler. Although he didn't intend to kick over the water cooler, nonetheless his kick was intentional and so he was responsible (but probably less so than his partner).

Another very similar distinction is between de re and de dicto, which can be broadly considered as distinguishing general intent from specific intent. The list of basic and specific intent crimes in English law is based more on policy than principle. However, there is a logical distinction between crimes with a *mens rea* satisfied by proof of negligence and recklessness (basic intent) and crimes with a minimum *mens rea* of knowledge or intent. Lord Diplock in *Caldwell* quoted with approval Lord Elwyn-Jones LC in *Majewski* who stated that:

> self-induced intoxication is no defence to a crime in which recklessness is enough to constitute the necessary mens rea.

The Law Commission stated in 1995:

> It is apparent . . . that there is no general agreement on the test which should be applied in order to distinguish offences of basic and of specific intent.

Coles and Jang argue that intoxication cannot affect a person's intent (Coles and Jang, 1996). The main effect of alcoholic intoxication is disinhibition, which does not affect intent in the eyes of the law (although it can nonetheless prevent the formation of a specific intent). It could be argued that the same principles should apply to risk-taking such as a sexsomniac sharing a bed with a stranger, or a sleepwalker drinking alcohol when he knows it triggers his sleepwalking. An English case that demonstrates the doctrine is *Heard (Lee)*, where the defendant whilst intoxicated had intentionally rubbed his penis against a police officer's leg. It was held that sexual assault was a crime of basic intent, and so it was only required that the defendant intentionally committed the *actus reus.* Voluntary intoxication was not a defence. This demonstrates that "basic intent" is the same as "general intent", and so the basis of the decision hinges on the de re/de dicto distinction. His only defence would have been if his touching had been completely accidental or involuntary. Hughes LJ stated:

> Because the offence is committed only by intentional touching, we agree that the judge's direction that the touching must be deliberate was correct. To flail about, stumble or barge around in an unco-ordinated manner which results in an unintended touching, objectively sexual, is not this offence. If to do so when sober is not this offence, then nor is it this offence to do so when intoxicated. It is also possible that such an action would not be judged by the jury to be objectively sexual, on the basis that it was clearly accidental, but whether that is so or not, we are satisfied that in such a case this offence is not committed. The intoxication, in such a situation, has not impacted on intention. Intention is simply not in question.
>
> (para 23)

However, the sense that his touching was intentional is slightly different from that in *Attorney-General's Reference (No. 4 of 2000).* This is because the minimum *mens rea* for sexual assault is recklessness, whereas the minimum *mens rea* of causing death by dangerous driving is negligence.

Wittgenstein defines actions as characterized by the absence of surprise (about the action, not the consequences). Thus, Wittgenstein would agree that the bus driver's depression of the accelerator was an action, even though the consequences were unwanted. This definition works well for examples like "Alien Hand Phenomenon", "Utilization Behaviour" and "Environmental Dependency Syndrome" where actions occur without conscious desires but in response to environmental cues. Certainly, many of the actions during sleepwalking are reactions to the environment (although in this case the person has impaired consciousness). The earliest jurists when pronouncing on the lack of responsibility for acts committed during sleep added the proviso that the sleeper must not be shown to have planned these acts, e.g. by placing a weapon to hand prior to falling asleep. I have not come across any cases where this was an issue, and if there was any preparation it would raise questions about whether the episode was a genuine automatism or not. This would follow the precedent of *Gallagher*, who had drunk whiskey for "Dutch courage" before killing his wife.

The neuroscientist Blakemore considers there is no difference between such actions and intentional actions:

> All our actions are the product of the activity of our brains. It seems to me to make no sense (in scientific terms) to try and distinguish sharply between acts that result from conscious intention and those that are pure reflexes or that are caused by disease or damage or damage to the brain. We feel ourselves,

usually, to be in control of our actions, but that feeling is in itself a product of the brain, whose machinery has been designed, on the basis of its functional utility, by natural selection.

(Blakemore, 1998)

He specifically rejects the folk psychology on which the law relies. It is the experience of humanity that these actions *feel* very different. However, he acknowledges that the two spheres of descriptive science and normative attribution of responsibility have little in common.

Moore discusses the effects of unconscious mental states on responsibility (Moore, 1979). It has been posited in the past that sleepwalkers are acting on unconscious desires. The expert witnesses I interviewed generally concluded that sleepwalkers were not acting on unconscious desires, but even if they were, they should not be held criminally responsible. Reznek talks about "Quearthlings", who are able to instruct their sleeping selves to perform acts during sleepwalking by reciting the instructions over and over. Following the precedent of *Gallagher*, the Quearthling would be held criminally responsible (Reznek, 1997). If the sleepwalker's rumination on an intention to cause harm resulted in that harm being acted out during sleepwalking, this would pose the question of whether or not they should be found criminally responsible.

There is an interesting contrast between the approaches to purportedly "repressed desires" and desires that the actor is consciously aware of, but which they suppress by an act of will or conscience.

In the case of *Kingston*, the accused had paedophilic tendencies and committed a sexual assault. He claimed he had been drugged without his knowledge. The victim of the offence was also drugged, and Kingston's co-defendant had videoed Kingston having sex with the boy for the purposes of blackmailing Kingston. The jury heard evidence about Kingston's collection of hardcore pornography, which was allowed because it established a propensity for homosexual acts. The ratio of Kingston is that he was still able to form the requisite *mens re*a for indecent assault. It is not explicitly stated how the video evidence showed that Kingston had formed the *mens rea* for indecent assault, although it is asserted in cross-examination that "You are obviously enjoying yourself". Are Kingston's actions distinguishable from those of a sexsomniac except by the principle of "*In somno voluntas non erat libera*"? What exactly does it mean to "form the *mens rea*" in this case?

Kingston argued before the Court of Appeal:

> A vital distinction exists between *mens rea* and intent. Intent is only *mens*. The use of the term intent in modern authorities rather than evil intent effectively leaves offences requiring general intent only as offences of strict liability save in cases where it is clear that the *actus reus* was not willed.
>
> A distinction exists between voluntary intoxication, which is culpable, and involuntary intoxication, which is excusable. Excusable intoxication may be of three degrees: (1) a relaxation of inhibitions so that acts are committed or permitted which would not be committed if the person's mind

> were unaffected . . . contrast *Reg. v. Davies* [1983] Crim.L.R. 741); (2) a dulling of the mind and its functions so that a person cannot tell right from wrong . . .; and (3) an effective paralysis of the higher mind, namely, automatism, or no capacity to form intent. All three states should excuse the actions of the person affected. In regard to state (3) there has always been a requirement for *mens rea* in all offences except those of strict liability. There has never been any doubt that an intoxicated man may lack the necessary specific intent, implicit in the act of becoming intoxicated attracting culpability: see *Reg. v. Majewski* [1977] A.C. 443.

This argument was continued before the House of Lords Appellate Committee:

> Even if the trial judge were right in equating *mens rea* with intent, his direction is still unsatisfactory. The jury could still be asked: did the accused intend the alleged acts. That is unsatisfactory for there are very few cases where a person does not intend his acts.
>
> If intent is used in place of *mens rea* there must be a need to distinguish between the higher mind (the seat of reason, conscience, operative fear of retribution) and the lower mind (the basic motor/instinctive control of the body): see Jerome Hall, *General Principles of Criminal Law*, 2nd edn (1960), p. 468. The Court of Appeal rejected an analysis of intent in terms of the higher and lower mind in favour of maintaining a distinction between intent and *mens rea*.

Kingston's argument hinges on the lack of culpability for intoxication which caused his lapse in controlling his paedophilic urges, thus making his intentional action or mens distinct from the *mens rea*. As Lord Taylor put it:

> the purpose of the criminal law is to inhibit by proscription and by penal sanction antisocial acts which individuals may otherwise commit. Its unspoken premise is that people may have tendencies and impulses to do those things which are considered sufficiently objectionable to be forbidden. Having paedophiliac inclinations and desires is not proscribed; putting them into practice is. If the sole reason why the threshold between the two has been crossed is or may have been that the inhibition that the law requires has been removed by the clandestine act of a third party, the purposes of the criminal law are not served by nevertheless holding that the person performing the act is guilty of an offence. A man is not responsible for a condition produced "by stratagem or the fraud of another". If, therefore, drink or a drug, surreptitiously administered, causes a person to lose his self-control and for that reason to form an intent which he would not otherwise have formed, it is consistent with the principle that the law should exculpate him, for the operative fault is not his. The law permits a finding that the intent formed was not a criminal intent or, in other words, that the involuntary intoxication negatives the *mens rea*.

The House of Lords ruled that the formation of *mens rea* was the deciding issue, and whether the intoxication was voluntary or not is irrelevant to this. The simple commission of a voluntary act was sufficient for liability. They quoted with approval the Court of Appeal in *Sheehan*:

> the mere fact that the defendant's mind was affected by drink so that he acted in a way in which he would not have done had he been sober does not assist him at all, provided that the necessary intention was there. A drunken intent is nevertheless an intent.

This makes it clear that the lack of culpability for involuntary intention is irrelevant to the issue of intent. It was only necessary to prove that he intentionally committed the act (thus constituting the *actus reus*), because indecent assault where the act is unequivocally indecent is a crime of basic intent (where the act is equivocal as regards decency, it is an act of specific intent). As the defence argued:

> The use of the term intent in modern authorities rather than evil intent effectively leaves offences requiring general intent only as offences of strict liability save in cases where it is clear that the *actus reus* was not willed.
>
> (Court of Appeal)

This appears to make crimes of general or basic intent effectively crimes of strict liability (with the probable exception of accidental actions, as per Attorney-General's Reference (No 4 of 2000) – see above). The comments of Lord Simon in *Morgan* seem to support this: "By 'crimes of basic intent' I mean those crimes whose definition expresses (or, more often, implies) a *mens rea* which does not go beyond the *actus reus*". However, his further explanation makes it clear that he is referring to the de re/de dicto distinction, where only crimes of ulterior (or specific) intent require an intention in acting, rather than simply intentionally acting. It also means there is little practical difference between voluntary and involuntary intoxication unless the involuntary intoxication is so profound as to result in automatism. This ruling emphasizes that voluntary intoxication is not a defence per se to crimes of specific intent, so the question is not whether or not the intoxicated person could form the necessary *mens rea*, but whether or not they did. Evidence of the effects of intoxication may support the argument that he did not. This ruling could be construed as meaning that the sexsomniac cannot argue lack of *mens rea* when he has committed an unequivocally indecent act; he must argue automatism. Schopp states:

> The problematic cases of automatism are those in which the defendant acted in such a manner as to indicate that he not only knew what he was doing he acted in that way for the purpose of performing the act constituting the objective elements of the offence.
>
> The defendant's mental states at the time of the offence are usually inferred on the basis of evidence regarding his behavior and speech . . . Automatism

> cases sometimes involve acts done in a skilful, coordinated manner, apparently for the purpose of achieving some specific end . . . Other defendants have not only performed the act constituting the offense in an apparently purposeful manner; they have engaged in preliminary behavior apparently intended to arrange circumstances in such a manner as to facilitate the offence. For example, one defendant called the victim over to the window, ostensibly to see an animal swimming in the water below, then struck the victim with a mallet and threw him from the window. [refers to case of Charlson]
>
> These events simply do not provide evidence from which to infer the defendant did not know what they were doing . . . these actors apparently selected a projected act-tree as their action-plan precisely because it was expected to produce an act-tree including the behavior constituting the offense. Unless this appearance is seriously misleading, these defendants knew what they were doing, and they performed their offenses purposely. Thus, neither a failure-of-proof defence regarding the culpability element nor the "nature and quality" disjunct of the McNaughtan test would apply.
>
> (Schopp, 1991)

Actions during parasomnias that are satisfying the appetite for either food or sexual satisfaction can be seen as fulfilling a desire and therefore intentional. Indeed, Schopp and Moore would consider the sleep eater or sexsomniac to be acting intentionally, but not voluntarily. Alternatively, it can be argued that despite appearances the sexsomniac is not intentionally acting and so he can argue lack of *mens rea*. Sleep experts would no doubt argue there is a compelling case that for parasomnias, appearances are seriously misleading. Again this is by recourse to the principle of "*In somno voluntas non erat libera*".

It is also difficult to reconcile this decision with cases like *R v. T*, who by the same criteria had clearly formed the *mens rea* for robbery. Here the defendant had been saying "I'm ill, I'm ill" during the course of a robbery. She had been raped a few days prior to this incident, and was diagnosed with post-traumatic stress disorder. The distinction between *Kingston* and another case of involuntary intoxication, *Hardie* (see below), appears to rest largely on the effect of diazepam on judgment of risk in *Hardie* where the requisite minimum *mens rea* was objective recklessness.

Disinhibition

The issue of whether the connection between intention and *mens rea* was affected by disinhibition was the deciding factor in the case of *Kingston.* Kingston's argument was that he would not have acted on his paedophilic urges if he had not been drugged, and in support of this contention he had not offended prior to this. The legal arguments were heavily dominated by issues of policy, with fears that an acquittal would "open the floodgates" of defendants claiming to have been involuntarily drugged. The ratio however was that despite the involuntary intoxication he was still able to form the requisite *mens rea* and on the basis of the video evidence did so. The decision of the House of Lords Appellate Committee is controversial, and many consider that the case was wrongly decided. It has the appearance of punishing bad character (see below re justification of act requirement).

Contrast this case with *Hardie* where the trial judge held that "voluntary self-administration of the drug was irrelevant as a defence since its effect could not negative *mens rea*", but the Appeal Court quashed his conviction stating that:

> under section 1(2) of the Act of 1971 a defendant's state of mind had to be considered only when he did the relevant act and the requirements of the subsection were established if the defendant when doing that act created an obvious risk that property would be destroyed and life endangered and gave no thought to the possibility of either risk; that, in considering his state of mind, the self-administration of a sedative or soporific drug, even in excess, did not automatically raise a conclusive presumption that its effects could not negative mens rea in the way that self-induced intoxication by alcohol or dangerous drugs could; that the trial judge had misdirected the jury that the effects of such a drug leading to a defendant's incapacity were irrelevant; and that, accordingly, the conviction had to be quashed since the jury should have been directed that if they concluded that by taking the drug a defendant could not appreciate the risks to property and persons from his actions, they should consider whether the taking of the drug was itself reckless.

However, the Appeal Court held in *McGhee* (rolled-up appeal with *Coley*) that a combination of temazepam and alcohol taken for the relief of tinnitus and causing disinhibition could not amount to automatism – Hughes LJ stated emphatically that "Disinhibition is exactly not automatism."

The fact that involuntary intoxication makes a choice harder is irrelevant – as Fitzjames Stephen put it, "If the impulse was resistible, the fact that it proceeded from disease is no excuse at all."

The trial judge directed the jury in *Hardie* that "an intoxicated intent was still an intent". It is not clear why diazepam could negate *mens rea* but temazepam (another benzodiazepine which has an identical effect) could not. It has been suggested that *Hardie* was decided *per incuriam*, as the effect of diazepam was misunderstood. Certainly, the decision to distinguish diazepam from "dangerous drugs" was opaque.

Crosby (2010) suggests that Kingston could be excused based on character theory. Although it could be argued that it was bad character that he was attracted to young boys, it could also be said that he showed good character in normally resisting in such urges – thus his offending was "out of character". Involuntary intoxication was mooted as an excuse in Hale's (1736) *Pleas of the Crown*, who classified "induced witlessness" as an excuse when induced by a negligent physician or "the contrivance of his enemies". Kingston could not be a clearer instance of incapacity produced by "the contrivance of [ones] enemies" – he was allegedly given the drugs in an attempt to blackmail him. Sullivan's "destabilization" defence would apply where "D is blamelessly destabilised by exceptional circumstances to such an extent that he acts in a way that he would not otherwise have done" (Crosby, 2010).

This would only be applicable in cases of "good character" – the absence of relevant convictions. Horder (1993) suggests an alternative solution to the problem of involuntary intoxication might be the extension of the diminished responsibility plea. Denno (2003) makes a similar suggestion. Diminished responsibility applies to a range of offences in California and South Africa, reducing the category of the crime (Wasik, 1982). This would be an alternative to the general/specific intention distinction made in English law.

This is an area where the Law Commission's proposed test for capacity would bring some welcome clarity. They suggest that the criminally responsible defendant should have the ability:

- rationally to form a judgment about the relevant conduct or circumstances;
- to understand the wrongfulness of what he or she is charged with having done; or
- to control his or her physical acts in relation to the relevant conduct or circumstances.

(Law Commission, 2013)

Arguably those who are sufficiently disinhibited will be unable to rationally form a judgment about the relevant conduct or circumstance – they are no longer effective practical reasoners. Similarly, the parasomniac may be able to perform complex motor tasks, but they have no access to the executive functions required to be criminally responsible as per the Law Commission's test.

Alcohol and sleepwalking: the legal question

There is widespread concern about the acquittal of individuals who are intoxicated on the basis of flimsy medical evidence in some cases. The exact reasons for this are not known, but may include a combination of these factors:

- the confusing law on automatism
- the standard and burden of proof for non-insane automatism and lack of *mens rea* defences
- the nature of some of the expert evidence on the probability of alcohol causing sleepwalking
- problems with the directions to the jury
- lack of application of the strict law on alcohol and culpability
- reluctance to apply the special verdict
- reluctance to convict intoxicated defendants for serious crimes.

There is probably no need for legislation to solve most of these problems. *Burgess* provides the precedent for sleepwalking being considered an insane automatism.

Since sleepwalking is an insane automatism, once the defendant has been found to be a sleepwalker, any examination of the cause of the particular episode is irrelevant to the legal question. Fault is irrelevant to insanity, whereas prior fault is an important bar to the defence of automatism.

There is an issue that the intoxicated individual is considered to have the *mens rea* for crimes of basic intent merely by the fact of voluntarily becoming intoxicated. There is mismatch between the fault element and the label (and also the punishment), and the Butler Committee (1975) suggested an alternative of "dangerous intoxication" to remedy this. The Law Commission in 1995 recommended there be no defence "where the automatism is caused partly by voluntary intoxication and partly by some other factor" (Law Commission, 1995).

This doctrine would remove the difficulties for the jury in determining criminal responsibility where both alcohol and another trigger for sleepwalking are operating in a particular case. An example of this is *Pooley*, where Judge Tyrer directed the jury that if alcohol was the sole trigger for his sleepwalking, then this was self-inflicted and not an excuse (*Bucks Herald*, 2007). Regardless of the scientific support for a link, there is a compelling policy argument for not considering alcohol-related parasomnic episodes as an excuse. It is also a perfectly ethical position to consider that the accused is entitled to argue any defence that the law allows, that the expert witness is there to assist the jury, and that it is for the jury to decide rather than the expert witness.

6 Expert evidence

This chapter is concerned primarily with the legal rules on expert evidence, but also deals with some particular issues with medical science. Expert evidence is central to the defences of automatism and insanity, as these issues are nearly always outside the jury's expertise. The expert witness's role is to assist the court – in the case of trial by indictment, specifically to assist the jury. The courts do not want "trial by experts" to take over from trial by jury, and so expert evidence must provide a basis for the opinion given so that jurors can weight and evaluate conflicting expert opinions. Where experts agree, the accused may not be subjected to a criminal trial. However, this diversion would avoid the possibility of measures to reassure the public, such as a supervision order and/or a Sexual Harm Prevention Order.

Expert evidence is a particular issue with automatism for a number of reasons. Firstly, with certain conditions such as sleepwalking, the lack of the requisite *mens rea* and *actus reus* will be assumed once the presence of the condition has been proven to the satisfaction of the jury. This makes the expert witness more influential than in the typical insanity defence, where the diagnosis is usually relatively unimportant as the degree of impairment is the crucial factor.[1] It is not whether or not the person suffers from schizophrenia that is important, but the effect of this disorder on their ability to know the nature of their actions (or less commonly their ability to know right from wrong). This makes automatism due to certain disorders effectively a status defence. Secondly, the medical practitioners who specialize in the relevant medical conditions usually do not have the same experience and expertise as forensic psychiatrists (with the possible exception of neuropsychiatrists). They will be less familiar with the demands of the criminal courts, especially with regards to criminal responsibility. They also tend to be more opposed to the use of the special verdict. Thirdly, there is no functional assessment to guide either expert witnesses or jurors, equivalent to the *McNaughtan Rules.*

1 This is not the case in some jurisdictions, where the presence of certain psychiatric disorders is sufficient for the insanity defence. In Norway, for example, the diagnosis of a psychotic illness fulfils the criteria for legal insanity. Also the Durham rule only required that the conduct was the product of a mental disorder.

These three issues will be examined further. Fourthly, the best witness to the accused's behaviour will often be the victim. The expert witness instructed by the defence is often not permitted to interview the victim.

Forensic psychiatrists have frequent exposure to the criminal courts; the preparation of medicolegal reports is a major part of their professional duties. They understand that the presence of a particular disorder does not automatically provide an excuse on the basis of causation of the behaviour or mere diminution of culpability. This issue tends to be problematic for expert witnesses outside of forensic psychiatry/psychology. There are many examples in the literature where a striking character change has occurred when the accused developed a particular condition. If the "but for" test were applied, the accused would not be held responsible. Morse describes this as the "fundamental psycholegal error", which is "to believe that causation, especially abnormal causation, is per se an excusing condition" (Morse, 2006b).

It is not the case in law that even where a dramatic personality change can be clearly attributed to a medical disorder that this automatically provides an excuse. An example of this is the patient with a brain tumour that produced a distinct change in behaviour (described in Chapter 4) (Burns and Swerdlow, 2003). There have been a vast number of excuses that have been argued in American courts, as detailed in Dershowitz's polemic about criminal defences in the USA, *The Abuse Excuse* (1994), which is concerned with expert evidence being perverted to defeat the ends of justice. The examples he cites include "Super Bowl Sunday Syndrome", "Urban Survival", and "Black Rage". The most famous example of all is the "Twinkie Defense" which entered the public consciousness, and indeed legal mythology, as the archetypal exploitation of junk science by unethical lawyers who claimed that over-consumption of Twinkies made Dan White kill Harvey Milk (Pogash, 2003). In fact, it has been widely misrepresented; the over-consumption of junk food was presented as the effect of White's mental state rather than the cause. This tendency has prompted terms like the "disappearing defendant" (Morse, 2006b).

Although it is a possibility that a jury could find that the accused was criminally responsible even though the illegal act occurred during an episode of sleepwalking (without other reasons for assigning guilt), there have been no reports of this happening. This means that the defence of automatism when caused by parasomnia effectively becomes a status defence. If the jury accept that the defendant was sleepwalking, they must acquit him. The aphorism "*In somno voluntas non erat libera*" (A sleeping person has no free will) has been accepted by the courts – at least until recently (see further below). This acceptance of the lack of capacity on the part of the accused gives the expert witness in such cases much more power than the forensic psychiatrist in a case where insanity is being pleaded. Although he may advance an opinion on the ultimate issue of whether or not the defendant is insane, the jury decides the issue. They can and do reject the unanimous opinion of experts instructed by both defence and prosecution. However, some expert witnesses have found the issue of whether or not parasomnic episodes involves a total loss of control has been argued in court. This demonstrates that the bipartite definition of automatism by Denning in *Bratty* is not being applied, and that the definition of "total loss of voluntary control" is not limited to driving cases.

The lack of a meaningful definition of automatism also contributes to the first issue. Although it is stated that as a matter of law, automatism requires a total loss of voluntary control, this has never been satisfactorily defined. A complete lack of neuromuscular control would be incompatible with virtually all *actus rei* (except where a loss of all control is culpable e.g. driving offences). The person would be unable to walk or talk. There are disorders where the sufferer has no intent at all, such as epilepsy, various movement disorders, and rare conditions such as alien hand syndrome. However, there are no recorded cases of liability in those circumstances. In the civil case of *Roberts v. Ramsbottom*, a driver was found liable for damages to vehicles despite suffering a stroke. By contrast, Tarleton was not found liable for demolishing a house during a hypoglycaemic episode (*Mansfield v. Weetabix*).

Further, medicolegal automatism typically involves an episodic disorder that involves reduced or absent consciousness. This limits the ability of the expert witness to determine the mental state of the defendant by direct questioning. The sole witness may be the complainant, who cannot be considered impartial. If the sole witness is the victim of a homicide, then it becomes very difficult to determine the mental state of the accused at all. The diagnosis of a sleepwalking episode can be difficult even for a medical expert. Mahowald asserts:

> [You] can prove someone is a sleepwalker . . . But that is only Part 1 of a two-part question. The second question is whether he was sleepwalking on the night of the murder. Only God can answer that.
>
> (Stryker, 1999)

In the absence of divine inspiration, the jury has to provide an answer.

The press coverage demonstrates that the public are fascinated by the idea that someone can commit crimes in their sleep. Expert witnesses trying to explain the state of automatism from other causes such as hypoglycaemia often draw an analogy with sleepwalking (Bell, 2010). For example, Prof Marks in the case of *Clarke (Trevor Norman)* stated that hypoglycaemia cause the defendant to "behave as an automaton able to perform certain habitual tasks but unable to appreciate their social consequences".[2]

A recent cinematic release about somnambulistic homicide was *Side Effects* (2013). The film deals well with some of the issues surrounding sleep disorders and the potential responsibility of prescribers for illegal acts triggered by adverse drug reactions. The basic plot is that a fictitious drug that can cause sleepwalking is blamed for a homicide (see Chapter 3 re the "Ambien defence"). The film-makers had clearly done their research, even if there are some minor quibbles (for example, the defence attorney describes a case that resembles *Falater*, except in this instance there is an acquittal).

2 From Professor Marks' medical report on Mr Clarke; permission was given to access this and quote from it.

One particular exchange that illustrated an important issue in forensic sleep disorders and automatism more generally occurred between Dr Banks, one of the protagonists, and his wife. She asks “Did the person do the thing? Are they guilty?“ and he replies “In this case, those are two very different things”. There was also a good discussion in court of legal responsibility and consciousness. During his testimony, Dr Banks compares the mental state of a sleepwalker with an insect:

Dr Banks (DB):	What makes us human, what differentiates us from let’s say insects, is that we have consciousness, an awareness of what we’re thinking and what we’re doing. If for example I’m hungry, I’m consciously aware of that, and so I go to the fridge and I make myself a sandwich.
Defence Attorney (DA):	So you intend to make a sandwich.
DB:	Yes.
DA:	So what you’re saying is that to have intent, you must also have consciousness?
Prosecution Attorney:	Objection Your Honour. The question calls for a legal conclusion, not a medical one.
Judge:	Overruled. You may continue.
DB:	Consciousness provides a context or meaning for our actions – if that part of you doesn’t exist, then basically we are functioning much like an insect where you just respond instinctively without a thought to what your actions mean.
DA:	And that part, that meaning to action, does that exist when we’re asleep?
DB:	No.
DA:	So without consciousness, how do we prove intent?
DB:	I don’t believe we can. (Personal transcript of DVD 49–51 mins)

That comparison is interesting, as it could be argued that mammals are a better example as their functioning is closer to humans. The point that motor functions are separate and distinct from the faculties that make us human and morally and legally responsible is well made. However, an expert witness would not be asked to comment on legal questions like this in reality.

There are some general principles that apply in all cases of automatism, partly because the mental condition of the accused at the time of the offence is generally so difficult to establish:

- Any disorder such as sleepwalking or epilepsy had presented before the index episode
- The crime is motiveless and out of character
- The behaviour demonstrated should not be goal-orientated, and there should be no evidence of planning

- The accused should have reduced or absent consciousness
- Confusion and bewilderment on the part of the accused, with no attempts to conceal the crime.

For some disorders, particularly parasomnias, it is common for sufferers not to receive a formal medical diagnosis for some years, and failure to seek medical help prior to arrest has no probative value (the NHS could not cope with every person who ever sleepwalked). There does need to be some independent corroboration of the disorder; this is crucial for legal reasons, but in the case of parasomnias, the sufferer himself will often be unaware of his behaviour. For many of the disorders that cause medicolegal automatism, there will be amnesia but it is not necessary.

It is for the jury to decide the facts of the case, and so it is not for the expert witness to state for example whether or not the accused had a motive or attempted to conceal the crime. Certain acts are ambiguous. Were there efforts to clean up attempts to conceal the crime or not? Was the accused lying or confabulating? Often the jury will be presented with expert evidence that differs in at least one significant particular. It is doubtful that there is a solution that can mould the messy business of expert evidence into the reliable "black box" that the legal system might be more comfortable with. As Gilson put it:

> law has a high expectation of science and scientists in this regard owing to the objectivity, rigour and precision extolled in its methods. It is disappointed when its evidence is doubtful, experts disagree or prove unreliable.
> (Gilson, 2012)

A lawyer sent me his opinion online of expert evidence regarding automatism:

> So here is my in-depth analysis of automatism, which I offer free, gratis and for nothing. Every so often some dozy twat of a driver falls asleep at the wheel and crashes into another vehicle, perhaps causing a death or two. When prosecuted, he will then try his hardest to argue that he didn't fall asleep at the wheel, no, perish the thought, he was suffering from narcolepsy or a rare attention deficit disorder or an unexplained quasi-epileptic attack. And after all, nobody can possibly see what was going on in his mind at the time and there are many rare neurological disorders of an intermittent nature. He may then find a gullible neurologist willing, for a fee, to prepare a convincing report that will enable the jury to acquit because there is a reasonable doubt.[3]

The case of *MacBrayne* would lend a certain amount of support to this cynical and pejorative view (Lazzari, 2011).

3 Personal communication from user with nym "The Todal" on uk.legal newsgroup on usernet.

Complex behaviour

Where the behaviour is complex, issues arise about whether or not it is compatible with medicolegal automatism, regardless of what mental state the accused was in at the time. Where sleepwalking behaviour is sufficiently complicated, the courts may not rely on the principle of "*in somno voluntas non erat libera*" (although sleepwalking actually arises out of sleep as such). They may fall back onto the formulation of a total loss of voluntary control. The problems with this definition have been recited in previous chapters. Certainly, the accused with particularly complex behaviour needs careful evaluation.

The folk psychological beliefs held by jurors may lead them to make erroneous conclusions about the compatibility of certain actions with parasomnia, and this is one of the major tasks of an expert witness to correct these and why they need to be clinicians with extensive experience of patients with parasomnia. Many motor tasks associated with parasomnias seem incompatible with sleep to the layperson, but the level of consciousness, presence or absence of executive function and duration are much more important. Thus, a list of the features of an episode is useful, especially where the particular acts may be ambiguous or their interpretation heavily dependent on context. This enables the jury to reach its own, possibly different, conclusions. For example, driving a highly familiar route is compatible with automaticity, but navigating an unfamiliar one is not. The difficulty with basing an evaluation of criminal responsibility on the compatibility of the behaviour with a particular medical condition is that the features of many of these conditions are still not fully elucidated. For example, it was once thought that penile erection was incompatible with sleepwalking. We now know this is not the case. Pressman considered that the ability to navigate shown by *Falater* (see Appendix D) ruled out sleepwalking, but it is now recognized this ability is preserved (Cartwright, 2000; Mitrovic and Katic, 2013). Weiss and del Busto noted:

> Parasomnias can be considered both mysterious and paradoxic. Actions during sleep can range from simple to complex, raising a fundamental question as to the nature of consciousness, often believed to be a mystery. In addition, these behaviors seem paradoxic, because they seem directed and purposeful and yet occur during a state of relative unconsciousness. One must ask, "What physical actions are possible during a sleeping state?" before judging whether free will was compromised or even absent. Whether those behaviors can be considered purposeful, voluntary, or culpable is a matter for evolving jurisprudence.
>
> (Weiss and del Busto, 2011)

Another forensic sleep expert stated:

> the behaviours that a lot of these people exhibit are really extraordinary, and if you take regular sleepwalking, ones that do not have forensic implications, the behaviours can be extraordinary, you don't have to extrapolate very far

> from the clinical complex sleepwalking population to the forensic behaviour. The behaviours can be extraordinarily protracted and extraordinarily complex, and sometimes they end up with medicolegal consequences, but often the ones that don't are still as impressive.
>
> (Rumbold, 2015)

To an extent, the literature is not helpful, as the considerable number of case reports generally highlight rare and extreme instances of parasomnia. An example is the case of Parks; individually, the aspects of the episode were possible during sleepwalking (although rare manifestations), but collectively the possibility of the entire episode representing sleepwalking is more and more remote with each complex behaviour. Some sleep experts believe that more complex behaviour occurs during a confusional arousal at the end of a sleepwalking episode, but confusional arousals are short-lived.

Some sleep experts believe that the longer sleep behaviours represent a merging of parasomnia with a psychogenic dissociative episode. Others believe that these episodes e.g. Kenneth Park's homicidal bout are purely dissociative in nature. One expert commenting on the possibility that Parks' episode was a sleep-related fugue stated:

> it probably makes more sense in terms of the complexity of driving a car and handling all of that that you're looking at something other than sort of "normal" sleepwalking. It doesn't fit that, for that length of time and that complexity of movement.
>
> (Butler cited in Rumbold, 2015))

Several experts differentiated "common or garden" sleepwalkers from the patients with more complex and problematic behaviour who often had extensive psychopathology. In the latter cases, the special verdict is very definitely more appropriate.

Assessment of forensic parasomnic episodes

There are specific criteria published to guide the assessment of forensic parasomnias. The medical science and/or phenomenology is arguably not sufficiently advanced to be dogmatic about many of the criteria. An historical example is the exclusion of sleepwalking in the presence of an erection in Fenwick's guidelines published in 1987 (prior to the recognition of sexsomnia in 2003). Table 6.1 lists the features of a forensic parasomnic episode from the review article by Morrison, Rumbold and Riha.

Duties of an expert witness

An expert witness's primary duty is to the court, as per Part 33.2 of the Criminal Procedure Rules: Expert's duty to the court:

Table 6.1 Features that support or refute a parasomnia defence

Strongly supports defence	*Supports defence*	*Neutral*	*Refutes defence*	*Strongly refutes defence*
Reliable eye witness account absolutely consistent with parasomniac behaviour		"Accused didn't appear to be asleep"		Reliable eyewitness account totally inconsistent with parasomniac behaviour
Unable to identify close relatives and friends		Mumbled conversations		
		Minor intoxication	Major intoxication[4]	Alcohol-related episode where alcohol known trigger
	Confused behaviour	Complex learned behaviour such as driving		Evidence of planning
	Difficulty navigating obstacles	Navigating familiar environments	Navigating unfamiliar environments	Evidence of working memory or higher cortical function
	Sexual activity with bed partner			Seeks out partner for sexual activity
	Reaction to confrontation, victim nearby			Seeks out victim
	No motive or advantage from event		Clear motive	

(continued)

Table 6.1 (continued)

Strongly supports defence	*Supports defence*	*Neutral*	*Refutes defence*	*Strongly refutes defence*
	Activity contrary to waking sexual orientation, no evidence of sexual arousal (sexual offences)		Sexual attraction	
	Shock and horror at actions, inconsolable	Denial		
Previously diagnosed parasomnia behaviour in keeping with episode	Personal and family history of parasomnias and/or sleep disorders, especially when verified by several parties	Parasomnia or sleep disorder was diagnosed retrospectively		No previous history of parasomnia
	Out of character		Consistent with character	
		Total amnesia or very fragmented memories		Clear memory for events
	Roused with difficulty and confused on arousal		No change in state when confronted and responds appropriately to situation	
	Immediately identifies behaviour as parasomnia			Attempts to cover up illegal act (see above)
		Lack of specific findings on video-PSG		

(Morrison, Rumbold and Riha, 2014)

4 Some would say major intoxication is a strong rebuttal.

1 An expert must help the court to achieve the overriding objective by giving objective, unbiased opinion on matters within his expertise.
2 This duty overrides any obligation to the person from whom he receives instructions or by whom he is paid.
3 This duty includes an obligation to inform all parties and the court if the expert's opinion changes from that contained in a report served as evidence or given in a statement.

Rix describes in greater detail the duties of a psychiatrist acting as an expert witness (most of which is applicable to forensic sleep experts). He states

> A psychiatrist who acts as an expert witness is:
>
> - a citizen
> - a doctor
> - a psychiatrist
> - an expert witness.
>
> (Rix, 2011)

There are tensions between these different roles. As a citizen and expert witness, there is a duty to assist the administration of justice. The doctor may be unused to a consultation where it has to be explained to the person being examined that there is no confidentiality, and where the focus is not the examinee's best interests. He may also feel a duty to protect the interests of the defendant as a doctor – some of the interviewees seemed to identify with the plight of the defendant. The expert witness should have no commitment to either the defendant or complainant.

Rix also describes the drawbacks of being too ready to change a professional opinion without good reason:

> If you acquire a reputation among barristers as a "hired gun" you may have some short term gains but when the barristers are sitting as recorders or have been elevated to the bench you should be not surprised if your opinions carry little weight with them.

The best efforts of an expert to avoid conscious bias may not eliminate the issue of partiality – a recent study showed that expert opinions were biased towards the side that had instructed them. The expert witness's freedom to express an opinion that helps the court, rather than their client, was until 2011 protected by immunity from civil action. However, in *Kaney v. Jones* this immunity was partially revoked, at least for experts instructed by the party. The ruling is hard to square with the maxim that the expert's duty is to the court. The majority argued that that the expert's duties to the court and to his client were not incompatible. Lord Dyson asserted:

> There is no conflict between the duty owed by an expert to his client and his overriding duty to the court. His duty to the client is to perform his function

> as an expert with the reasonable skill and care of an expert drawn from the relevant discipline. This includes a duty to perform the overriding duty to assist the court. Thus the discharge of the duty to the court cannot be a breach of duty to the client. If an expert gives an independent and unbiased opinion which is within the range of reasonable expert opinions he will have discharged his duty both to the court and his client.

Baroness Hale dissented, arguing:

> it is impossible to say what effect the removal of immunity will have, either on the care with which the experts give their evidence, or upon their willingness to do so. It is certainly possible that it will reduce any tendency to act as a "hired gun" and that would be a very good thing; but it is also possible that it will increase the pressure on an expert to stick to her previous opinion for fear of being sued if she retracts or modifies it. It is possible that it will have no effect at all upon the willingness of experts to give evidence; it is also possible that, in certain fields at least, it will reduce their willingness to do so, or even to become involved in the particular field of practice at all.

This decision may make experts more reticent about changing their opinion, and so make joint meetings a pointless exercise. The other effect of *Kaney v. Jones* is an apparent greater willingness to permit parties to instruct a fresh expert, as happened in *Stallwood v. David*. This should only apply in very limited circumstances according to Teare J who states:

> where a court is asked for permission to adduce expert evidence from a third expert in circumstances where the applicant is dissatisfied with the opinion of his own expert following the experts' discussion it should only do so where there is good reason to suppose that the applicant's first expert has agreed with the expert instructed by the other side or has modified his opinion for reasons which cannot properly or fairly support his revised opinion, such as those mentioned in the note in the White Book to which I have referred. It is likely that it will be a rare case in which such good reason can be shown. Where good reason is shown the court will have to consider whether, having regard to all the circumstances of the case and the overriding objective to deal with cases justly, it can properly be said that further expert evidence is "reasonably required to resolve the proceedings".

McDuff J in *Singh v. O'Shea* disagreed with this restrictive approach, stating:

> As a matter of principle the court has a wide discretion and a judge case managing a case uses that wide discretion to ensure that expert evidence shall be restricted to that which is reasonably required to resolve the proceedings. The judge was exercising that discretion in the court below when he made his decision.

Whether this same approach would be taken in criminal trials is uncertain.

Admissibility

The English courts have been traditionally quite liberal about the inclusion of expert evidence. The requirements as laid out in the Australian case of *Bonython* (cited with approval in English cases) are:

- whether the subject matter of the opinion is such that a person without instruction or experience in the area of knowledge or human experience would be able to form a sound judgment on the matter without the assistance of a witness possessing special knowledge or experience in the area
- whether the subject matter of the opinion forms part of a body of knowledge or experience which is sufficiently organized or recognized to be accepted as a reliable body of knowledge or experience, a special acquaintance with which by the witness would render his opinion of assistance to the court
- whether the witness has acquired by study or experience sufficient knowledge of the subject to render his opinion of value in resolving the issues before the court.

The breadth of this definition has been criticized. On the other hand, it has the effect of excluding expert testimony in matters deemed to be the realm of the jury, like provocation (*R v. Turner*) which are considered to come under "common knowledge" or the veracity of a witness (unless the witness is abnormal). As seen below, it can include the identification of the defendant where special technology is required. The effect of *Turner* is that experts can testify in general about the effects of a sexual assault (for example, post-traumatic stress disorder) in order to counter possible jury biases based on "rape myths", but they cannot attest to the veracity of the particular complainant as this would be considered "oath-helping", or compurgation. This is also the reason why the expert witness must find corroborating evidence of a disorder. For example, where a defendant claims to be a sleepwalker, the expert witness must find a bed partner or other bystander that has witnessed an episode rather than simply taking the defendant's word for it. In effect, an expert witness can provide "group character testimony".

Reliability criteria and the gatekeeper function

The test in English law for admissibility accords with the long-standing Frye test adopted in the USA, which requires that the findings or technique "be sufficiently established to have gained general acceptance in the particular field in which it belongs" (*Frye v. United States*). The application of this test has often been found wanting, as the example of ear-print testing demonstrates (*Dallagher*). However the USA requirements have evolved, with a trio of cases transforming the criteria for admissibility of scientific and technical evidence – *Daubert v. Merrell-Dow Pharmaceutical, Inc, General Electric Co. v. Joiner*, and *Kumho Tire*

Co. v. Carmichael. These cases led to the amendment of Rule 702 of the Federal Rules of Evidence. This states that:

> A witness who is qualified as an expert by knowledge, skill, experience, training, or education may testify in the form of an opinion or otherwise if:
>
> (a) the expert's scientific, technical, or other specialized knowledge will help the trier of fact to understand the evidence or to determine a fact in issue;
> (b) the testimony is based on sufficient facts or data;
> (c) the testimony is the product of reliable principles and methods; and
> (d) the expert has reliably applied the principles and methods to the facts of the case.

Rule 702 focuses on the methodology rather than the conclusion of the expert. It has been assumed by some commentators to be a stricter test than Frye, but in this author's opinion it is not, as the general acceptance requirement is abolished. FRE 403 could in theory be more helpful in excluding unreliable evidence:

> Although relevant, evidence may be excluded if its probative value is substantially outweighed by the danger of unfair prejudice, confusion of the issues, or misleading the jury, or by considerations of undue delay, waste of time, or needless presentation of cumulative evidence.

This conclusion is shared by Brown and Murphy where they state

> we argue that Rule 403, rather than the Daubert (or similar) rules governing scientific evidence, provides both (a) the necessary individualized assessment of claims and (b) room to allow the technology, as well as the public understanding of the technology, to improve and adapt, rather than being defined by Daubert (or similar) rulings that may be categorically and too broadly applied.
>
> (Brown and Murphy, 2010)

However, Edmond et al. note:

> Techniques deemed admissible under Rule 702 might, in theory, run afoul of Rule 403. Courts reluctant to tangle with complex reliability debates might go directly to Rule 403 to make a determination on the admissibility of evidence . . . Because many jurisdictions maintain an explicit reliability standard, once expert opinion evidence is deemed admissible, and therefore implicitly reliable, there is limited scope for subsequently finding that the evidence will create unfair prejudice. ***Admissibility standards (such as Rule 702), in effect, almost always trump exclusionary discretions (such as Rule 403).*** (italics mine)
>
> (Edmond et al., 2013)

The Law Commission's preference is for an enhanced gatekeeper modelled on Rule 702. Expert opinion could be excluded if it was not sufficiently reliable, based on the following considerations:

(a) the opinion is soundly based, and
(b) the strength of the opinion is warranted having regard to the grounds on which it is based.

Reasons for excluding an opinion for being insufficiently reliable would include:

(a) the opinion is based on a hypothesis which has not been subjected to sufficient scrutiny (including, where appropriate, experimental or other testing), or which has failed to stand up to scrutiny;
(b) the opinion is based on an unjustifiable assumption;
(c) the opinion is based on flawed data;
(d) the opinion relies on an examination, technique, method or process which was not properly carried out or applied, or was not appropriate for use in the particular case;
(e) the opinion relies on an inference or conclusion which has not been properly reached.

The relevant facts for deciding these questions are detailed further by the Law Commission:

(a) The extent and quality of the data on which the opinion is based, and the validity of the methods by which they were obtained.
(b) If the opinion relies on an inference from any findings, whether the opinion properly explains how safe or unsafe the inference is (whether by reference to statistical significance or in other appropriate terms).
(c) If the opinion relies on the results of the use of any method (for instance, a test, measurement or survey), whether the opinion takes proper account of matters, such as the degree of precision or margin of uncertainty, affecting the accuracy or reliability of those results.
(d) The extent to which any material upon which the opinion is based has been reviewed by others with relevant expertise (for instance, in peer-reviewed publications), and the views of those others on that material.
(e) The extent to which the opinion is based on material falling outside the expert's own field of expertise.
(f) The completeness of the information which was available to the expert, and whether the expert took account of all relevant information in arriving at the opinion (including information as to the context of any facts to which the opinion relates).
(g) Whether there is a range of expert opinion on the matter in question; and, if there is, where in the range the opinion lies and whether the expert's preference for the opinion proffered has been properly explained.

(h) Whether the expert's methods followed established practice in the field and, if they did not, whether the reason for the divergence has been properly explained.

(Law Commission, 2009)

Most importantly in the application of this test, if there is any doubt about whether expert testimony is opinion or fact, it should be considered to be opinion. Whether or not this would make a substantial difference to the quality of biomedical expert evidence is debatable, although it would certainly seem capable of excluding the alcohol provocation test (APT). The correct application of these criteria requires a level of scientific literacy which is arguably often lacking in the judiciary. There is a large role for expert opinion for two major reasons, both epistemological: firstly, that medical knowledge may be limited in a particular field; secondly, that certain assessments are judgments, which can be based on current knowledge but never ascertained with any precision. Whether or not an episode was parasomnia is a matter of opinion for both these reasons.

Some commentators have asserted that expert evidence must follow the principles of evidence-based medicine. This assertion is incorrect. It is for the courts to determine what evidence is admissible. Just as with clinical medicine, the courts often have to make decisions in the face of inadequate and unreliable evidence. Evidence that has no value in enabling the jury to come to a decision will be excluded, but the fact that a test is not 100 per cent or even 80 per cent reliable will not automatically lead to its exclusion. A fact that is determinative of guilt or innocence by itself is proof, not evidence. The collection of several pieces of evidence may amount to proof.

The Court of Appeal in *Luttrell* didn't consider it necessary that:

> the methods used are sufficiently explained to be tested in cross-examination and so to be verifiable or falsifiable.

Additionally it was stated that:

> [t]he fact that an expert may be wrong is no reason to deprive the jury of such assistance as may be gleaned from the evidence.

The case involved the admissibility of lip reading evidence. The court regarded its reliability as affecting not just admissibility of the evidence but also the weight that evidence should be given (which is an issue for the jury to decide). The Court of Appeal was satisfied that the lip reading evidence was sufficiently reliable to be admissible. The jury can be instructed about the weight that should be put on the evidence:

> Transcription by expert lip reading could provide intelligence and corroborative evidence, but, because of her [Jessica Rees] inaccuracies, her evidence

was unlikely to be capable of standing alone. There was potential for unreliability in such evidence.

(p. 530)

Difficulties with biomedical evidence

The range of actions possible during a parasomnia episode is reasonably well described, but it may be either incomplete or over-inclusive. Medicine does present particular difficulties in this regard as much of the scientific research is observational. Le Fort, the French surgeon who classified three types of mid-face fractures, only used his club on the facial skeletons of cadavers – clearly it would be unethical to inflict injuries on living human subjects (Patterson, 1991). These same difficulties do not apply to the physical sciences. Generally, "natural experiments" have to be relied on to determine the causation or likely effect of injuries or other lesions, like the unfortunate accident of Phineas Gage. Gage was an American railroad worker who had a tamping iron enter below his eye socket and exit through the top of his skull. He miraculously survived but his behaviour dramatically changed (there is some debate about the degree of impairment he suffered) (Damasio et al., 1994; Kean, 2014). These natural experiments only take us so far however, and the actual lesion is difficult to define precisely (whereas experimental lesions in animal experiments for example can be precisely delineated). The retrospective assessment of a parasomnic or epileptic episode is intrinsically subjective, as the accused's brain state cannot be determined in the absence of electroencephalographic monitoring.

Cartwright's hypothesis that a sleepwalker can be "primed" is an example of a theory which, if shown to be correct, would dramatically widen the spectrum of behaviours possible during somnambulism (Cartwright, 2004). The strongest assertion that an expert can validly advance about a parasomnic episode is that it is consistent with a particular parasomnia. They can also comment on the other circumstantial factors that will support automatism, such as a lack of motive and behaviour contrary to the accused's character. These statements neither would nor should be excluded by a *Daubert*-type test.

Application of expert evidence on forensic sleep disorders

Both the quality of the observational data supporting an association between alcohol and sleepwalking, and the interpretation of polysomnographic data during an alcohol provocation test (APT), may well be brought into question. The support in the literature for the APT is not robust, with insufficient data from polysomnography on the effect of alcohol in sleepwalkers.

Pressman believes that a *Daubert*-type test would exclude testimony about the effect of alcohol on sleepwalking, stating:

> the hypothesis of alcohol-induced sleep-walking has no valid evidence-based scientific support and should be considered "junk science."

Whilst it might exclude the use of the APT, it probably would not exclude expert witnesses giving their opinion on alcohol and sleepwalking based on their professional experience. Again it can be argued that it should not – if we accept sleepwalkers' accounts of what triggers their sleepwalking, we must accept sleepwalkers' accounts of the effect of alcohol. Such testimony is absolutely appropriate, and does not fall into the *ipse dixit*[5] fallacy (nor run foul of compurgation). Wynne comments that in the legal sphere, deconstruction of expert opinion can end in deconstruction of the basis of a field of knowledge. Thus if some experts deconstruct the attribution of sleepwalking episodes to alcohol consumption, they also deconstruct the entire basis for categorizing parasomnic episodes. It must be emphasized that there is an important distinction between a lack of evidence for an effect, and evidence for a lack of an effect. There are recent publications that support the association of alcohol consumption with sleepwalking episodes in some individuals.

The courts and junk science

It might be thought self-evident that the minimal requirement of the admissibility test is the exclusion of junk science. The term "junk science" suggests that it is easy to differentiate between "good" and "bad" science. It has, however, proven remarkably difficult for the courts to distinguish between the two. As Mercer (2002) states:

> The difficulty in actually defining simple legal rules for demarcating real science from junk science, and plausibly dismissing numerous scientific controversies and popular concerns with new science and technology as merely "junk science"-led paranoia, has been difficult to convert into sustainable policies. Implementing simple demarcation criteria between science and non-science have proved more difficult in practice than advocates have anticipated.

The Law Commission's proposals contain a number of references to peer review and established practice, proving the point. Moreover, it could be suggested that the most important distinction is how the science is used. Science can be valuable and proven, but nonetheless have greater prejudicial than probative value in the courtroom. Currently this can be excluded on a discretionary basis. The exercise of this discretion has not been studied. This author has come across several examples of evidence of very dubious value being admitted. For example, the finding of a three-second run of non-sustained ventricular tachycardia in a driving case was used to support a cardiac cause for a driving error. This finding was not reproduced on other tests including a repeat ambulatory ECG. The defendant's heart was structurally normal on echocardiography. This finding is very common,

5 He himself said it; the fallacy of bare assertion.

and by itself was not sufficient to establish a cardiac cause for the episode on the balance of probabilities.

Also, evidence can be excluded under Section 78 of the Police and Criminal Evidence Act 1984:

> In any proceedings the court may refuse to allow evidence on which the prosecution proposes to rely to be given if it appears to the court that, having regard to all the circumstances, including the circumstances in which the evidence was obtained, the admission of the evidence would have such an adverse effect on the fairness of the proceedings that the court ought not to admit it.

Both these measures only apply to prosecution evidence. In *Robb* it was noted that:

> if the Crown are permitted to call an expert witness of some but tenuous qualifications the burden of proof may imperceptibly shift and a burden be cast on the defendant.

These doctrines mean that the defence can rely on significantly weaker expert evidence, which is an issue observed with the parasomnia defence. The Appeal Court showed great faith in ability of cross-examination to refute dubious scientific evidence when it added that:

> the appellant had ample opportunity to meet and rebut Dr Baldwin's evidence, if he could.

In *Luttrell*, the court commented that:

> evidence might be so lacking in "prima facie reliability" that it has no probative force or its probative force is too slight to influence a decision: *R v. Clarke* [1995] 2 Cr.App.R. 425, 432.

In the case of *Clarke (Robert Lee)*, an expert in facial mapping gave evidence as to whether the defendant was the man on the video images captured by security cameras, as there were no eye witnesses to the bank robbery. The judge ruled that this evidence was admissible and

> [t]he matter was left to the jury on the basis that it was for them to assess that expert evidence and to decide whether the technique was reliable and whether it reliably demonstrated that the appellant was the man on the photographs taken in the bank.

This puts great responsibility on the laypersons in the jury. This is arguably a matter for the field of science and technology studies rather than just the courts and scientists to resolve. Any judgment of the probative value of evidence versus its prejudicial value cannot ignore societal influences. For example, the feminist argument against the "sexsomnia defence" is partially based on the perception that science which exonerates the accused is more likely to be believed within a "rape culture", regardless of its intrinsic scientific worth.

R v. Turner is an example of the exclusion of psychiatric evidence in relation to the partial defence of provocation. However, there is rather more to *Turner* than just this aspect of "common knowledge". The decision in *Turner* was also based on the low probative value of the psychiatric testimony, accompanied by the danger of the jury being misled about the objective standard for provocation. The use of expert evidence could add nothing to the jury's deliberations, which are guided by their knowledge of the "reasonable man". On the other hand, cases like *Emery* demonstrate circumstances where the jury may require the help of psychologists or psychiatrists to understand the vulnerability of an individual to duress. Mitchell, Mackay and Brookbanks (2008) argue it is unjust that individuals that have certain conditions are held to the same standards as the general population, arguing:

> The term "undesirable characteristics" is rather ambiguous and refers to two fundamentally different groups of individuals. First, there are those who share the same basic values as ordinary citizens but they suffer from a mental abnormality or personality trait. Dressler's argument is that such cases breach what he calls the "oxymoron principle", that the jury should not, for example, be asked to consider how the "reasonable paranoid" would have reacted. But this problem only arises because of the misguided use of the reasonable or ordinary person test. The second major group of persons with "undesirable characteristics" do not share the same basic social values as the vast majority of ordinary citizens. The American Model Penal Code describes such characteristics as reflecting "idiosyncratic moral values". Dressler cited by way of an example an assassin who believes it is right to kill political leaders. Horder spoke of a racist who believes "it is the gravest of insults for a coloured person to speak to a white man unless spoken to first". Unless such characteristics reflect a condition which brings the individual within a recognised category of legal excuse – some form of mental abnormality is perhaps the most obvious, but some individuals in this group will almost certainly have no excuse of this or any other sort which the law currently recognises – they should be excluded because they would effectively contradict the criminal law's attempt to maintain social values.

Redmayne (2001) stresses that:

> evidence which falls victim to the balancing process is nearly always, as in Turner, of minimal probative value, and that often the dangers of admitting it would be significant.

These criteria apply in this author's opinion to the APT. The weak claims that can be made for the APT can be contrasted with the dangers of admitting it in evidence. It is common knowledge that parasomnias are rare, but alcoholic intoxication and blackouts are relatively common; further, they are foreseeable consequences of alcohol consumption. The admission of the APT carries with it the arguably incorrect inference that it can tell the jury something about the episode in question.

There is an assumption that the jury is able to deal effectively and logically with these weighting exercises. This assumption seems difficult to sustain in the light of the award of $1 million to a woman who claimed that she had lost her psychic powers during a CT scan. Donald Elliott, general counsel of the Environmental Protection Agency in the case, is quoted as saying that the law:

> extends equal dignity to the opinions of charlatans and Nobel Prize winners, with only a lay jury to distinguish between the two.

On the other hand, it has been suggested that the "CSI effect" leads to jurors familiar with CSI and similar TV shows being more likely to reject evidence that does not meet their raised expectations of the reliability of forensic science. There is not good evidence for a straightforward relationship, and the "CSI effect" does not necessarily lead to a greater tendency to acquit.

Psychological and psychiatric testimony should include consideration of the possibility of malingering, exaggeration or functional overlay, and the steps taken to detect it, both in the clinical assessment and in any tests performed. This should reduce the prejudicial value of such testimony. The expert's opinion about the accused's character or guilt is irrelevant to the jury, and the courts are keen to exclude testimony that is based on these assessments which subvert the purpose of the jury. There is some evidence that expert witness testimony is in some instances influenced by these "gut reactions". This is impossible to eliminate entirely, but its encroachment into testimony is be resisted as "a form of charlatanism that could mislead the court into according too much weight to the evidence" (Roberts, 1996).

Despite all these safeguards, a review by Edmond et al. (2013) found that the test for admissibility makes little difference to what evidence is accepted in court. They quote Moriarty and Saks who state:

> The single most important observation about judicial [gate-keeping] of forensic science is that most judges under most circumstances admit most forensic science. There is almost no expert testimony so threadbare that it will not be admitted if it comes to a criminal proceeding under the banner of forensic science . . . . The applicable legal test offers little assurance. The maverick who is a field unto him- or herself has repeatedly been readily admitted under Frye, and the complete absence of foundational research has not prevented such admission in Daubert Jurisdictions.

They compared the US, England and Wales, Australia and Canada, all common law jurisdictions. They noted the lack of evidence for reliability for many forms of forensic science, most notably fingerprinting (c.f. the Scottish case of *McKie* where a latent print from a crime scene was misattributed to a police officer). This points to a far more fundamental problem with how the courts deal with science, which admissibility rules can do little to address.

The approaches that focus on the process and reliability of evidence have much to commend them. However, in certain areas where there has been little research, this may present an insurmountable barrier to any evidence being adduced at all. This is particularly so in medicine for the reasons stated above. Gilson describes the demonstration by a prosecution expert witness of the force required to cause the injuries seen in the Louise Woodward case as "nothing less than a spectacle" (the defence rightly objected to the proposed use of a doll to demonstrate this) (Gilson, 2012). The degree of force required to produce shaken baby syndrome is simply not known. Rule 702 might exclude any testimony about shaken baby syndrome given that no testimony would be "based on sufficient facts or data" or "the product of reliable principles and methods". Some commentators might consider that this would be entirely appropriate. It is this author's belief that enhanced admissibility rules should not be applied universally, and particularly in the very cases which the courts are concerned about. The exclusion of scientific evidence simply because of the existence of controversy would be to the detriment of the criminal justice system.

Peer assessment may ensure that the opinion is mainstream, but excluding opinions simply on this basis is intuitively wrong – the orthodox opinion is often proved to be wrong over time. The peer review process may be unduly influenced by politics and in a small area of expertise affected by the close relationships of all those involved. Like accreditation, it may do nothing to challenge assumptions that inform expert opinion that may be simply perpetuated in the process of professional training. Certain memes may persist long after they have been discredited. The current situation regarding alcohol and sleepwalking is a good example of the difficulties.

Gilson analyses in his monograph the more general difficulties that law and science have. The court wants scientific expertise to assist the legal decision-making process, rather than the court having to adjudicate in a scientific dispute. An example of this is Pressman's appeal for the courts to exclude the alcohol provocation test (APT) from expert evidence. Gilson comments about these difficulties that:

> Ironically in this predicament, law that operates only under legal/illegal codes is pressed for true/false conclusions, which constitutes a serious abuse of its processes. In terms of science, neither is it equipped for this, nor in law's terms should there be such expectation, given that the opinion of an expert specifically is meant to inform tribunals and inquiries so that they can arrive at reliable conclusions. In the event, law has adapted its normal procedures to enable it to test the reliability of experts rather than true/false contentions in science but is still without a universal guarantee of certainty.
>
> (Gilson, 2012)

However, there are many who disagree with this stark portrayal of a law-science chasm. The courts have no difficulties dealing with other types of ambivalent and unreliable evidence e.g. eye witness testimony, as *Turnbull* demonstrates. The trial process is entirely about giving weight to contradictory pieces of evidences in order to come to a conclusion. As Wynne put it:

> Science, like life in general, involves creating adequate conclusions from inadequate premises.
>
> (Smith and Wynne, 1989)

This indubitably applies to the criminal trial also.

As seen with FRE Rule 702 and other enhanced gatekeeper tests, the law concerns itself with the processes involved rather than the conclusions. It cannot adjudicate on what is true and false, nor even what is good and bad science. It is important not to fall into the trap of "scientism"; that is to believe that only scientific methods can establish objective and meaningful knowledge and practices. Similarly, it should be understood it is impossible to totally "depoliticize" science to ensure reliable scientific opinion. Wynne and Smith describe the problems with using legal processes:

> Policy makers put forward the extreme formality of legal processes - what Tribe calls the law's "rituals of precision" – as an antidote to the procedural imprecision and inconsistency invariably found whenever science is subjected to detailed scrutiny. This development follows from the widespread belief, which we question, that a lack of consistency in scientific knowledge must be due to a lack of procedural rigour.
>
> (Smith and Wynne, 1989)

In essence, they reject the basis for the application of the principles of evidence-based medicine to expert evidence. The effect of prior assumptions, beliefs and/or policy goals can be seen in the different interpretations of ambivalent evidence of child abuse. An example is the different interpretations of maternal actions on covert video surveillance of mothers suspected of child abuse (Munchhausen syndrome by proxy aka factitious or induced illness) (Morley, 1998).

Also, the law wishes to prevent psychologists and psychiatrists straying into areas that are the province of the jury (and therefore of folk psychology). Expert evidence seen as bolstering a witness's credibility is excluded as per *Robinson*. This might seem to exclude the use of such testimony to support counterintuitive phenomena, as Colman and Mackay note in the case of *Neeson* (Colman and Mackay, 1991). There has been resistance to the use of expert testimony to combat "rape myths", which is a prime example of expert testimony that would serve policy ends well (Ellison, 2005). However, since *Turner*, the courts have clarified that expert evidence is admissible where the condition "is complex and . . . is not known by the public at large" (*Emery*). The parasomnia defence is an area where the folk psychology of the jury is drawn on to an extent – the sleepwalker cannot be held responsible because he is asleep. However, expert testimony is permitted to demonstrate that, counterintuitively, the parasomniac can be asleep whilst performing various complex tasks. The same would apply for most conditions causing medicolegal automatism.

Some experts believe that the adversarial system is responsible for many of the issues, and propose the use of a single expert (Rumbold, 2015). An *amicus curiae* can be appointed in civil litigation, but such an appointment is not possible in criminal trials, where it would infringe on the defendant's right to an independent defence. Wynne points out the problems of this solution:

> critics of the adversary process argue that it introduces artificial polarization into scientific discourse, demeaning science in public by encouraging unseemly (and by implication, false) conflict. They argue that experts should be assigned to the court (as happens, for example, in France) not to competing parties, and that issues of technical fact can be resolved by expert consensus processes outside legal cross-examination. Defenders of the adversary system argue that this is elitist and unreliable: left to themselves scientists are insufficiently precise, and prone to unseen bias. They believe that the truth can therefore be revealed only by exposing through adversary cross-examination which side of an expert disagreement is introducing covert, extraneous bias (including values or opinions) or incompetence.
>
> (Smith and Wynne, 1989)

This author is of the view that the opinion of certain experts was demonstrably value-laden e.g. with regard to alcohol and sleepwalking, and so concurs that the adoption of a single expert would introduce these biases into the trial. It could not be a substitute for scientific debate.

Controversies in expert evidence: alcohol and sleepwalking

One of the most contested areas of the sleepwalking defence is the role of alcohol in triggering sleepwalking. The academic literature on alcohol and sleepwalking is problematic. Where expert witnesses extensively cite self-authored review articles, they replace the *ipse dixit* fallacy with the *ipse scribit* fallacy.[6] If peer review of the academic literature was influenced by a group of experts with a particular opinion, this would further complicate the application of the literature in expert testimony. There is evidence that this is the case with the issue of alcohol and sleepwalking – this author has had reports of it, and also personal experience when submitting a co-authored paper for peer review. Not only is it difficult to publish articles linking alcohol and sleepwalking, also it is even difficult to get a major sleep journal to accept letters and short notes about the debate. This makes it even harder to mobilize the scientific community to obtain robust data to refute or support the hypothesis.

6 He himself wrote it; the same fallacy as *ipse dixit* but in print.

The latest version of the diagnostic criteria for sleep disorders, the ICSD-3, again demonstrates the dominance of one body of opinion. It is now stated that:

> Disorders of arousal should not be diagnosed in the presence of alcoholic intoxication. The behavior of the alcohol-intoxicated individual may superficially resemble that of the sleepwalker. However, the sleepwalker is typically severely cognitively impaired, but with only limited motor impairment. The alcohol-intoxicated individual's level of cognitive functioning may be reduced, but not absent, whereas motor behavior is often severely impaired.
> (American Academy of Sleep Medicine, 2014)

There are some eminent forensic sleep experts who dissent from this assertion, for example Cartwright. The ICSD-3 should be treated as an expression of the opinion of the authors, rather than scientific fact. Such documents can be extremely influential, and might lead to the exclusion of all alcohol-induced parasomnias. However, the courts have not attached great significance to other diagnostic manuals e.g. the *Diagnostic and Statistical Manual of Mental Disorders*. The fact that a disorder is listed or not listed is irrelevant to the legal issues. When expert witnesses who contributed to the ICSD-3 cite it in expert evidence, they are arguably committing the *ipse scribit* fallacy.

Prominent North American sleep experts believe that there is no good evidence that alcohol triggers forensic sleepwalking episodes (whether violent or sexual behaviour) at all (Pressman et al., 2007, 2013). The Sleep Forensics Associates group refuse to testify in cases involving significant alcohol ingestion. Schenck states this position is based on the policy issue that it is impossible to distinguish alcoholic intoxication from sleepwalking (Rumbold, 2015). They also point to a lack of research and to studies that show that alcohol consumption has a clinically insignificant effect on the amount of slow wave sleep. The basis of the claim that this effect is clinically insignificant is not entirely clear, but the comparison is made with the effect on slow wave sleep of sleep deprivation (a recognized trigger for sleepwalking and other NREM parasomnias).

Most British experts agree that alcohol appears to precipitate sleepwalking in some sleepwalkers on the basis that a small minority of sleepwalkers report an association. The sceptics contend that factors associated with alcohol consumption such as a late night and stress may in fact be responsible for the apparent connection. Also, the patients and eyewitnesses will be often unable to distinguish alcohol-related episodes from true parasomnias – the effects of alcohol on the brain are remarkably similar to that seen in the limited studies of sleepwalking. The major difference is the effect of alcohol on the cerebellum, which will cause unsteadiness and slurring of speech. All of those agree that as greater amounts of alcohol are consumed, it is increasingly likely that the behaviour is related to alcohol intoxication rather than sleepwalking. The discussion at the medicolegal seminar on automatism at Keele confirmed this consensus, with the caveat that most sleepwalkers report alcohol has either no effect on or reduces their sleepwalking. A recently published case-control study also found an association, with

12 per cent of sleepwalkers reporting that alcohol exacerbated their sleepwalking (Lopez et al., 2013). Ebrahim reviewed the literature on alcohol and sleep and came to a different conclusion to Pressman et al. (Ebrahim et al., 2013). There are other experts who agreed with Ebrahim about some of the problems with Pressman's review, particularly the selection of more generic papers on alcohol and sleep that did not address the relevant questions. Ebrahim argues that only nine out of the 19 studies are relevant. The majority (seven) of these nine studies show significant increase in slow wave sleep for the first two to four hours of sleep (which is the relevant period for NREM parasomnias). Another relevant point is that since the effect occurs in a minority of sleepwalkers, studies of the general population of sleepwalkers may be inappropriate anyway.

This weak positive association between sleepwalking and alcohol consumption means that when large amounts of alcohol are consumed, the experts in the Sleep Clinic Group rely on the alcohol provocation test (APT) to prove that alcohol is a relevant trigger for sleepwalking for the defendant. The procedure involves a three-night sleep study. The first night's results are "discarded" – its purpose is to acclimatize the subject to the test conditions (see comments above about the issues with this). The second night is the "diagnostic baseline" night, to see what occurs during sleep in the absence of alcohol. The third night is the alcohol challenge night, where the subject consumes the amount of alcohol that will achieve the blood alcohol levels calculated to have been present during the episode of harmful behaviour. The presence of parasomnias or parasomnia-related signs is considered to indicate a capacity to respond to alcohol consumption with a parasomnia episode.

On the other hand, a negative APT neither rules out alcohol as a trigger nor a parasomnic episode as the cause of the behaviour. The extent of variation across different nights for the same subject makes the designation of the second night as a "baseline" questionable. The proponents of the APT state that the case report by Hartmann validates the test.

Hartmann performed polysomnography for four nights in total. Patient P. H. consumed two typical cocktails on nights two to four of four non-consecutive nights of polysomnography with the following result:

> On Night 2, 1½ hours after sleep onset, he began talking and cursing in his sleep, disconnected himself from the electrodes, got up, and wandered down the hall; he looked confused and could not be awakened for a time by the technician. This episode was very similar to some of P. H.'s milder sleepwalking episodes as described by his wife.

Abstinence from alcohol led to full resolution of his nocturnal wandering (Hartmann, 1983). The difficulty with this case report is that we do not know what stage of sleep this behaviour arose from, so we cannot be sure this was sleepwalking. It has been stated that a "sleepwalking" episode during polysomnography is a ground to suspect malingering. One of the experts who formerly used the APT now disavows its use.

The main basis of the sceptic's position is the scientific data on the effect of alcohol on sleep, although there are other policy and legal justifications. There are several criticisms of the APT listed in the review of alcohol and sleepwalking by Pressman et al.:

1 This test was specifically created for legal purposes and has never been used in clinical settings.
2 This test lacks any data regarding its sensitivity, as there are no reports of the effects of alcohol at any dose on clinically diagnosed sleepwalkers.
3 This test lacks any data on its specificity, as it has never been tested on normal controls or patients with other types of sleep disorders.
4 There are no normative data on which to base clinical or forensic decisions.
5 The basic premise of alcohol testing that alcohol increases SWS [slow wave sleep] and arousal threshold is supported by only six of 19 published research studies.
6 No episodes of sleepwalking have been reported during alcohol studies.
7 At the time of the criminal act most defendants were chronic alcohol users, but at the time of the sleep study they have been abstinent for months or years. The alcohol provocations thus cannot be a "recreation".
8 Administering a large quantity of alcohol to someone who is no longer tolerant to large quantities of alcohol is potentially dangerous.
9 Other factors present at the time of the crime cannot be duplicated including:

   a sleep quantity and patterns for at least 1 week;
   b stress levels;
   c use of other legal or illegal drugs.

10 Trigger for episode unknown
11 Other people, including victims not present in sleep laboratory.
12 Sleep laboratory is sound shielded.
13 Sleep laboratory is absolutely dark.
14 Numerous electrodes and sensors placed on patient may disrupt sleep.
15 Sleep laboratory practices can disrupt usual sleep patterns.
16 Abstinent alcoholics have very poor quantity and quality of sleep.
17 Abstinent alcoholics have frequent arousals in sleep.
18 Administration of alcohol may result in an increase in SWS in abstinent defendants whose SWS has not dropped to very low levels.
19 Administration of alcohol to individuals whose baseline level of SWS during abstinence has remained low may not show any increase in SWS.
20 Administration of alcohol is known to increase the severity of OSA and cause a change from simple snoring to sleep apnea. Sleep apnea is associated with frequent arousals from sleep. Frequent arousals from sleep may reduce SWS.
21 Presence of arousals or HSDWs [hypersynchronous delta waves] is not diagnostic of sleepwalking.

(Pressman et al., 2007)

Also it is not possible to "fail" the APT e.g. a negative result does not rule out parasomnia. Arousals seen on video-PSG in the intoxicated patient may not have the same significance as arousals in the non-intoxicated patient. What is uncontroversial is that alcohol may exacerbate OSAHS and upper airways resistance syndrome, by relaxing the muscles in the upper airways. Where these conditions trigger parasomnia, it seems an entirely defensible conclusion that alcohol will exacerbate that parasomnia.

The role of large amounts of alcohol and the use of the APT is a particular concern for Pressman and colleagues. Their review emphasizes the lack of solid evidence that alcohol increases the likelihood of sleepwalking; however, they provide no positive evidence to support the conclusion that a certain level of alcohol consumption rules out sleepwalking as a defence. However, Pressman et al. (2007) do not disapprove of testimony based on clinical experience about the effect of alcohol on sleepwalking, especially if qualified – simply expert testimony containing claims there is scientific evidence to prove that alcohol can trigger sleepwalking. They also disagree with the use of the APT, in which they are not alone.

Alcoholic blackout is an important differential diagnosis for sleepwalking (White, Jamieson-Drake and Swartzwelder, 2002; Jnr, 2004; van Oorsouw et al., 2004). Alcohol and Z-drugs have an almost identical effect on the brain as sleepwalking, except alcohol affects the cerebellum more (leading to slurred speech and unsteadiness), and both alcohol and Z-drugs affect memory more than motor skills. Some sleep experts believe it is impossible to reliably distinguish clinically alcohol intoxication from sleepwalking or sexsomnia (presumably in the lack of the cerebellar signs mentioned above). It would also be a reasonable position to take that alcohol-induced sleepwalking ought not to be an excuse, being a consequence of alcoholic intoxication as per *Finegan v. Heywood* (albeit a rare consequence).

Although the number of criminal cases where sleepwalking is part of the defence remains small, the issue of alcohol is a significant component in these cases Many of the criminal cases reported in the press (over 40 per cent) have involved alcohol (Rumbold, 2015). There was an acrimonious exchange in the literature over a paper reporting the case of *Lowe*. *Lowe* killed his father after consuming a considerable amount of alcohol (blood alcohol at the time of the offence was estimated to be 215mg/dl). This was the most contentious aspect of the case, with Pressman asserting that the amount of alcohol involved made the defence of sleepwalking "untenable". Pressman criticized the APT used as unvalidated. He also points out the atypical features of the case – prolonged assault, seeking out his victim and attempts to conceal his crime by mopping up blood. Pressman is a leading advocate for evidence-based medicine with reference to forensic sleep expert testimony. Evidence-based medicine is not a requirement of the criminal courts, and the application of its principles is particularly problematic in the case of forensic sleep disorders, because there is a dearth of good quality research. He dismisses the observational data supporting an association as weak, since it is not proven that any episodes after alcohol consumption are parasomnic. This same caveat applies to most data about parasomnia episodes. For example, the known sleepwalkers who drive automobiles were not being monitored during episodes.

Characterization of the actions of the putative sleepwalker according to the current incomplete understanding arguably contradicts *Daubert* and evidence-based principles. In addition, it appears that the position of some of the critics is not that alcohol cannot trigger sleepwalking per se, but rather that it cannot be proven to trigger violent sleepwalking and that it should not support the defence of sleepwalking: "In our opinion, claims of alcohol-induced sleepwalking violence or sleep sex lack any reliable scientific basis" (Pressman et al., 2013). Note the precise language used – that there is no experimental evidence that alcohol causes sleepwalking violence or sleep sex. As noted previously, the position of Pressman and Sleep Forensic Associates have changed over time. Expert 29 stated to me:

> we feel very strongly that alcohol really precludes the use of sleepwalking as a defence – which is not to say that it might not actually be, but you just can't tell. If there's that much alcohol involved, if you just look statistically at the violence, alcohol causes a lot more violence than sleepwalking does. And so I think that alcohol just should preclude the consideration of sleepwalking as a defence.
>
> (Rumbold, 2015)

Pressman states:

> the hypothesis of alcohol-induced sleep-walking has no valid evidence-based scientific support and should be considered "junk science". In cases of severe alcohol intoxication, no other explanation for behaviors is required. In most jurisdictions voluntary intoxication is not a complete defense for criminal behavior and in many it provides no justification whatsoever. A suggestion – or legal defense in which alcohol intoxication is reported to cause sleepwalking – often appears to be a way of trying to sidestep the fact that the alcohol intoxication was voluntary and sometime reckless.
>
> (Pressman, 2011a)

He finishes by quoting a review article by himself and Mahowald and Schenck: "Claims of alcohol-induced parasomnias presented solely to circumvent the laws of voluntary intoxication should be understood for what they are and rejected" (Pressman et al., 2007).

Certainly, if it is impossible to distinguish alcohol intoxication from sleepwalking, this position is understandable. This emphasizes the potential importance of the APT, if it could truly distinguish between the two conditions.

The users of the APT argue that their position has been misrepresented. They respond that they are not purporting to be able to recreate the conditions nor the events of the evening. A positive APT simply means that the accused had the potential to have a particular reaction to alcohol. It does not prove that he had that reaction on the night in question. It helps to distinguish the acknowledged minority where alcohol exacerbates sleepwalking from the majority where it does not. What is even more controversial than alcohol as a trigger for sleepwalking is the possible effect of alcohol on the quality of sleepwalking episodes. The dissenters believe that alcohol can make sleepwalking episodes more complex. They too do not believe that alcohol should be an excuse where the accused knows that it triggers sleepwalking and harmful behaviour. The experts who support the link between alcohol and sleepwalking also complain that it is very difficult to get articles discussing the role of alcohol in forensic sleepwalking episodes to be accepted by the major journals. This author encountered difficulty when submitting a co-authored review article – the section about any possible link between alcohol and sleepwalking had to be removed before it would be accepted for publication.

The position that alcohol consumption should preclude the sleepwalking defence is based more on dogma than scientific fact. These assertions by expert witnesses encroach into the jury's remit. There are two distinct issues here. Whether or not alcohol triggers sleepwalking is a descriptive question. Whether or not alcohol-triggered putative sleepwalking episodes should be an excuse in criminal law is a normative question. The former is an issue for medical science to answer. The latter is a question for the law to answer. However, the policy concerns about the use of sleepwalking to excuse crimes committed whilst simply intoxicated are extremely valid. Most putative sexsomnia cases involve alcohol, where the accused would not be able to rely on any other defence. The fact that the defence only needs to raise a reasonable doubt in the mind of the jury enables tenuous claims of sleepwalking to procure acquittals.

These differences of opinion between expert witnesses have led to General Medical Council (GMC) involvement in some cases, although it is the courts that are the experts in deciding what the duties of expert witnesses are, and whether particular experts have fulfilled them or not. In this respect, it is perhaps regrettable that the decision of Judge Collins in the High Court in *Meadow* was overturned. He ruled that the GMC should not invoke disciplinary proceedings unless a trial judge commented on the quality of expert evidence given. Trial judges have criticized medical expert witnesses on rare occasions, with Sedley LJ describing Dr Donegan's evidence as "junk science" in *Re B (A Child) (Immunisation: Parental Rights)*, an appeal from the Court of Protection relating to MMR vaccination. However, judges would be loath to criticize an expert witness merely on the basis of contested science, because this might dramatically affect the range of opinions experts might volunteer.

The Court of Appeal in *Meadow* disagreed with Judge Collins, ruling that the GMC was able to adjudicate where such issues impacted on fitness to practice. It is unclear when, if ever, a doctor's expert witness work would impact on their fitness to practice. The fact that expert witnesses from overseas are not members of UK organizations and so not subject to UK professional regulation is a bone of contention with some who have been the subject of complaints. There are registers and organizations for expert witnesses but there are no mandatory requirements for registration or membership.

The presumption of innocence may justify the requirements for medical expert evidence for the prosecution being different from those for the defence. For example, theories about a criminal cause for certain childhood injuries supporting a prosecution for child abuse need to meet certain standards to satisfy the presumption of innocence. The defendant on the other hand may be entitled to use less solid evidence to raise reasonable doubt in the minds of the jury. Fanciful and far-fetched theories should not be admitted, but lack of a rigorous research base should not be the sole ground for excluding exculpatory evidence. Another significant difference is that not uncommonly in child abuse cases there may be dispute about whether or not there was a crime – the post-mortem findings may be non-specific where smothering is suspected, for example. In sleepwalking cases the illegal act is usually not disputed, and the issue is simply one of criminal responsibility.

7 Commentary and conclusions

Automatism is a rarely used defence, although it is difficult to ascertain accurately how often it is argued. The defence of automatism is in fact at least three separate defences – denial of the *actus reus*, denial of the *mens rea*, and the insanity defence. These three defences have a combination of different standards for culpability along with different standards and burdens of proof. This makes the law confusing even for the judiciary and legal profession.

The essential difference between automatism and insanity ought to be based on the need for social control measures. The law has attempted to draw a bright line in the sand between conditions requiring social control measures and those that do not. This is probably an impossible task. The medical science that would enable a precise assessment of future risk is not currently available. Unfortunately, the surrogate measures used by the judiciary are unsatisfactory, particularly for the medical expert witnesses. Education on the basis of the legal doctrines would be likely to improve the quality of expert evidence. Ultimately, much of the case law has roots in policy issues, and this explains why the automatism defence as it stands lacks a convincing justification in jurisprudence or medical science. Further, there is the issue of the application of the case law, which is honoured more in the breach than the observance as previously noted.

The judiciary continues to evince reluctance to instructing the jury to consider the insanity defence. Defendants are also resistant to pleading insanity. There are several possible reasons for these attitudes, not least the stigma still associated with the label of insanity. The Law Commission voiced concerns over the use of medical conditions to argue lack of *mens rea* in their discussion document. This would seem a reasonable basis for a prosecution application for the insanity defence to be considered by the jury. The lack of this capability permits the elision of this important mechanism for ensuring public safety. This could be combined with other reforms that would eliminate some of the most unsatisfactory issues, including the name of the defence.

Legal automatism suffers from the lack of a satisfactory definition. Total loss of voluntary control seems quite clear, but it seems far too high a threshold for avoiding criminal responsibility, particularly when performing a task such as driving where less than total loss of control can have fatal consequences. The reform of automatism proposed by the Law Commission has much to commend it (although currently, the prospects of it becoming law seem remote). However, even then it would not provide a defence to the unfortunate diabetic driver who becomes hypoglycaemic through no fault of his own.

Reform of the law in this area has been considered on several occasions. The Butler Committee proposed that non-insane automatism be restricted to:

> transient states not related to other forms of mental disorder and arising solely as a consequence of a) the administration, maladministration or non-administration of alcohol, drugs or other substances or b) physical injury.
>
> (Butler Committee, 1975)

This definition covers among other conditions iatrogenic hypoglycaemia and delirium tremens. They also proposed the defence of "not guilty on evidence of mental disorder". The Law Commission rejected the expansion of the definition proposed by the Butler Committee, which would have included cases like *Clarke (Trevor Norman)*. They were concerned that:

> this might be to subject too many acquitted persons to a possibly stigmatising and distressing verdict and to inappropriate control through the courts' disposal power.
>
> (Law Commission, 1989)

Interestingly, this type of expansion is what the Law Commission now proposes (see below).

The Butler Committee also recommended flexibility of disposal, which was implemented by the Criminal Procedure (Insanity and Unfitness to Plead) Act 1991. The Law Commission's Draft Criminal Code proposed that "mental disorder" should include:

> a state of automatism (not resulting only from intoxication) which is a feature of a disorder, whether organic or functional and whether continuing or recurring, that may cause a similar state on another occasion
>
> (Clause 34)

Clause 33(1) states that a person will not be convicted:

> if he acts in a state of automatism, that is, his act:
>
> (i) is a reflex, spasm, or convulsion; or
> (ii) occurs while he is in a condition (whether of sleep, unconsciousness, impaired consciousness or otherwise) depriving him of effective control of the act.

Both bodies proposed that incapacity due to a condition likely to recur should come under a new mental condition defence to ensure social control. Additionally, both proposals would ensure that the diabetic driver would have recourse to a mental condition defence (albeit via different means). The most recent Law Commission proposals which are in the same vein are discussed below in detail.

Policy issues

Many of the concerns raised in public and parliamentary debate are based on reasonable policy grounds. As Hart states:

> Any increase in the number of conditions required to establish criminal liability increases the opportunity for deceiving courts of juries by the pretence that some condition is not satisfied.
>
> (Hart, 1968)

The main difficulty with the special verdict is the term "insanity", which would require statutory change. There are valid objections to the expansion of the remit of the special verdict. One objection is increased cost – the risk of recurrence of harmful behaviour is extremely low, so supervision and treatment are not cost-effective from a harm prevention perspective. Another objection concerns the potential for state abuse of powers for social control, which echoes the concerns of the Law Commission above. A final objection relates to the impact of the special verdict; despite being nominally an acquittal, being not found not guilty by reason of insanity has the same effect as a conviction as regards the Sex Offenders' Register and it is discoverable on an enhanced criminal records check.

Another thorny issue is the admissibility test for expert evidence. Some of the evidence permitted in court to support automatism and insanity has little probative value. This is not an issue confined to mental condition defences; there are other well-known areas where scientific evidence is highly contested. This is exacerbated by the current burden and standard of proof for automatism.

The Law Commission's discussion document on reform of the law on insanity and automatism contained solutions to many of these issues (Law Commission, 2013). The Law Commission's proposals for a new mental condition defence (which would cover many conditions considered as legal automatism) omit any mention of voluntariness per se. They acknowledge many difficulties with the insanity and automatism defences:

- the law lags behind psychiatric understanding, and this partly explains why, in practice, the defence is underused and medical professionals do not apply the correct legal test;
- the label of "insane" is outdated as a description of those with mental illness, and simply wrong as regards those who have learning disabilities or learning difficulties, or those with epilepsy;
- the case law on insane and non-insane automatism is incoherent and produces results that run counter to common-sense.

The Law Commission proposes a new test for capacity, which would cover all the circumstances where a medical condition was the basis for arguing a lack of *mens rea*. The accused must be able:

- rationally to form a judgment about the relevant conduct or circumstances;
- to understand the wrongfulness of what he or she is charged with having done; or
- to control his or her physical acts in relation to the relevant conduct or circumstances.

Further, once the evidential burden had been satisfied, the burden of proof would be on the prosecution to prove that the accused had the requisite capacities beyond reasonable doubt. The new special verdict for the defendant acquitted on the basis of the proposed statutory defence would be "not criminally responsible by reason of recognized medical condition". Thus both psychiatric and medical conditions will be assessed by the same functional test. The defence of automatism would be retained, but for very limited circumstances; the "spasms, convulsions, and reflex acts" mentioned by Mackay (Mackay, 1995), when not caused by a chronic condition as per *Pull* (who had multiple sclerosis), and other rare occurrences like a head injury or a swarm of bees attacking.

There are two suggestions that this author finds problematic. Firstly, the requirement for the prosecution to prove beyond a reasonable doubt that the defendant lacked the relevant capacities would potentially perpetuate the current problems with weak expert evidence being sufficient to procure an acquittal. Alternatively, this issue could be solved by an effective reform of admissibility criteria along with judicial training in the evaluation of scientific evidence (although this has been attempted in the past with little success (Edmond et al., 2013)). Secondly, the requirement for a total loss of the relevant capacities still excludes the problematic diabetic driver cases, such as the cases of *Broome v. Perkins*, *Watmore v. Jenkins* and *R v. Clarke (Trevor Norman)*. This requirement could be replaced with "effective loss of control".

Unfortunately, statutory reform is not high on the political agenda because of the low number of cases involved. There are no current moves to legislate for the Law Commission's proposed reforms – therefore there is a strong argument for more modest reform in the short term that does not require legislation. As was suggested in the Law Commission's Draft Criminal Code, simply changing the definition of automatism from "total loss of control" to "effective loss of control" would eliminate some of the problematic decisions with diabetic drivers. This could be achieved through the common law. Instructions to the judiciary about the greater use of the special verdict in cases of parasomnia would mean that weak medical evidence would be less likely to secure an acquittal. The possible reforms are clear, and all that is needed is the political will.

Glossary

As this text is intended for the use of both legal and medical practitioners, relevant legal and medical terms are explained below.

Legal

Actus reus (plural *actus rei*) Literally "guilty [or blameworthy] act", the actus reus is the conduct element of the crime. The *actus reus* depends on the offence. The actus reus requires that the act be voluntary, although with some crimes the voluntary act may not be simultaneous with the harm. An example is where the person drives whilst being aware of a condition like epilepsy which during the course of the journey causes him to lose control. Here the voluntary act is starting the journey, even the involuntary actions which caused the crash occurred later. Legally, driving is seen as a continuing act.

Automatism Legal automatism has been defined in similar terms in several different cases. All the definitions mean either involuntary or unconscious behaviour. It has variously been defined as:

"total destruction of voluntary control" (Lord Taylor CJ in *Attorney-General's Reference (No. 2 of 1992)*)

"acting involuntarily in the sense that his actions are independent of his will, and therefore not subject to any conscious control" (Tompkins J in *R v. Campbell*)

"an act which is done by the muscles without any control by the mind such as a spasm, a reflex action or a convulsion; or an act done by a person who is not conscious of what he is doing such as an act done whilst suffering from concussion or whilst sleepwalking" (Lord Denning in *Bratty v. Attorney General for Northern Ireland*);

"the mind does not go with what is being done" (Viscount Kilmuir L.C. in *Bratty v. Attorney General for Northern Ireland*);

"all the deliberative functions of the mind must be absent" (North P. in *R v. Burr*).

The US Model Penal Code excludes from criminal liability:

A reflex, convulsion, movements during unconsciousness or sleep, conduct during hypnosis or due to hypnotic suggestion, and any movement that otherwise is not the product of the effort or determination of the actor, either conscious or habitual.

Burden of proof The burden of proof in criminal trials is on the prosecution – they have to prove the accused's guilt. The defence has the burden of proof with the insanity defence. The prosecution has the burden of proof with the sane automatism defence (once the evidential burden has been satisfied).

Evidential burden In sane automatism, the defence must present sufficient evidence for the defence to put before the jury. Generally medical evidence is required.

Illegal act The illegal act is generally the actus reus e.g. homicide, although a further requirement relevant to crimes of strict liability is that the act be voluntary. An act does not constitute a crime without the necessary mental element and voluntariness.

Mens rea (plural *mentes reae*) Literally "guilty [or blameworthy] mind", the mens rea is the mental element of the crime. *Mens rea* may be categorized as intention (or purpose), knowledge, recklessness and negligence (US Model Penal Code Section 2.02). A crime of strict liability requires no *mens rea*, just an *actus reus*.

US Model Penal Code Section 2.02
General Requirements of Culpability:

(1) Minimum Requirements of Culpability. Except as provided in Section 2.05, a person is not guilty of an offense unless he acted purposely, knowingly, recklessly or negligently, as the law may require, with respect to each material element of the offense.
(2) Kinds of Culpability Defined.

(a) Purposely.

A person acts purposely with respect to a material element of an offense when:

(i) if the element involves the nature of his conduct or a result thereof, it is his conscious object to engage in conduct of that nature or to cause such a result; and
(ii) if the element involves the attendant circumstances, he is aware of the existence of such circumstances or he believes or hopes that they exist.

(b) Knowingly.

A person acts knowingly with respect to a material element of an offense when:

(i) if the element involves the nature of his conduct or the attendant circumstances, he is aware that his conduct is of that nature or that such circumstances exist; and

(ii) if the element involves a result of his conduct, he is aware that it is practically certain that his conduct will cause such a result.

(c) Recklessly.

A person acts recklessly with respect to a material element of an offense when he consciously disregards a substantial and unjustifiable risk that the material element exists or will result from his conduct. The risk must be of such a nature and degree that, considering the nature and purpose of the actor's conduct and the circumstances known to him, its disregard involves a gross deviation from the standard of conduct that a law-abiding person would observe in the actor's situation.

(d) Negligently.

A person acts negligently with respect to a material element of an offense when he should be aware of a substantial and unjustifiable risk that the material element exists or will result from his conduct. The risk must be of such a nature and degree that the actor's failure to perceive it, considering the nature and purpose of his conduct and the circumstances known to him, involves a gross deviation from the standard of care that a reasonable person would observe in the actor's situation.

Obiter dictum/dicta (plural) Literally a "saying by the way". It is an observation on a legal question arising out of a case, but not one that applies to the actual decision. It is persuasive, but is not binding, for other judges.

Objective standard The standard of the reasonable man, or the "man on the Clapham omnibus". An example of an objective standard is dangerous driving, which is assessed by the standards of the reasonable man, not the standards of the defendant. Compare subjective standard.

Ratio or *ratio decidendi* The reason for the legal decision in a case. Compare *obiter dicta.*

Section 12 psychiatrist A psychiatrist approved under Section 12 of the Mental Health Act 1983, whose opinion is necessary for a hospital order to be made.

Special verdict The statutory special verdict must be returned by a jury (so trial by indictment in a crown court). The jury returns a verdict of not guilty by reason of insanity, and the accused is acquitted but subject to the disposal powers of the Criminal Procedure (Insanity and Unfitness to Plead) Act 1991 (as modified by the Domestic Violence, Crime and Victims Act 1984). The verdict is "not guilty by reason of insanity". The result of a successful insanity defence in a summary trial (magistrates court) is a plain acquittal. This is due to the operation of the common law insanity defence.

Strict liability offence Strict liability offences only require an actus reus, not a mens rea. This makes automatism one of the few defences available, since automatism is a denial of actus reus. Many driving offences are strict liability, on the ground that their main purpose is to protect the public.

Subjective standard A subjective standard relies on the individual perspective or assessment. An example of a subjective standard in law is recklessness. The defendant is assessed on the risks as he saw them. Some legal tests are a mixture of objective and subjective standards. The test for the level of force required in self-defence is objective, but the assessment of the risk posed to the defendant is subjective.

Medical

AASM American Academy of Sleep Medicine (www.aasmnet.org/). Its website states: "Headquartered in Darien, IL, the American Academy of Sleep Medicine (AASM) is the only professional society dedicated exclusively to the medical subspecialty of sleep medicine. As the leading voice in the field of sleep medicine, the AASM sets standards and promotes excellence in health care, education and research. Established in 1975 as the Association of Sleep Disorders Centers, 10,000 physicians, researchers and health care professionals and 1,500 sleep centers are currently members of the American Academy of Sleep Medicine. Members specialize in studying, diagnosing and treating disorders of sleep and daytime alertness such as insomnia, narcolepsy and obstructive sleep apnea."

Alien hand phenomenon Aka the alien hand syndrome, the alien limb syndrome and the alien limb phenomenon. There is a number of alien hand phenomena associated with different neuropathologies. It can affect upper or lower limbs, with complex reflex movements or dyspraxias.

Alters These are alternative personalities to the host personality in dissociative identity disorder (aka multiple personality disorder).

Automatism Medical automatisms are: Stereotyped non-purposeful behaviour occurring during psychomotor seizures.

Body Mass Index (BMI) A measurement which is used as a proxy for body fat measurement, it is calculated by the weight in kilogrammes divided by the height in metres squared. The normal range is 18.5–25. A high BMI or collar size (17 or over) is associated with obstructive sleep apnoea/hypopnoea syndrome, because obesity increases the tendency of the airway to obstruct.

Continuous positive airway pressure (CPAP) A treatment used for obstructive sleep apnoea/hypopnoea syndrome (OSAHS). A snug-fitting mask provides constant pressure to prevent collapse of the upper airway due to relaxed muscles and the pressure of the soft tissues of the neck. The mask may go over the mouth and nose or the nose only. It is very effective for the treatment of OSAHS, but the main problem is toleration of the treatment. Compliance with treatment can be monitored, and is required for HGV drivers, for example.

Electrocardiogram (ECG) The electrocardiogram or ECG (EKG in USA) is a recording of the electrical activity of the heart.

Electroencephalogram (EEG) The electroencephalogram or EEG is a recording of the electrical activity of the brain. Different electrode combinations look at different parts of the brain.

Environmental dependency syndrome The individual affected by environmental dependency syndrome relies on cues from his environment to adjust his behaviour or to accomplish certain tasks.

Evidence-based medicine Evidence-based medicine has been defined as "the judicious use of the best current available scientific research in making decisions about the care of patients". It involves four steps:

- formulate a clear clinical question from a patient's problem
- search the literature for relevant clinical articles
- evaluate (critically appraise) the evidence for its validity and usefulness
- implement useful findings in clinical practice.

One characteristic is reference to meta-analyses and databases of systemic reviews such as the Cochrane Collaboration. Attention is paid not just to the published evidence but also the quality of that evidence. The different grades of evidence (according to the Centre for Evidence-Based Medicine) are:

1a) Systematic review (with homogeneity) of Level 1 diagnostic studies; or a clinical decision rule with 1b studies from different clinical centres
1b) Validating cohort study with good reference standards; or clinical decision rule tested within one clinical centre
1c) Absolute SpPins and SnNouts (An Absolute SpPin is a diagnostic finding whose specificity is so high that a positive result rules-in the diagnosis. An Absolute SnNout is a diagnostic finding whose sensitivity is so high that a negative result rules-out the diagnosis)
2a) Systematic review (with homogeneity) of Level >2 diagnostic studies
2b) Exploratory cohort study with good reference standards; clinical decision rule after derivation, or validated only on split-sample or databases
3a) Systematic review (with homogeneity) of 3b and better studies
3b) Non-consecutive study; or without consistently applied reference standards
4) Case-control study, poor or non-independent reference standard
5) Expert opinion without explicit critical appraisal, or based on physiology, bench research or "first principles".

General Medical Council (GMC) The General Medical Council is the professional regulatory body for the medical profession in the UK. Until 2012 the GMC provided panels and ran disciplinary proceedings, but this is now the purview of the Medical Practitioners Tribunal Service (see below) since June 2012.

Hypoglycaemia Blood glucose of less than 2.2 mmol/l, accompanied by symptoms, and relieved by administration of glucose. The symptoms of hypoglycaemia are divided into symptoms of adrenaline release, and symptoms directly caused by low blood glucose. The symptoms caused by adrenaline release are the following syndromes:

Kleine-Levin syndrome A syndrome of excessive sleepiness and cognitive and mood changes. It is often associated with increased appetite and libido. It is cyclical, with patients usually completely normal between episodes. It is sometimes referred to as "Sleeping Beauty" syndrome.

Klüver-Bucy syndrome A syndrome of hypersexuality, plus hyperphagia, visual problems and other deficits. The effects are due to the location of the lesion in the brain, and have several possible causes.

Malingering This is the deliberate simulation of a condition for a secondary gain e.g. monetary gain or escaping criminal punishment.

Medical Practitioners Tribunal Service (MPTS) The MPTS was launched in June 2012. According to their website:

> The establishment of the MPTS is part of GMC's wider programme of reform of medical adjudication. It was set up to: provide better separation between the GMC's complaints and investigation functions and adjudication, and to take over responsibility for the day to day management of hearings, panellists and their decisions.
>
> The MPTS is funded by the GMC but we are accountable directly to Parliament, to which we will report on an annual basis. We will report to the Council of the GMC twice a year.
>
> (Available at www.mpts-uk.org/about/1603.asp; accessed 15 August 2014)

Obstructive sleep apnoea/hypopnoea syndrome (OSAHS) (Related terms obstructive sleep apnoea/hypopnoea (OSAH), obstructive sleep apnoea (OSA), obstructive sleep apnoea syndrome (OSAS)). Obstructive sleep apnoea/hypopnoea syndrome (also known as obstructive sleep apnoea syndrome) is a syndrome of reduced or absent breathing during sleep causing excessive daytime sleepiness. It is characterized by collapse of the upper airway (throat) during inspiration. Various substances will exacerbate this by relaxing the muscles e.g. alcohol and sedatives.

Parasomnia "unpleasant or undesirable behavioral or experiential phenomena that occur predominantly or exclusively during the sleep period" and "a group of sleep disorders broadly defined as undesirable physical or experiential events that occur within entry into sleep, within sleep, or during arousals from sleep" (AASM – Mahowald and Bornemann, 2005 and American Academy of Sleep Medicine, 2005).

Parasomniac A sufferer from parasomnia.

Polysomnography (PSG) Polysomnography – a procedure used for the diagnosis of sleep disorders which involves monitoring of brain activity, breathing, heart rate, movement of legs, eyes and chest. The exact number of electrodes varies between units, particularly the number of electroencephalogram leads. Often simultaneous video recording takes place.

Rapid eye movement (REM) sleep A form of sleep characterized by paralysis of most of the muscles, except the eye muscles and the muscles of respiration. This is when complex dream mentation occurs.

Sleep-disordered breathing This is an umbrella term covering:

- OSAHS (see earlier)
- Central or mixed apnoea
- Upper airway resistance syndrome (UARS)
- Snoring.

Utilization behaviour Utilization behaviour is similar to environmental dependency syndrome, except that it is the use of a particular tool or object, which is triggered by its presence within sight of the sufferer. If, for example, the person sees a toothbrush, he will involuntarily start to brush his teeth.

Video-polysomnography (video-PSG) The combination of video recording of the patient with polysomnography. Used in diagnosing sleep disorders by monitoring the patient, usually during a night's sleep. Sometimes the patient is deliberately sleep-deprived to improve the diagnostic accuracy. Arousals during sleep, by a sudden loud sound for example, will also help the diagnosis of disorders of arousal. The procedure takes about an hour to set up, because of the application of a number of sensors and testing of them. Different units may have slightly different protocols, particularly the number of EEG electrodes used. Analysis is time-consuming, and some units use computerized analysis. This is not considered sufficiently reliable for forensic use.

Bibliography

Recommended reading

Eigen, J.P. (2003) *Unconscious Crime: Mental Absence and Criminal Responsibility in Victorian London*. Baltimore, MD: The Johns Hopkins University Press.

Mackay, R. (1995) *Mental Condition Defences in the Criminal Law*. Oxford: Clarendon Press.

Meynen, G. (2016) *Legal Insanity: Explorations in Psychiatry, Law, and Ethics*. Springer.

Rix, K. J. B. (2011) *Expert Psychiatric Evidence*. London: RCPsych Publications.

Walker, N. (1968) *Crime and Insanity in England (Volume One): The Historical Perspective*. Edinburgh: Edinburgh University Press.

Schopp, R. (1991) *Automatism, Insanity and the Psychology of Criminal Responsibility*. Cambridge: Cambridge University Press.

Young, S., Kopelman, M. and Gudjonsson, G. (eds.). *Forensic Neuropsychology in Practice*. 1st Ed. Oxford: Oxford University Press

References

Agargun, M. Y. et al. (2001) "Characteristics of patients with nocturnal dissociative disorders", *Sleep and Hypnosis*, 3(4), pp. 131–134.

Allen, V. (2013) "Justice has betrayed me, says victim as judge free attacker who claims he is a sexomniac", *Daily Mail*.

American Academy of Sleep Medicine (2005) *International Classification of Sleep Disorders: Diagnostic and Coding Manual*. 2nd edn. Westchester, IL: American Academy of Sleep Medicine.

American Academy of Sleep Medicine (2014) *International Classification of Sleep Disorders*. 3rd edn. Darien, IL: American Academy of Sleep Medicine.

American Law Institute (1985) Model Penal Code: Official Draft and Explanatory Notes: Complete Text of Model Penal Code as Adopted at the 1962 Annual Meeting of the American Law Institute at Washington, D.C., May 24, 1962. Philadelphia, PA: The Institute.

Anscombe, G. E. M. (1957) *Intention*. Oxford: Blackwell.

Arenson, K. J. (2013) "Thabo Meli Revisited: The Pernicious Effects of Result-driven Decisions", *Journal of Criminal Law*, 77, p. 41.

Ashworth, A. (2009) *Principles of Criminal Law*. 6th edn. Oxford: OUP.

Banerjee, D. and Nisbet, A. (no date) "Sleepwalking", *Sleep Medicine Clinics*, 6, pp. 401–415.

Bassetti, C. et al. (2000) "Research Letter: SPECT during sleepwalking", *Lancet*, 356 (5 August), p. 484.

Bayne, T. (2013) "Agency as a Marker of Consciousness", in Clark, A., Kiverstein, J. and Vierkant, T. (eds). *Decomposing the Will*. New York: Oxford University Press, p. 160.

BBC News (2014) "'Sleep driving' jockey Tom Queally banned", 17 November, available at www.bbc.co.uk/news/uk-england-suffolk-30088748.

Beard, G. M. (1881) *Nature and Phenomenon of Trance ("Hypnotism," or "Somnambulism")*. New York: GP Putnam's Sons.

Bell, D. S. (2010) "Nocturnal hypoglycaemia presenting as somnambulism", *Diabetologia*, 53(9), pp. 2066–2067. doi: 10.1007/s00125-010-1842-5.

Bentley, P. (2013) "'Sexsomniac', 40, is cleared of raping a 21-year-old at Butlins because he had 'no control over his actions while asleep'", *Daily Mail*.

Bird, J., Newson, M. and Dembny, K. (2009) "Epilepsy and automatism", in Young, S., Kopelman, M. and Gudjonsson, G. (eds). *Forensic Neuropsychology in Practice*. Oxford: Oxford University Press, p. 165.

Bjorvatn, B., Grønli, J. and Pallesen, S. (2010) "Prevalence of different parasomnias in the general population", *Sleep Medicine*, 11(10), pp. 1031–1034. doi: http://dx.doi.org/10.1016/j.sleep.2010.07.011.

Blakemore, C. J. (1998) *The Mind Machine*. London: BBC Books.

Bonkalo, A. (1974) "Impulsive acts and confusional states during incomplete arousal from sleep: criminological and forensic implications", *Psychiatr Q*, 48, pp. 400–409.

Brooke, C. (2007) "Police shot diabetic in coma with Taser – because they thought he was suicide bomber", *Daily Mail*, November. Available at: www.dailymail.co.uk/news/article-494199/Police-shot-diabetic-coma-Taser--thought-suicide-bomber.html.

Broughton, R. et al. (1994) "Homicidal Somnambulism: A Case Report", *Sleep*, 17(3), pp. 253–264.

Brown, T. and Murphy, E. (2010) "Through a scanner darkly: functional neuroimaging as evidence of a criminal defendant's past mental states", *Stanford Law Review*, 62(April), p. 1119.

de Bruxelles, S. (2009) "Man with rare sleep illness who killed his wife of 40 years during nightmare is declared innocent", *The Times*.

Buchanan, P. R. (2011) "Sleep Sex", *Sleep Medicine Clinics*, 6(4), pp. 417–428.

Bucks Herald (2007) "Man Cleared of Rape after Sleepwalking Defence", *Bucks Herald*.

Burke, J. (2016) "Oscar Pistorius begins murder term after trial that held mirror to South Africa", *The Guardian*, July. Available at: www.theguardian.com/world/2016/jul/06/oscar-pistorius-begins-murder-term-after-trial-held-mirror-south-africa.

Burns, J. M. and Swerdlow, R. H. (2003) "Right Orbitofrontal Tumor With Pedophilia Symptom and Constructional Apraxia Sign", *Archives of Neurology*, 60, pp. 437–440.

Butler Committee (1975) "Report of the committee on mentally abnormal offenders", Home Office Department of Health and Social Security, Cmnd, 6244.

Calisher, C. H. (2008) "What do we know about anything?", *Croatian Medical Journal*, 49(3), pp. 436–440.

Can LII (2014) *R. v. S.H., 2014 ONCA 303, 310 CCC (3d) 455. CanLII*. Available at: www.canlii.org/en/on/onca/doc/2014/2014onca303/2014onca303.html?searchUrlHash=AAAAAQAVZGlzZWFzZSBvZiBicmFpbiBtaW5kAAAAAAE&resultIndex=1.

Cartwright, R. (2000) "Sleep-related violence: does the polysomnogram help establish the diagnosis?", *Sleep Medicine*, 1, p. 331.

Cartwright, R. (2004) "Sleepwalking Violence: A Sleep Disorder, a Legal Dilemma, and a Psychological Challenge", *American Journal of Psychiatry*, 161(7), p. 1149.

Cartwright, R. (2010) *The Twenty-four Hour Mind*. New York: Oxford University Press.

Cartwright, R. D. and Guilleminault, C. (2013) "Defending Sleepwalkers with Science and an illustrative case", *Journal of Clinical Sleep Medicine*, 9(7), p. 721.

Chevreul, M. E. (1854) *De la Baguette Divinatoire et du Pendule Dit Explorateur (On the Divining Rod and the So-called Exploratory Pendulum)*. Paris: Maillet-Bachelier.

Chung, S. A. et al. (2010) "Frequency of Sexsomnia in sleep clinic patients", *Sleep*, 33(Abstract Supplement), p. A226.

Coles, E. M. (2000) "Scientific Support for the Legal Concept of Automatism", *Psychiatry, Psychology and Law*, 7(1), pp. 33–50.

Coles, E. M. and Jang, D. (1996) "A Psychological Perspective on the Legal Concepts of 'Volition' and 'Intent'", *Journal of Law and Medicine*, 4(August), p. 60.

Colman, A. M. and Mackay, R. D. (1991) "Excluding expert evidence: a tale of ordinary folk and common experience", *Crim. L.R.*, (Nov), p. 800.

Cooke, R. (2010) "Revealed: the real Mo Mowlam", *The Observer*.

Crocker, A. G. et al. (2015) "The national trajectory project of individuals found not criminally responsible on account of mental disorder in Canada. Part 2: the people behind the label", *Canadian Journal of Psychiatry. Revue Canadienne de psychiatrie*, 60(3), pp. 106–116.

Crosby, C. (2010) "Culpability, Kingston and the Law Commission", *Journal of Criminal Law*, 74(5), pp. 434–471.

D'Agostini, A. et al. (no date) "Challenging the myth of REM sleep behavior disorder: No evidence of heightened aggressiveness in dreams", *Sleep Medicine*, 13, p. 714.

Daily Record (2011) "Paedophile who claimed he was asleep when he molested two girls jailed for three years", *Daily Record* (8 June). Available at: www.dailyrecord.co.uk/news/scottish-news/paedophile-who-claimed-he-was-asleep-when-he-molested-1104968.

Dagan, Y. and Katz, G. (no date) "A Case of Atypical Antipsychotic-induced Somnambulism: A Class Effect", *Journal of Clinical Psychiatry*, 74(4), p. 370.

Daily Mail (2011) "'Stephen Davies' (a correction)", *Daily Mail*.

Damasio, H. et al. (1994) "The Return of Phineas Gage: Clues About the Brain from The Skull of a Famous Patient", *Science*, 265(5162), p. 1102.

Dauvilliers, Y. et al. (2007) "REM Sleep Characteristics in Narcolepsy and REM Sleep Behavior Disorder", *Sleep*, 30(7), pp. 844–849.

Davidson M. J. and Walters, S. (1993) "United States v. Berri: The Automatism Defense Rears Its Ugly Little Head", *The Army Lawyer*, (October), p. 17.

Dawson, D. and Reid, K. (1997) "Fatigue, alcohol and performance impairment", *Nature*, 388(6639), p. 235.

Denno, D. W. (2003) "A Mind to Blame: New Views on Involuntary Acts", *Behavioral Sciences and the Law*, 21, pp. 601–618.

Dershowitz, A. M. (1994) *The Abuse Excuse*. New York: Little, Brown & Company.

Doghramji, K., Bertoglia, S. M. and Watson, C. (2013) "Chapter 31: Forensic Aspects of the Parasomnias", in Kothare, S. V and Ivanenko, A. (eds). *Parasomnias: Clinical Characteristics and Treatment*. New York: Springer, p. 463.

Dolan, A. (2012) "Jail for rapist who said he was sleepwalking", *Daily Mail*.

Dubber, M. D. and Hornle, T. (2014) *Criminal Law: A Comparative Approach*. Oxford: Oxford University Press.

Duff, R. A. (1986) *Trials and Punishments*. Cambridge: Cambridge University Press.

DVLA (2004) *DIAB1 Online Medical Questionnaire*. Available at: www.gov.uk/government/uploads/system/uploads/attachment_data/file/693660/diab-medical-questionnaire.pdf.

Eadie, M. J. (2002) "The Epileptology of Theodore Herpin (1799–1865)", *Epilepsia*, 43(10), p. 1256.

Ebrahim, I. O. et al. (2013) "Alcohol and Sleep I: Effects on Normal Sleep", *Alcoholism: Clinical and Experimental Research*, 37(4), pp. 539–549. doi: 10.1111/acer.12006.

Ebrahim, I. O. and Fenwick, P. (2008) "Sleep-related automatism and the law", *Medicine, Science and the Law*, 48(2), p. 124.

Ebrahim, I. O. and Shapiro, C. M. (2010) "Medico-legal consequences of parasomnias", in Thorpy, M. J. and Plazzi, G. (eds). *The Parasomnias and Other Sleep-Related Movement Disorders*. Cambridge: Cambridge University Press, p. 84.

Edmond, G. et al. (2013) "Admissibility compared: The reception of incriminating expert evidence (i.e. forensic science) in four adversarial jurisdictions", *University of Denver Criminal Law Review*, 3(1), p. 31.

Eigen, J. P. (1995) *Witnessing Insanity: Madness and Mad-Doctors in the English Court*. New Haven, CT: Yale University Press.

Eigen, J. P. (2003) *Unconscious Crime: Mental Absence and Criminal Responsibility in Victorian London*. Baltimore, MD: The Johns Hopkins University Press.

Eigen, J. P. (2004) "Delusion's odyssey: Charting the course of Victorian forensic psychiatry", *International Journal of Law and Psychiatry. Pergamon*, 27(5), pp. 395–412. doi: 10.1016/J.IJLP.2004.06.003.

Eigen, J. P. (no date) "An Inducement to Morbid Minds", in Dubber, M. D. and Farmer, L. (ed.). *Modern Histories of Crime and Punishment*. Stanford: Stanford University Press.

Ekirch, A. R. and Shneerson, J. M. (2011) "Nineteenth-Century Sleep Violence Cases: A Historical View", *Sleep Medicine Clinics*, 6(4), p. 483.

Ellison, L. (2005) "Closing the credibility gap: the prosecutorial use of expert witness testimony in sexual assault cases", *International Journal of Evidence & Proof*, 9(4), p. 239.

Faraday, M. (1853) "Experimental investigation of table turning", *Atheneum*, (July), p. 801.

Fenwick, P. (1987) "Somnambulism and the Law: A Review", *Behavioral Science and the Law*, 5(3), pp. 343–357.

Fenwick, P. and Fenwick, E. (1985) *Epilepsy and the Law – A Medical Symposium on the Current Law*. London: Royal Society of Medicine.

Fitzjames, S. J. (1883) *A History of the Criminal Law of England*. Moscow: Ripol Classic Publishing House.

Gilson, C. G. (2012) *The Law-Science Chasm: Bridging Law's Disaffection with Science as Evidence*. New Orleans: Quid Pro, LLC.

Guardian, The (1998) "News in brief: Disabled driver cleared", *The Guardian*.

Guilleminault, C. et al. (2002) "Atypical Sexual Behavior During Sleep", *Psychosomatic Medicine*, 64, pp. 328–336.

Guilleminault, C., Moscovitch, A. and Leger, D. (1995) "Forensic sleep medicine: nocturnal wandering and violence", *Sleep*, 18, pp. 740–748.

Hale, M. (1736) *History of the Pleas of the Crown* (Vol 1). In the Savoy: London.

Hall, J. (1960) *General Principles of Criminal Law*, 2nd edn. Indianapolis: The Bobbs Merrill Company.

Hansard (2008) Rape (Defences), House of Commons Debate.

Hart, H. L. A. (1968) *Punishment and Responsibility*. Oxford: Clarendon Press.

Hartman, D. et al. (2001) "Is there a dissociative process in sleepwalking and night terrors?", *Postgraduate Medical Journal*, 77, p. 244.

Hartmann, E. (1983) "Two Case Reports: Night Terrors With Sleepwalking – A Potentially Lethal Disorder", *Journal of Nervous and Mental Disease*, 171(8), p. 503.

Hawthorne, R. (2011) "Strict criminal liability: a principled approach", *Cambridge Student Law Review*, 6, p. 33.

Herring, J. (2006) *Criminal Law Text, Cases and Materials*. 2nd edn. Oxford: Oxford University Press.

Herring, J. (2010) *Criminal Law: Text, Cases and Materials*. 4th edn. Oxford: OUP.

Holmes, O. W. (1881) *The Common Law*. Boston: Little, Brown and Company.

Home Office (2005) Circular 24 (The Domestic Violence, Crime and Victims Act 2004.

Horder, J. (1993) "Pleading involuntary lack of capacity", *Cambridge Law Journal*, 52, p. 298.

Horne, J. (2011) "Focus on Sleep-Related Fatal Vehicle Crashes", *Journal of Homicide and Major Incident Investigation*, 7(1), p. 121.

Horne, J. A. and Baulk, S. D. (2004) "Awareness of sleepiness when driving", *Psychophysiology*, 41(1), pp. 161–165.

Horne, J. A. and Reyner, L. A. (1995) "Sleep related vehicle accidents", *BMJ*, 310(6979), p. 565.

Howell, M. J., Schenck, C. H. and Crow, S. J. (2009) "A review of nighttime eating disorders", *Sleep Medicine Reviews*, 13(1), p. 23.

Husak, D. (2006) "Rethinking the Act Requirement", *Cardozo Law Review*, 28, pp. 2437–2360.

Husain, A. M., Miller, P. P. and Carwile, S. T. (2001) "REM sleep behavior disorder: Potential relationship to post-traumatic stress disorder", *Journal of Clinical Neurophysiology*, 18, p. 148.

Hyman, R. (1999) "The Mischief-Making of Ideomotor Action", *The Scientific Review of Alternative Medicine*, Fall-Winter, Amherst, NY: Prometheus Books.

James, W. (1890) *Principles of Psychology*. New York, NY: Holt.

Jamieson, A. (2008) "Victim speaks out after man cleared of rape while sleepwalking", *Daily Mail*.

Jnr, R. P. G. (2004) "Commentary: Alcoholic blackout and allegation of amnesia during criminal acts", *Journal of the American Academy Psychiatry and the Law*, 32, p. 371.

Johns, M. W. (1991) "Daytime sleepiness, snoring, and obstructive sleep apnea. The Epworth Sleepiness Scale", *Sleep*, 14(6), pp. 540–545.

Jones, T. (1995) "Insanity, automatism, and the burden of proof on the accused", *Law Quarterly Review*, 111, pp. 475–516.

Joubert, P. M. and van Staden, C. W. (2016) "Behaviour that underpins non-pathological criminal incapacity and automatism: Toward clarity for psychiatric testimony", *International Journal of Law and Psychiatry*. *Pergamon*, 49, pp. 10–16. doi: 10.1016/J.IJLP.2016.04.007.

Judicial Studies Board (2010, March) *Crown Court Bench Book*.

Kales, A. et al. (1980) "Hereditary factors in sleepwalking and night terrors", *British Journal of Psychiatry*, 137, pp. 111–118.

Kean, S. (2014) "Phineas Gage neuroscience's most famous patient", *Science*, 11, p. 32.

Koster, O. (2008) "'How could the man who "raped" me be cleared because he was sleepwalking'", *Daily Mail*.

van der Kruijs, S. J. M. et al. (2012) "Functional connectivity of dissociation in patients with psychogenic non-epileptic seizures", *Journal of Neurology, Neurosurgery & Psychiatry*, 83(3), pp. 239–247. doi: 10.1136/jnnp-2011-300776.

Labelle, M.-A. et al. (2013) "Psychopathologic correlates of adult sleepwalking", *Sleep Medicine*, 14, p. 1348–55.

Langelüddeke, A. (1955) "Crimes committed during sleep", *Nervenarzt*, 26, p. 28.

Lanham, D. (no date) "Larsonneur Revisited", *Criminal Law Review*, p. 276.

Law Commission (1989) A Criminal Code for England and Wales.

Law Commission (1995) Legislating the Criminal Code: Intoxication and Criminal Liability.

Law Commission (2009) The Admissibility of Expert Evidence in Criminal Proceedings in England and Wales.

Law Commission (2013) Criminal Liability: Reforming Insanity and Automatism.

Law Commission (2013) Criminal Liability: Insanity and Automatism A Discussion Paper 23. Available at: www.lawcom.gov.uk/app/uploads/2015/06/insanity_discussion.pdf.

Lazzari, A. (2011) "Norfolk solicitor found not guilty in death crash trial", *Eastern Daily Press*, 5 May.

Levy, N. and Bayne, T. (2004) "Doing without deliberation: automatism, automaticity, and moral accountability", *International Review of Psychiatry*, 16(3), p. 209.

Lisper, H. O., Laurell, H. and Loon, J. Van (1986) "Relation between time to falling asleep behind the wheel on a closed track and changes in the subsidiary reaction time during prolonged driving on a motorway", *Ergonomics*, 29(3), pp. 445–453.

Lopez, R. et al. (2013) "Functional Impairment in Adult Sleepwalkers: A Case-Control Study", *Sleep*, 36(3), p. 345.

Mackay, R. D. (1988) "Post-Hinckley insanity in the U.S.A", *Criminal Law Review*, (February), p. 88.

Mackay, R. D. (1995) *Mental Condition Defences in the Criminal Law*. Oxford: Clarendon Press.

Mackay, T. R. R. D. (2013) "Case Comment R. v Coley; R. v McGhee; R. v Harris: insanity – distinction between voluntary intoxication and disease of mind caused by voluntary intoxication", *Criminal Law Review*, 11, pp. 923–929.

Mackay, R. and Mitchell, B. (2006) "Sleepwalking, Automatism and Insanity", *Criminal Law Review*, (Oct), pp. 901–905.

MacNish, R. (1890) *The Philosophy of Sleep*. Glasgow: W. R. M'Phun.

Magnin, E. et al. (2014) "Conversion, dissociative amnesia, and Ganser syndrome in a case of "chameleon" syndrome: Anatomo-functional findings", *Neurocase*. Routledge, 20(1), pp. 27–36. doi: 10.1080/13554794.2012.732081.

Mahowald, M. W. and Bornemann, M. A. C. (2005) NREM sleep-arousal parasomnias", in Kryger, M. H., Roth T. and Dement, W. C. (eds). *Principles and Practice of Sleep Medicine*. 4th edn. Philadelphia, PA: Elsevier Saunders, pp. 889–896.

Mahowald, M., Bornemann, M. C. and Schenck, C. (2007) "Finally – sleep science for the courtroom", *Sleep Medicine Review*, 11(1), pp. 1–3.

Mahowald, M. W., Bornemann, M. A. C. and Schenck, C. H. (2009) "Behavior and Parasomnias (RSBD)", in Stickgold, R. and Walker, M. (eds). *The Neuroscience of Sleep*, Cambridge, MA: Academic Press, p. 18.

Mahowald, M. W., Schenck, C. H. and Bornemann, M. A. C. (2005) "Sleep-related Violence", *Current Neurology and Neuroscience Reports*, 5, pp. 153–158.

McSherry, B. (2003) "Voluntariness, Intention and the Defence of Mental Disorder: Toward a rational approach", *Behavioral Science and the Law*, 21, pp. 581–599.

McSherry, B. (2004) "Criminal responsibility, 'fleeting' states of mental impairment, and the power of self-control", *International Journal of Law and Psychiatry*, 27(5), pp. 445–457. doi: 10.1016/j.ijlp.2004.06.002.

Mega, M. (2016a) "'Sexsomnia' soldier who dodged rape trial after claiming he was sleep-walking later attacked two women", *Daily Mirror*, May. Available at: www.mirror.co.uk/news/uk-news/sexsomnia-soldier-who-dodged-rape-8075111.

Mega, M. (2016b) "Rape victim whose attacker dodged jail using 'sexsomnia' excuse hits out as he is finally locked up", *Daily Record*, June. Available at: www.dailyrecord.co.uk/news/real-life/rape-victim-whose-attacker-dodged-8222936.

Mega, M. (2016c) "Rapist soldier avoided jail for years after claiming he attacked women in his sleep", *Daily Mirror*, 18 June. Available at: www.mirror.co.uk/news/uk-news/rapist-soldier-avoided-jail-years-8226537.

Mercer, D. (2002) "The intersection of Sociology of Scientific Knowledge (SSK) and law: Some themes and policy reflections", *Law Text Culture*, 6, p. 137.

Mitchell, B., Mackay, R. D. and Brookbanks, W. J. (2008) "Pleading for provoked killers: in defence of Morgan Smith", *Law Quarterly Review*, 124, pp. 675–705.

Mitrovic, M. and Katic, L. (2013) "Sleepwalking Movement Behaviour: A Study on (Somnambular) Perception of Space", in *V. Dubrovnik Conference on Cognitive Science.*

Molaie, M. and Deutsch, G. K. (1997) "Psychogenic Events Presenting as Parasomnia", *Sleep*. Oxford University Press, 20(6), pp. 402–405. doi: 10.1093/sleep/20.6.402.

Moldofsky, H. et al. (1995) "Sleep-Related Violence", *Sleep*, 18(9), pp. 731–739.

Moore, M. S. (1979) "Responsibility and the unconscious", *Southern California Law Review*, 53, p. 1563.

Moore, M. S. (1993) Act and Crime: The Philosophy of Action and its Implications for the Criminal Law. Oxford: Oxford University Press.

Moore, M. S. (2013) "Intention as a Marker of Criminal Culpability and Legal Punishability", in Duff, R. A. and Green, S. P. (eds). *Philosophical Foundations of Criminal Law*. Oxford: Oxford University Press, p. 179.

Morley, C. (1998) "Concerns about using and interpreting covert video surveillance", *BMJ*, 316(7i44)(23 May), p. 1603.

Moran, R. (1981) *Knowing Right from Wrong: The Insanity Defence of Daniel McNaughtan*. New York: The Free Press.

Morris, N. (1951) "Somnambulistic homicide: Ghosts, spiders, and North Koreans", *Res Judicatae*, 5, p. 29.

Morrison, I., Rumbold, J. M. M. and Riha, R. L. (2014) "Medicolegal aspects of complex behaviours arising from the sleep period: A review and guide for the practising sleep physician", *Sleep Medicine Reviews*, 18(3). doi: 10.1016/j.smrv.2013.07.004.

Morse, S. J. (1985) "Excusing the crazy: the insanity defense reconsidered", *South California Law Review*, 58, p. 777.

Morse, S. J. (2004) "New neuroscience, old problems", in Garland, B. (ed.). *Neuroscience and the Law: Brain, Mind, and Scales of Justice*. New York: Dana Press.

Morse, S. J. (2006a) "Criminal Responsibility and the Disappearing Person", *Cardozo Law Review*, 28(6), pp. 2545–2576. Available at: http://heinonline.org/HOL/Page?handle=hein.journals/cdozo28&id=2561&div=83&collection=journals.

Morse, S. J. (2006b) "Brain Overclaim Syndrome and Criminal Responsibility: A Diagnostic Note", *Ohio State Journal of Criminal Law*, 3, p. 397.

Mortati, K.(2012) "A patient with distinct dissociative and hallucinatory fugues", *BMJ Case Reports*. doi: 10.1136/bcr.11.2011.5078.

Nielsen, T., Svob, C. and Kuiken, D. (2009) "Dream-enacting behaviors in a normal population", *Sleep*, 32(12), pp. 1629–1636.

Nofzinger, E. A. and Wettstein, R. M. (1995) "Homicidal Behavior and Sleep Apnea: a Case Report and Medicolegal Discussion", *Sleep*. Oxford: Oxford University Press, 18(9), pp. 776–782. doi: 10.1093/sleep/18.9.776.

O'Reilly-Fleming, T. (1992) "From beasts to bedlam: Hadfield, the Regency crisis, M'Naghten and the 'mad' business in Britain, 1788–1843", *Journal of Psychiatry and Law*, 20, p. 167.

Ohayon, M., Caulet, M. and Priest, R. (1997) "Violent Behavior During Sleep", *Journal of Clinical Psychiatry*, 58, pp. 369–376.

Ohayon, M. M. et al. (1997) "An International Study on Sleep Disorders in the General Population: Methodological Aspects of the Use of the Sleep-EVAL System", *Sleep*, 20(12), pp. 1086–1092.

Oxford Mail (2011) "Jurors take just 20 minutes to convict killer Sean Freaney", *Oxford Mail*.

van Oorsouw, K. et al. (2004) "Alcoholic blackout for criminally relevant behavior", *Journal of the American Academy of Psychiatry and the Law*, 32, p. 364.

Old Bailey (1853) "R v Sarah Minchin", *The Proceedings of the Old Bailey*, 13 June, p. 725.

Otmani, S. et al. (2005) "Effect of driving duration and partial sleep deprivation on subsequent alertness and performance of car drivers", *Physiology and Behaviour*, 84(5), pp. 715–724.

Parsons, M. (no date) "Fits and Other Causes of Loss of Consciousness Whilst Driving", *Quarterly Journal of Medicine*, 58(227), p. 295.

Pasick, A. (2000) "An Unconscious Love Life – 'Sleepsexers' Remember Nothing in the Morning", *Fox News*, 13 January, available at www.rense.com/ufo6/sleepsex.htm.

Patterson, R. (1991) "The Le Fort fractures: René Le Fort and his work in anatomical pathology", *Canadian Journal of Surgery*, 34(2), pp. 183–184.

Pilon, M., Montplaisir, J. and Zadra, A. (2008) "Precipitating factors of somnambulism: Impact of sleep deprivation and forced arousals", *Neurology*, 20(10 June), p. 2284.

Plante, D. T. and Winkelman, J. W. (2008) "Parasomnias: Psychiatric Considerations", *Sleep Medicine Clinics*, 3, pp. 217–229.

Ploog, D. W. (2003) "The place of the Triune Brain in psychiatry", *Physiology & Behavior*. Elsevier, 79(3), pp. 487–493. doi: 10.1016/S0031-9384(03)00154-9.

Podolsky, E. (1961) "Somnambulistic homicide", *Medicine, Science and the Law*, 1, p. 260.

Pogash, C. (2003) "Myth of the 'Twinkie defense' / The verdict in the Dan White case wasn't based on his ingestion of junk food". Available: http://www.sfgate.com/health/article/Myth-of-the-Twinkie-defense-The-verdict-in-2511152.php.

Pressman, M. R. et al. (2007) "Alcohol-induced sleepwalking or confusional arousal as a defense to criminal behavior: a review of scientific evidence, methods and forensic considerations", *Journal of Sleep Research*, 16, pp. 198–212.

Pressman, M. R. (2011a) "Preface: Common Misconceptions About Sleepwalking and Other Parasomnias", *Sleep Medicine Clinics*, 6(4), p. xiii.

Pressman, M. R. (2011b) "Sleep and Drug-Impaired Driving Overlap Syndrome", *Sleep Medicine Clinics*, 6(4), p. 441.

Pressman, M. R. (2011c) "Sleep Driving and Z-Drugs: sleepwalking variant or misuse of drugs?", *Sleep Medicine Reviews*, 15, p. 285.

Pressman, M. R. et al. (2013) "Alcohol, sleepwalking and violence: lack of reliable scientific evidence", *Brain*, 136(2), p. e229.

Pressman, M. R., Mahowald, M. W. and Schenck, C. H. (2005) "Sleep terrors/Sleepwalking – Not REM Behavior Disorder", *Sleep*, 28, p. 278.

Pressman, M. R., Mahowald, M. H., Schenck, C. H., Cramer Bornemann, M. A., Monplaisir, J. Y., Zadra, A., Pilon, M., Grunstein, R., Buchanan, P. R. and Tachibana , N. (2009) "Sleep-related automatism and the law (letter to the editor)", *Medicine, Science and the Law*, 49(2), pp. 139–143.

Press Complaints Commission (2011) "Stephen Davies and Eleanor Parker v The Guardian about Accuracy", 27 September.

Purton, M. (2011) "Orpington mum launches e-petition to raise awareness of sleep apnoea after son injured and his fiancee killed in crash". Available at www.newsshopper.co.uk/news/9193032.Campaign_to_raise_awareness_of_sleep_disorder_after_fatal_crash/ Aug 12 2011.

Redmayne, M. (2001) *Expert Evidence and Criminal Justice*. Oxford: Oxford University Press.

Reyner, L. A. and Horne, J. A. (1998) "Falling asleep whilst driving: are drivers aware of prior sleepiness?", *International Journal of Legal Medicine*, 111(3), p. 120.

Reznek, L. (1997) *Evil or Ill? Justifying the Insanity Defence*. Abingdon: Routledge.

Rix, K. J. B. (2011) *Expert Psychiatric Evidence*. London: RCPsych Publications.

Rix, K. J. B. and Clarkson, A. (1994) "Depersonalization and intent", *Journal of Forensic Psychiatry*, 5, p. 409.

Roberts, P. (1996) "Will you stand up in court? On the admissibility of psychiatric and psychological evidence", *Journal of Forensic Psychiatry*, 7(1), pp. 63–78.

Robinson, P. H. (1993) "Should the Criminal Law Abandon the Actus Reus–Mens Rea Distinction?", in Shute, S., Gardner, J., and Horder, J. (eds) *Action and Value in Criminal Law*. Oxford: Clarendon Press, pp. 187–211.

Rosenthal, J. M. et al. (2001) "The effect of acute hypoglycemia on brain function and activation: a functional magnetic resonance imaging study", *Diabetes. American Diabetes Association*, 50(7), pp. 1618–26. doi: 10.2337/DIABETES.50.7.1618.

Rumbold, J. M. M. (2015) *The parasomnia defence: expert evidence in criminal trials, Keele University*. Keele Research Depository, Keele University. Available at: http://eprints.keele.ac.uk/2501/.

Rumbold, J. and Wasik, M. (2011) "Diabetic drivers, hypoglycaemic unawareness, and automatism", *Criminal Law Review*, pp. 863–872.

Ryle, G. (1970) *The Concept of Mind*. London: Penguin.

Saks, E. R. (2001) "Multiple Personality Disorder and Criminal Responsibility", *Southern California Interdisciplinary Law Journal*, 10(2), p. 185.

Salkeld, L. (2007) "'Sexsomniac' RAF man sobs as he is cleared of raping girl in his sleep", *Daily Mail*. Available at: www.dailymail.co.uk/news/article-473525/Sexsomniac-RAF-man-sobs-cleared-raping-girl-sleep.html.

Sasai, T., Inoue, Y. and Matsuura, M. (2012) "Do patients with rapid eye movement sleep behavior disorder have a disease-specific personality?", *Parkinsonism & related disorders*, 18(5), pp. 616–618. doi: http://dx.doi.org/10.1016/j.parkreldis.2011.12.010.

Schenck, C. H. et al. (1986) "Chronic behavioral disorders of human REM sleep: a new category of parasomnia", *Sleep*, 9, pp. 293–308.

Schenck, C. H. et al. (1989) "Dissociative disorders presenting as somnambulism. Polysomnographic, video and clinical documentation (8 cases)", *Dissociation*, 11, p. 194.

Schenck, C. H. (2005) *Paradox Lost: Midnight in the Battleground of Sleep and Dreams*. Minneapolis: Extreme Nights LLC.

Schenck, C. H., Hurwitz, T. D. and Mahowald, M. W. (1993) "REM sleep behavior disorder: an update on a series of 96 patients and a review of world literature", *Journal of Sleep Research*, 2, pp. 223–231.

Schenck C. H. and Mahowald, M. W. (1995) "A Polysomnographically Documented Case of Adult Somnambulism With Long-Distance Automobile Driving and Frequent Nocturnal Violence: Parasomnia With Continuing Danger as a Noninsane Automatism?", *Sleep*, 18(9), pp. 765–772.

Schenck C. H. and Mahowald, M. W. (1998) "An Analysis of a Recent Criminal trial Involving Sexual Misconduct with a Child, Alcohol Abuse and a Successful Sleepwalking Defence: arguments supporting two proposed new forensic categories", *Medicine, Science and the Law*, 38(2), pp. 147–152.

Schopp, R. F. (1991) *Automatism, Insanity and the Psychology of Criminal Responsibility*. Cambridge: Cambridge University Press.

Selby, K. E., Morrison, I. and Riha, R. L. (2012) "Psychiatric Comorbidity in Arousal Disorders: Chicken or Egg?", *The Journal of Neuropsychiatry and Clinical Neurosciences*. American Psychiatric Association, Arlington, VA, 24(3), pp. E36–E36. doi: 10.1176/appi.neuropsych.11070173.

Shapiro, C., Trajanovic, N. and Fedoroff, J. (2003) "Sexsomnia – A New Parasomnia?", *Canadian Journal of Psychiatry*, 48(5), pp. 311–317.

Siclari, F. et al. (2010) "Violence in sleep", *Brain*, 133, pp. 3494–3509.

Siddiqui, F., Osuna, E. and Chokroverty, S. (2009) "Writing emails as part of sleepwalking after increase in Zolpidem", *Sleep Medicine*, 10, p. 262.

de Sio, F. S. (2006) "Razionalità, identità, controllo: le condizioni soggettive dellarespon-sabilità", *Rivista di Filosofia*, XCVII(1), p. 33.

Slobogin, C. (2006) *Minding Justice: Laws that Deprive People with Mental Disability of Life and Liberty*. Cambridge, MA: Harvard University Press.

Smart, A. (1987) "Criminal responsibility for failing to do the impossible", *Law Quarterly Review*, 103(Oct), pp. 532–563.

Smith, J. C. (no date) "Driving without due care and attention – diabetic", *Criminal Law Review*, (Apr), p. 271.

Smith, R. and Wynne, B. (eds) (1989) *Expert Evidence: Interpreting Science in the Law*. London: Routledge.

Somers, W. A. and Weller, M. (1991) "Differences in the medical and legal viewpoint illustrated by R v Hardie", *Medicine, Science and the Law*, 31(2), pp. 152–156.

Stimpson, S. C. (1994) "State v. Cowan: The Consequences of Montana's Abolition of the Insanity Defense", *Montana Law Review*, 55, p. 503.

Stradling J. R. and Davies, R. J. O. (2004) "Sleep 1: Obstructive sleep apnoea/hypopnoea syndrome: definitions, epidemiology and natural history", *Thorax*, 59, pp. 73–78.

Stryker, J. (1999) "Sleepstabbing: The strange science of sleep behavior and one verdict: Guilty!", *Salon*, 8 July.

Sullivan, G. R. (1996) "Making Excuses", in Simester, A. P. and Smith, A. T. H. (eds). *Harm and Culpability*. Oxford: Clarendon Press, p. 134.

Tassinari, C. A. et al. (2006) "Central pattern generators for a common semiology in fronto-limbic seizures and in parasomnias. A neuroethologic approach", *Neurological Sciences*, 26(3 Supplement), p. s225.

Telegraph (2007) "Hotels train staff for naked sleepwalkers", *Telegraph*, 25 October.

Terzaghi, M. et al. (2009) "Evidence of Dissociated Arousal States During NREM Parasomnia from an Intracerebral Neurophysiological Study", *Sleep*, 32(3), pp. 409–412.

Thorpe, B. (1840) *Ancient Laws and Institutes of England*. London: George E. Eyre and Andrew Spottiswoode.

The Times (1961) "US Sergeant is Cleared of Murder".

Twisty (2005) *Raper's Delight, I Blame The Patriarchy*. Available at: http://blog.iblamethepatriarchy.com/2005/12/01/rapers-delight/.

Vasagar, J. (2002) "REM guitarist cleared of air rage", *The Guardian*, 6 April. Available at: www.theguardian.com/uk/2002/apr/06/world.jeevanvasagar.

Vetrugno, R. et al. (2006) "Nocturnal eating: sleep-related eating disorder or night eating syndrome? A videopolysomnographic study", *Sleep*, 29(7), p. 949.

Vincent, N. (2013) *The Stilnox defence: automatism or amnesia?* Available at: http://nicolevincent.net/?p=385.

Virgo, G. (1993) "The Law Commission Consultation Paper on intoxication and criminal liability: Part 1: Reconciling principle and policy", *Criminal Law Review*, p. 415.

Walker, N. (1968) *Crime and Insanity in England (Volume One): The Historical Perspective.* Edinburgh: Edinburgh University Press.

Warren, R. E. and Frier, B. M. (2005) "Hypoglycaemia and cognitive function", *Diabetes, Obesity and Metabolism*, 7(5), pp. 493–503. doi: 10.1111/j.1463-1326.2004.00421.x.

Wasik, M. (1982) "Partial excuses in the criminal law", *Modern Law Review*, (September), p. 516.

Weiss, K. J. and del Busto, E. (2011) "Early American Jurisprudence of Sleep Violence", *Sleep Medicine Clinics*, 6(4), p. 469.

White, A. M. (2003) "What happened? Alcohol, memory blackouts, and the brain", *Alcohol Research & Health*, 27(186).

White, A. M., Jamieson-Drake, D. W. and Swartzwelder, H. S. (2002) "Prevalence and correlates of alcohol-induced blackouts among college students: Results of an e-mail survey", *Journal of American College Health*, 51, p. 117.

White, C. et al. (2012) "Diagnostic Delay in REM Sleep Behaviour Disorder (RBD)", *Journal of Clinical Sleep Medicine*, 8(2), p. 133.

Wigley, S. (2007) "Automaticity, Consciousness and Moral Responsibility", *Philosophical Psychology*, 20(2), p. 209.

Williams, G. (1982) "Offences and Defences", *Legal Studies*, 2, p. 232.

Williams, G. (no date) *Textbook of Criminal Law*. 2nd edn. Dallas, TX: Stevens.

Xu, M. (2009) "Sexsomnia: A Valid Defence to Sexual Assault?", *Journal of Gender Race & Justice*, 12, p. 687.

Yellowlees, D. (1878) "Homicide by a Somnambulist", *Journal of Mental Science*, 24(415–58).

Yeo, S. (2001) "Putting Voluntariness Back Into Automatism", *Victoria University of Wellington Law Review*, 32, pp. 387–406.

Appendices

A

Hansard 15th Oct 2008

Col 799

Rape (Defences)

12.32 pm

Harry Cohen (Leyton and Wanstead) (Lab): I beg to move,

That leave be given to bring in a Bill to amend the Sexual Offences Act 2003 to prohibit the use of a defence of sleepwalking in proceedings relating to the offence of rape; and for connected purposes.

I think of this as my rape and sleepwalking Bill, because it deals with what has become a loophole in rape law. My Bill says that it shall not be a defence for a defendant accused of an offence of rape to claim that he was sleepwalking or suffering from non-insane automatism or other similar condition when the offence was alleged to have taken place.

This matter came to my attention during a Select Committee on Work and Pensions visit to Australia to obtain evidence for our excellent carer's report. During the stopover at Hong Kong airport, I was reading in an Australian newspaper of an ongoing court case where the defendant, Leonard Spencer, was claiming as a defence for rape that he had been sleepwalking. I thought, no chance! To my amazement, on the journey back I saw a report in *The Australian* on 16 May that he had been acquitted on those grounds and that it was the first time in an Australian court that "sex-sleep" had succeeded as part of a defence.

The article said:

> It is not hard to imagine that more cases will come to light, as defence lawyers ask clients facing sex charges: "Do you have any strange episodes in your sleep?"

It should be pointed out that Spencer's lawyer, Jon Tippett QC, did not ask his client any such leading questions. It was the police, curiously, in what seemed a throwaway question, who asked Spencer whether he had sleep issues. Spencer, who was on medication for depression, replied that he did."

From then on, the sexsomnia angle was played strongly through the trial. The article continued: "Spencer did not deny being in the woman's bed. The defence argued that he did not remember being there. A person cannot be found guilty if there is no intent involved. That's why the sleeper defence is a ripper."

I was then astonished to see not only that the defence had been used internationally—the 2005 judgment of a Canadian man, Jan Luedecke, is one sexsomniac acquittal—but that the cases of two British men were also referred to. The first was that of London man James Bilton in 2005, and the second was from 2007, when RAF mechanic Kenneth Ecott was acquitted of raping a 15-year-old girl despite admitting to having committed the act. Some experts now think that those cases have set a precedent in the law.

I sought a House of Commons Library briefing on the subject, and it brought my attention to several other cases. In 1994, Robert Burnett, a prison officer from Newcastle upon Tyne, was found not guilty of attempted rape after the court accepted that he was sleepwalking at the time. In 2006, Terry Hind, a gay race trainer—I am not sure what that is—committed a sexual assault on another man in Scotland when sleepwalking and the jury gave the verdict of "not proven", which is part of the Scottish law. In 2006, Christopher Davies initially denied and then admitted sexually assaulting a woman, but was found not guilty because he was sleepwalking at the time. In 2007, David Pooley, a former RAF corporal, was found not guilty of rape after he successfully proved that he was suffering an episode of parasomnia, which can include sleepwalking.

The law provides defences of insanity and non-insane automatism. The distinction between the two is crucial. According to English criminal law, the former requires a disease of the mind and is decided on the balance of probabilities. When it results in a not guilty criminal verdict, other powers can be invoked, such as the provisions under the Mental Health Act 2007. In the cases of non-insane automatism, the onus is on the prosecution to exclude it beyond reasonable doubt, or the result is an outright acquittal. My Library briefing says:

> English law lacks a satisfactory method of dealing with defendants who, although lacking fault, pose a potential threat to the public . . . The law in this area was described in 1973 as a 'quagmire' and recent cases have only made matters worse.

As I have said, automania [sic] is increasingly being used as a defence in rape cases in the UK, Canada and Australia, and defendants are being acquitted. There must now be serious doubt that the Crown Prosecution Service would bring such a case to court if it thought that that defence would be used, as it has become extremely difficult to get a conviction.

Just 6 per cent of rape cases result in a conviction and such loopholes make a conviction even harder to obtain. That is a harsh injustice to the victims of rape and treats that serious crime as though it is of little consequence in the legal system. I think that the loophole has widened following recent cases. My briefing said:

> Automatism . . . is a complete defence (unless it is self-induced, for instance by voluntary taking of drugs and alcohol). In a couple of the recent cases, prior consumption of alcohol was admitted but the juries still deemed it not a factor in accepting the automatism defence.

There was one case of extreme violence back in 1991—the case of *Burgess*. The expert medical opinion presented evidence that sleepwalking was a mental abnormality and could deem the defendant legally insane. The judge accepted that, but the series of more recent cases to which I have referred have overridden that decision as far as rape is concerned. Rape is obviously not deemed to be serious enough. My Library briefing says that English law lacks a satisfactory method of dealing with defendants who, although lacking fault, pose a potential threat to the public, and the court will have a sentencing discretion including absolute discharge, guardianship and supervision only if a disease of the mind is established.

The law in this area is a case of political correctness gone mad. I think that it defies common sense. Sleepwalking is not a reasonable excuse for rape that should lead to acquittal. Dr Cosmo Hallstrom, a fellow of the Royal College of Psychiatrists, has said:

> People do sleepwalk and they do strange things in their sleep, but it usually is no more complex than grinding the teeth or smacking the lips—at most they may get up and make a cup of tea. I would think it was extremely difficult to perform such a complex manoeuvre as having sexual intercourse while asleep—especially if the other person is unwilling.

B

Legislation proposed by Rape (Defences) Bill

A Bill to amend the Sexual Offences Act 2003 to prohibit the use of a defence of sleepwalking in proceedings relating to the offence of rape; and for connected purposes.

BE IT ENACTED by the Queen's most Excellent Majesty, by and with the advice and consent of the Lords Spiritual and Temporal, and Commons, in this present Parliament assembled, and by the authority of the same, as follows:—

1 Amendment of the Sexual Offences Act 2003 in relation to rape

(1) Section 1 of the Sexual Offences Act 2003 (c. 42) (rape) is amended as follows.

(2) After subsection (3) insert—

"(3A) It shall not be a defence for a defendant accused of an offence under this section to claim he was—

(a) sleepwalking, or
(b) suffering from non-insane automatism or other similar condition when the offence was alleged to have taken place."

2 Short title

This Act may be cited as the Rape (Defences) Act 2008.

C

Early Day Motion 463

AUTOMATISM AS A DEFENCE IN LAW

Session: 2009–10

Date tabled: 14.12.2009

Primary sponsor: Cohen, Harry

That this House considers current UK law which provides sleepwalking as a defence for rape or murder to be grossly unreasonable following recent cases, including a not guilty verdict on a man who killed his wife; notes that the jury in this recent case were presented with the option of not guilty by way of insane automatism or not guilty due to non-insane automatism; further notes that sleep specialist Dr Chris Idzikowski is quoted in *The Guardian* on 5 December 2009 as saying that insane automatism is intrinsic to the person's behaviour, whilst non-insane automatism is used if a person has had a blow to the head, or is withdrawing from drugs, which creates the condition; further notes that the same article states that an estimated 10 million people in the UK have sleep problems; further notes that very many people at any one time suffer the effects of a blow to the head or withdrawal from drugs, prescription or otherwise; considers that those are not proper defences for rape or murder which warrant walking free without any consequence and if they are now deemed to be so, represent a massive legal loophole; further considers that anyone who kills or commits rape cannot be considered completely safe to walk free in the community without much more extensive tests to check that they will not act in the same manner again and that the seriousness of the act should require detention for such tests in all cases; and calls for a full-scale legal inquiry to consider this matter and to bring sense to UK law.

D

Material from the assessment of Scott Falater by Mark Pressman

List of Observed and Inferred Behaviors	*Cognitive Skills Required*
Start 9:15 PM??	
Defendant Statement	
Go upstairs to bed	
Change into pajamas	

1	Leave contact lenses in	Planning-needed them later??
2	Change from pajamas into undergarments?, Jeans, ASU t-shirt, socks, boots	Oriented to time, place
3	Descend stairs	
4	Retrieve knife	Oriented to place, planning, Memory
5	Locate mouthpiece and place in Mouth??	Oriented to place, planning, Memory
6	Locate and retrieve flashlight	Oriented to place and time (knew it was nighttime), planning, memory
7	Exit home	
8	Aim flashlight at pool pump	?
9	Stab wife 44 times	
10	Ignore cries of wife	unarousable vs. murderous intent Absence of social interaction vs. ignores wife's cries
11	Exit pool area and enter garage	planning, intent, oriented to place
12	Undress	
13	Locate keys to car	planning, intent, concealment
14	Unlock/open trunk of Volvo station Wagon	planning, intent, oriented to place
15	Locate Tupperware container, plastic Garbage bag? Already in place??	Advanced planning, intent, concealment
16	Place bloody jeans, ASU t-shirt undergarments, socks, boots knife, knife sheath, mouth piece in Tupperware container	Advanced planned, intent, concealment
17	Seal Tupperware container and Place in black plastic garbage bag	Planning, intent, concealment, double sealed, not visible.
18	Place garbage bag with Tupperware container in spare tire wheel well of car.	Ready for disposal?? Planning
19	Close wheel well and trunk of car	Tidy?
20	Put on pajamas. Pajamas ready in garage? Or walked naked through house to bedroom to find pajamas??	Advanced preparation/planning, oriented to place

21	Exit garage	
22	Go upstairs to bedroom	
23	Turn on bedroom light	Oriented to time
24	Exit bedroom to bathroom	
25	Turn off light in bedroom	Oriented to time
26	Wash blood off	Self awareness, aware of appearance
27	Clean cut on finger of right hand	Aware of pain, cut
28	Locate band aids	Aware of need for treatment, aware of proper treatment, memory where to find treatment
29	Remove band aid from wrapper	Excellent fine motor coordination
30	Place properly on right hand	Good motor coordination, planning
31	Turn bedroom light off	Oriented to time, very thrifty
32	Turn bathroom light off	Oriented to time, very thrifty
33	Go downstairs	
34	Enter kitchen area	
35	Washing hands (wringing motion of Hands)	
36	Enter room next to Arcadia doors	
37	Opened Arcadia doors partially and gestured to barking dog to be quiet – dog stopped barking	Social interaction. He didn't respond to wife's cries, but did respond to dog barking!
38	Exited Arcadia doors	
39	Walked over to body of wife	Memory, planning – neighbor saw her moving 5 minutes after stabbing, was she still alive??
40	Stood over body for several mins.	Planning??
41	Looked over shoulder in direction of neighbor	orienting to sound??, attention
42	Re-enters home via Arcadia doors	
43	Locates gloves	
44	Several minutes later exits garage door	
45	Pulls on gloves while walking	planning, good physical coordination
46	Walks towards wife's body	
47	Steps over body	

48	With back to pool, bends over, grabs wrists of victim and drags body to edge of pool without looking back excellent planning, maintained mental image of distance to pool –	did not fall in
49	Move to feet and grabs and with back to pool drags 6 ft. to pool's edge without looking back	excellent planning, maintained mental image of distance to pool – did not fall in
50	Move behind body	
51	Place arms under body	Good planning
52	Flip body into pool	
53	Move to edge of pool where body is floating	
54	Repeatedly hold head of victim under water	Victim still alive. Finish job??
55	Leave body in pool	
56	Walk to and enter garage	
57	Open trunk of car with key	Complete concealment of incriminating evidence
58	Open spare tire well	Complete concealment of incriminating evidence
59	Remove black garbage bag	" "
60	Place wet gloves in garbage bag	" "
61	Replace black garbage bag in spare tire well	" "
62	Close spare tire well cover	
63	Close car trunk	
64	Leave garage	
65	Go upstairs	
66	Come downstairs Arrested by police.	

E

Account of a Somnambulist Monk from Savarin's *Physiologie du Goût* (quotation in *Paradox Lost*):

> There was a monk . . . who was looked upon as a somnambulist. He used often to leave his cell, and when he went astray, people were forced to guide him back. Many attempts were made to cure him, but in vain. One evening I had not gone to bed at the usual hour, but was in my office . . . when I saw

this monk enter in a perfect state of somnambulism. His eyes were open but fixed and . . . he had a huge knife in his hand. He came at once to my bed, the position of which he was familiar with, and after having felt my hand, struck three blows which penetrated the mattress on which I laid . . . I saw an expression of extreme gratification pervaded his face. The light of two lamps on my desk made no impression, and he returned as he had come, opening the doors which led to his cell, and I soon became satisfied that he had quietly gone to bed . . . On the next day I sent for the somnambulist and asked him what he had dreamed of during the preceding night . . . "Father," said he, "I had scarcely gone to sleep when I had dreamed that you had killed my mother, and when her bloody shadow appeared to demand vengeance, I hurried into your cell, and as I thought stabbed you. Not long after I arose . . . I thanked God that I had not committed the crime I had meditated." I then told him what had passed, and pointed out to him the blows he had aimed at me . . .

F

Reform of the Law on Automatism and Insanity (an article I posted online on www.academia.edu/11329643/Reform_of_the_law_on_automatism_and_insanity written 9 April 2012).

The law on automatism and insanity is currently being examined by the Law Commission. Automatism has been described as a "quagmire . . . seldom entered nowadays save by those in desperate need of some kind of a defence" (Lawton LJ in *Quick*). The need for reform has been recognized for some time, and here are some of the suggestions that have been made.

Abolish the internal/external divide doctrine

Under this doctrine, automatism with an internal cause is deemed an insane automatism and therefore defined by the *McNaughtan Rules* and leading to the special verdict. If there is an external cause, it is deemed a sane (or non-insane) automatism and leading to a plain acquittal.

This doctrine is the most problematic for medical expert witnesses. Many medical conditions are a combination of a predisposition and a trigger, and therefore a combination of internal and external factors. The internal/external divide leads to anomalies, one notable example being in the case of a person with diabetes (*Quick*). If he either takes too much insulin, or neglects to eat or drinks alcohol, he may suffer a hypoglycaemic episode (low blood sugar) which being triggered by the administration of a drug is deemed to be a sane automatism. If he neglects his condition and fails to take sufficient insulin and becomes hyperglycaemic (high blood sugar), this is deemed an insane automatism, similarly if he suffers hypoglycaemia due to an insulin-secreting tumour.

The other difficulty with this distinction is directing the jury when either insane or sane automatism is a possibility. The terminology of "insane automatism" even confuses lawyers, as the direction below demonstrates.

If there is no distinction between the two, either all cases of automatism will have to be pleaded under the special verdict (or an alternative defence used e.g. lack of *mens rea*) or some other criterion will be used to distinguish between sane and insane automatism e.g. risk of recurrence or risk to the public. The criterion of dangerousness is used in Canada (see *Rabey* and *Parks*). This would provide a better rational to the decision, understandable as it was, in *R v. T.*

Change disposal powers

Judges have very flexible disposal powers in the Criminal Procedures (Insanity and Unfitness to Plead) Act 1991. However, those accused of homicide and acquitted by the special verdict must receive a hospital order, if they have a mental disorder. It is not known if sleepwalking would be considered a mental disorder (and this is one instance where the decision might be made on a case-by-case basis).

Restrict the ambit of (sane) automatism

The Butler Committee (1975) proposed restricting sane automatism to "transient states not related to other forms of mental disorder and arising solely as a consequence of (a) the administration, maladministration or non-administration of alcohol, drugs or other substances or (b) physical injury" (para 18.23). This would not eliminate the diabetic anomaly mentioned above. Other suggestions are to restrict it still further to "reflex, spasm or convulsions" as per the first part of Clause 33(1) of the Law Commission's Draft Criminal Code (this would make the definition of legal automatism and medical automatism virtually identical). This has been suggested in combination with widening the ambit of the insanity defence. This would have the arguable advantage of requiring the defence to prove the defendant was sleepwalking etc.

The problem with this approach is the stigmatizing label of "insanity". This is already an issue with epilepsy and other conditions. The solution which has been advocated for some time is to change the name of the defence. For example, in Canada it is now the defence of being "not criminally responsible on account of mental disorder" (NCRMD). Even this is not wholly satisfactory, given the number of physical complaints that can cause legal insanity.

Apply the partial defence of diminished responsibility or a similar third verdict to all offences.

It has been argued that in some conditions, sleepwalking included, although the sufferers are not fully culpable, neither do they have no responsibility for their actions. The partial defence of diminished responsibility currently only applies to homicide, resulting in a conviction for manslaughter rather than murder, but some commentators argue that this concept should be applied to all offences. Given the flexibility of disposal given to judges by the Criminal Procedure

(Insanity and Unfitness to Plead) Act 1991, the arguments for this option are much weaker now.

Partial abolition of the insanity defence

Some US states have "abolished" the insanity defence. This is only partial abolition, since defendants are still able to argue lack of *mens rea* due to their mental illness. Another option (used in England and Wales between 1883 and 1964) is the verdict "guilty but insane" and other variations e.g. "guilty but mentally ill", which in some cases are in addition to the special verdict.

The objection to the former option is the possibility that treatment may not be offered to either the acquitted or the convicted that are mentally ill. The objection to the latter option is unfair labelling of the mentally ill as criminals.

Altering the standard or burden of proof

The insanity defence is an anomaly, given that the burden of proof is on the defence. This was the case for the issues of accident, self defence and provocation prior to *DPP v. Woolmington* (Jones, 1995). Thus it has been argued that there should only be an evidential burden in insanity, the same as for same automatism.

US Federal law requires "clear and convincing evidence" of insanity of the defence, a higher standard than the balance of probabilities but less than beyond reasonable doubt.

Changing the definition of legal insanity

Various definitions are used in different jurisdictions. In the US, various states use the Model Penal Code definition (sometimes modified), the Durham rule or the *McNaughtan Rules* (often combined with a volitional limb). There has been a tendency away from the Durham test back to the *McNaughtan Rules*. It's unlikely that English law would change from the *McNaughtan Rules*. The most likely changes would be an expansion of the definition from "knowledge of the nature and wrongfulness of the act" to an "appreciation of the nature and wrongfulness of the act". Scotland adopted such a definition (not yet in force) in the Criminal Justice and Licensing (Scotland) Act 2010, s. 168 which states:

(1) A person is not criminally responsible for conduct constituting an offence, and is to be acquitted of the offence, if the person was at the time of the conduct unable by reason of mental disorder to appreciate the nature or wrongfulness of the conduct.

(2) But a person does not lack criminal responsibility for such conduct if the mental disorder in question consists only of a personality disorder which is characterised solely or principally by abnormally aggressive or seriously irresponsible conduct.

Changing the name of the defence

The label of "insanity" is very stigmatizing. Whether or not a simple name change would reduce the stigma is arguable. The Canadian equivalent is known as "not criminally responsible on account of mental disorder" (NCRMD). Some would argue that the stigma extends to any defence that denies criminal responsibility. That is unavoidable in some circumstances.

Case histories

Parks

Found not guilty of murder

The Parks case truly divides the expert witness community, and for this reason should not be held up as an archetypal forensic sleepwalking episode (although it is often used as such in discussions of legal philosophy, for example). In Toronto in 1987, Kenneth Parks (23) fell asleep at home watching *Saturday Night Live.* The next thing he knew he "woke up" over a woman with a "help me" look (Cartwright, 2010). The "woman" was his mother-in-law.

His level of consciousness gradually increased and he heard the kids upstairs screaming. He tried to reassure but all the children heard was animal grunting noises. When he realized he had a knife in his hands and that there were two people lying covered in blood, he drove to the police station saying "I just killed someone with my bare hands; Oh my God, I just killed someone; I've just killed two people; My God, I've just killed two people with my hands; My God, I've just killed two people. My hands; I just killed two people. I killed them; I just killed two people; I've just killed my mother- and father-in-law. I stabbed and beat them to death. It's all my fault". Only then did he realize that he had several severed tendons in his hand which required surgical repair.

In the interim period he had got up from the couch; put on his jacket and shoes; he went out the house without locking the door (which he was normally punctilious about); drove 23 km which would have required negotiating at least one set of traffic lights, depending on the route; entering his in-law's home; and strangling his father-in-law into unconsciousness and stabbing and beating his mother-in-law to death. His description of the events he recalled was consistent during several interviews.

Kenneth Parks was very close to his in-laws, especially his mother-in-law, having gone after their daughter when she ran away from home (before they were married). He was a "gentle giant" (larger than average stature is a feature of chronic sleepwalkers) not known for violence.

His acquittal was upheld in the Canadian Supreme Court, who held that since sleepwalking arose from the normal state of sleeping, it could not amount to legal insanity. It was also commented that the medical evidence was different to that presented in Burgess. The prosecution instructed no sleep experts to refute the defence of sleepwalking.

Falater

Found guilty of first degree murder

In Phoenix, Arizona, in 1997, Scott Falater went to bed, and was woken by the police at his door. When the detectives informed him that they were the Homicide Squad, he asked "Does that mean my wife is dead?" The facts of the case are that the defendant stabbed his wife 44 times and then returned to drown her in the pool. The neighbour, woken by dogs barking and a woman screaming, saw Falater motion to his dogs to stay down. He then rolled his wife into the pool, at which point the neighbour called the police. When the police arrived, he was not aware that his wife was dead and assumed the police were hunting for the assailant.

He had a strong history of sleepwalking and there were circumstances of sleep deprivation and considerable stress at work leading up to the episode where he killed his wife. He had no discernible motive, and this was totally out of character – he testified that his wife was his only friend. However, the episode had several atypical features. Falater returned to drown his wife, apparently still alive, after the frenzy of stabbing. There were efforts to conceal evidence, bloody clothing and the murder weapon being placed in a Tupperware container, put inside a rubbish bag and placed within the wheel-well of his car. A neighbour witnessed Falater signalling to his dog to lie down.

Pressman was the expert witness instructed by the State of Arizona in Falater, and he notes 65 details of the incident. Some of these are inconsistent with sleep-walking e.g. actions that demonstrated that working memory was functional (see Appendix D). Not all his conclusions are uncontroversial – there has been work on spatial perception in sleepwalking that suggests that the ability to navigate may be retained. It was also established that it was unlikely that the Tupperware box in which the bloody clothes and weapon were stashed was normally in the car boot, given the effect of the ambient temperature in Phoenix on the plastic used. He also maintained that there was a motive for murder (Yarmila Falater had genital warts which may have indicated marital infidelity). There were conflicting accounts about the state of their marriage.

During the night he had got up to fix the pool motor. Perhaps his wife Yarmila had disturbed him during a sleepwalking episode, but for whatever reason he stabbed his wife of 20 years 44 times, coming back later to drown her in the pool. He tidied away his tools, put them and the bloodied shirt and knife in a Tupperware container in the boot of the car, washed his face and went back to bed. A neighbour who saw Scott drown his wife called the police.

This case contains a number of features that seem to be inconsistent with sleepwalking. If the washing of the face and tidying away of the tools, knife and shirt are seen as covering up, this rules out sleepwalking. However, the washing of the face missed blood on the neck, the knife was not cleaned and part of the shirt was sticking out of the wheel well in the boot, enabling the police to find the evidence easily. If it was a cover-up, it was a very poorly organized one. On the other hand, it could be seen as an expression of Falater's normal behaviour – he was a very tidy man. Crucially, he made no effort to conceal the body at all. Although his wife may have triggered the initial violence by disturbing Falater, this could not have been the case when he later drowned her. The neighbour saw Falater motion to his dogs to keep down.

Falater was a devout Mormon and devoted to his wife. He stated of her "She was my best friend and the only woman I ever loved". In the months prior to the incident, Falater had been under considerable stress at work. The project he was working on was failing, and he was debating on what to tell his bosses. He asked his wife what to do, and she advised him to "Just tell them what they want to hear". As a Mormon he normally didn't consume any caffeinated beverages but he started taking caffeine tablets. He was also suffering sleep deprivation from the stress of his work situation. He was distraught on learning that his wife was dead.

Ultimately, the jury did not believe that the episode was sleepwalking, and returned a verdict of guilty. Mr Falater's son has qualified as an attorney and continues to pursue a gubernatorial pardon.

Lowe

Found not guilty by reason of insanity of murder

In Manchester in 2005, Jules Lowe (22) had gone drinking with his father after his father's partner had died. There was forensic evidence that suggested that Lowe had battered his father to death during a prolonged assault which had some features that were not indicative of a sleepwalking automatism. The defendant had had a considerable amount to drink; he may have sought out his victim; the episode lasted some time, involving at least four separate attacks in the night (Pressman, Mahowald and Schenck et al., 2009); and there were attempts to clear up the blood. Mr Lowe had no memory of the events and did not mention sleepwalking at all in his interviews to the police. It was only nine months later when a friend mentioned a TV programme about the actions possible during sleepwalking that Lowe mentioned to his solicitors that he was a sleepwalker and wondered if sleepwalking on the night in question was a possibility.

The defendant had a personal and family history of sleepwalking from at least adolescence, corroborated by several witnesses among his family and friends. The defendant had no motive and made no organized attempts at cover-up (like Falater, there were some ineffective attempts to clear up blood). The expert witnesses described the testing done in Broadmoor as "the most detailed scientific tests in British legal history". Lowe was described as "the first sleepwalking murder in the UK" by Ebrahim, apparently ignoring *Fraser* from the previous century, and the admittedly contentious *Boshears* (*The Times*, 1961).

An initial sleep study had proved technically inadequate and a further three-night study persuaded the initially sceptical prosecution expert (Dr Ebrahim) that this was in fact a case of parasomnia (whether a confusional arousal or sleepwalking). The case report published (Ebrahim and Fenwick, 2008) prompted heated discussion among the forensic sleepwalking community. It has been suggested that the amount of alcohol consumed by the defendant made the defence of sleepwalking untenable, and that the Alcohol Provocation Test used was inappropriate due to being unvalidated (Pressman, Mahowald and Schenck et al., 2009). The signs of an assault at four different loci were interpreted by the critics as signs of four separate assaults.

Lowe's father was known to be violent when drunk, so it is entirely plausible that he might have provoked an incident. Again like Falater, if there were attempts to cover up they were very poorly organized.

Lowe received a hospital order, and was released after ten months.

Thomas

Found not guilty of murder

In Aberporth in 2008, Brian Thomas and his wife were on holiday in their campervan. Mr Thomas had a strong history of sleep disorders – he had been a sleepwalker since childhood. However, he attributed erectile dysfunction to his medication for depression and Parkinson's disease, and so would periodically omit to take them so he could make love to his wife. One such occasion was the holiday with his wife in July 2008. He took their campervan to West Wales for a romantic break. Their sleep was disturbed by boy-racers in the car park where they were staying overnight. Later that night he had a dream that someone was on top of his wife in the campervan. He went to pull the man off by pulling at his neck. In the morning he realized he had in fact strangled his wife and called 999, stating "I think I've killed my wife. Oh my God. I thought someone had broken in, I must have been dreaming or something. What have I done?"

The prosecution accepted that Mr Thomas was not responsible for his actions, so the only issue at trial was whether the jury should find him not guilty by reason of insanity or just not guilty. Both the sleep experts agreed he had been suffering a sleep disorder, and when the forensic psychiatrist testified that there were no public safety concerns to justify a hospital order, the trial was halted and the judge directed the jury to acquit. The experts did not disclose the bulk of the details in court, to reduce the chance of "copycat" crimes.

The media coverage was universally sympathetic to Mr Thomas, who has no known motive and a well-established medical history. He was a "decent man and a devoted husband" according to Judge Nigel Davis. He had no motive, his brother stating "They were a loving couple and always like that together. He has always been a loving husband and a family man."

Reitz

Found guilty of murder

In the case of Stephen Reitz his actions were extremely violent, but not entirely out of character. He launched a frenzied attack on the married woman with whom he had been having an affair, stabbing and beating her to death. Their relationship had been volatile; he had been violent in the past towards his lover and once threated to "gut her like a fish". The assault had been sustained and frenzied. Reitz had a history of sleepwalking, which was corroborated by family and friends. He stated he had killed his girlfriend during a dream where he struggled with an intruder. He had consumed alcohol and cocaine that night. The wounds in his victim's neck were like those he inflicted on sharks (he was a commercial fisherman). During a sleep study pre-trial, he had a violent sleep terror. Nonetheless, the jury convicted him of first degree murder.

Ricksgers

Found guilty of murder (currently being appealed)

Michael Ricksgers shot his wife with a .357 Magnum. He suffered severe obstructive sleep apnoea, and he claimed that he shot his wife during a dream about an intruder. The prosecution argued that he was planning to leave his wife, and that the shot was aimed. He is serving life without parole. If he has have been wrongly convicted, his refusal to accept their guilt on grounds of their sleep disorder will likely thwart attempts to get parole.

Clarke (Trevor Norman)

Found guilty of causing death by dangerous driving

On 13 April 2006 the defendant Trevor Norman Clarke, who was 49 years old, and had suffered from type 1 diabetes for 30 years, was driving along a very familiar route, when he suffered a hypoglycaemic episode. The effect of that was to cause him to drive erratically for just over two miles. Bystanders noted that the driver looked "paranoid", "fidgety" and "out of it". He was seen to accelerate and then brake for no reason, to put on his windscreen wipers when there was no need, and to stop at a green light. Throughout this time he was swerving and weaving about the road. The defendant narrowly avoided a collision with another car only by the corrective action of the other driver. Throughout this bizarre driving the defendant appeared to be oblivious to other drivers sounding their horns. Eventually the defendant's car left the road and went on to a footpath where two boys were walking. The younger boy, who was just four years old, was struck by the car and gravely injured. He died two weeks later in hospital. The elder boy, the deceased's 14-year-old stepbrother, was also injured. The defendant was charged with causing death by dangerous driving.

At the first trial the jury was unable to reach a verdict, but at a second trial the jury convicted, and Clarke was sentenced to three years in prison. There was an appeal against sentence, when the penalty was reduced to one year. The appeal against sentence is reported but the full facts of the case were not rehearsed there. Mr Clarke's self-management of his condition generally, and on the day in question, was, in the opinion of almost everyone in the case, faultless. He had checked his blood glucose before setting off, and had eaten some food because his blood glucose was 4.4 mmol/l. This is as recommended by the DVLA guidelines. The advice to diabetics to test their blood sugar before setting out on a journey has been described by expert witnesses in another case as "a counsel of perfection", but that is what Mr Clarke did. Clarke had glucose tablets ready in the footwell of his vehicle, again as recommended. The self-management of his condition was described by his diabetic specialist (who was also an expert witness at both trials) as exemplary. On appeal against sentence the Court of Appeal observed that Clarke ". . . was almost obsessive about testing himself, testing his blood more frequently than is recommended". This view of Clarke's very careful self-management was not, however, shared by the prosecution expert witness, who said that the defendant's tight glycaemic control was negligent.

It is fair to say that Clarke's actions after the accident were somewhat odd, and capable of being interpreted either as evasiveness (as the prosecution contended) or as diabetic confusion (according to the defence). For example, he removed his sat nav from the windscreen – conduct seen by the prosecution as evidence against automatism, but interpreted by the defence as inappropriate behaviour and therefore evidence of hypoglycaemia. The defence experts testified that amnesia is universal in hypoglycaemia and often results in the sufferer trying later to fill in the gaps in their memory (confabulation). Clarke gave a misleading account of events to the police. At first he denied having suffered a hypoglycaemic attack, a denial which he later said was motivated by the desire to keep his driving licence. His medical condition certainly improved rapidly with glucose. Clarke's medical condition, and the fact that he had suffered a hypoglycaemic attack, was ultimately not in doubt. What remained contentious was the degree of impairment which it had caused and the defendant's responsibility for allowing the attack to happen.

Two experts appeared for the defence in *Clarke*, one a recognized world authority on hypoglycaemia (Professor Marks) and the other the head of the largest diabetes unit in the United Kingdom (Professor Barnett). The expert instructed by the prosecution was a geriatrician (Professor Livesley) who, according to the assessment of the trial judge, was not a specialist, but had long-term involvement in the control of diabetes. The two experts for the defence were agreed that Clarke was suffering from hypoglycaemic automatism and hypoglycaemic unawareness, and in their view his driving so erratically along a highly familiar route was entirely consistent with that diagnosis. There is evidence that Clarke was suffering hypoglycaemic unawareness. He had ambulatory monitoring of his glucose levels after the accident, which demonstrated 26 episodes of biochemical hypoglycaemia, of which Clarke was aware of only two. The prosecution expert pointed out that the reliability of this assessment depended on Clarke's veracity, but in support of his account, Clarke was noted by observers to be hypoglycaemic during a telephone call which he made to one of his doctors. In the opinion of the two defence experts Clarke had managed his condition in an exemplary manner and had taken all reasonable and proper precautions. In their view Mr Clarke's driving was "automatic behaviour", and Clarke had been unaware of the onset of the attack.

In contrast, the prosecution expert, Professor Livesley, said that he was "100 per cent certain that [Mr Clarke] was aware that he was suffering from hypoglycaemia and that he could have prevented the accident by stopping and by eating or taking glucose tablets". The central issue at the trial was thus whether the defendant at some stage had been aware that he was suffering a hypoglycaemic attack and had nevertheless continued to drive, or whether his medical condition, including his hypoglycaemic unawareness, impaired his cognitive ability to the extent that he was not so aware.

The jury rejected the evidence of Professors Barnett and Marks. Their verdict can only have been based on their acceptance that there had been a time (however brief) during which the defendant was aware of his deteriorating condition. The Court of Appeal said that the legal basis for the defendant's conviction must have been his (albeit brief or fleeting) awareness of the onset of the hypoglycaemic attack and his failure at that point to stop driving.

Rabey

Acquittal on the ground of automatism quashed.

The defendant developed strong feelings for a classmate, which were not reciprocated. He found comments by her in a letter that stated that she found other men exciting but he was nothing to her. When he next encountered her in the geology lab, after she stated that he was "just a friend", he hit her over the head with a rock and started choking her.

He was in an extreme state of emotional agitation, and had only a partial memory of these events. The behaviour was completely out of character, with no history of mental health issues. Expert witnesses concluded that this was a dissociative episode.

The appeal court found that this trigger was not consistent with automatism, because:

> the ordinary stresses and disappointments of life which are the common lot of mankind do not constitute an external cause; the emotional stress suffered by the defendant could not be said to be an external factor producing automatism within the authorities; the source of the dissociative state was the appellant's psychological or emotional makeup.

The trial judge acquitted him on the ground of automatism, but this was overturned on appeal.

Radford

The defendant shot a friend of his ex-wife. His wife was living with a female friend, whom he blamed for the break-up of their marriage. He went to the friend's house, armed with a rifle. He tried to get his ex-wife to leave in his car.

His victim, Nancy Grugan, came out of her house armed with a cricket bat. He took the rifle out of his car, and shot her seven times. The defendant described the incident in court:

> Nancy was screaming in the same manner as my wife, shouting "You leave my friend alone. You leave my friend alone." Out of the corner of my eye I notice that she was swinging some form of club and flailing her arms around.
>
> I noted with some relief that I would reach the gate before her but I think we reached it about the same time. I cannot accurately recall but I may have been struck by Nancy with the object that she was holding which I now understand to be a cricket bat. I am uncertain of this.
>
> I then became very detached from the situation as though I had gone into a sort of cocoon. I must have crossed the road being unaware of any traffic. My car reminded me of my old Army command vehicle. I approached my car and saw the rifle with its barrel jammed down between the front seat and the centre console. I can remember seeing it there as a long and black instrument and thinking to myself, "Good, that's good that I have got a long barrel weapon".
>
> I felt as though I had no control over the situation and I must have grabbed the weapon and walked back towards the side gate. Everything felt very queer. I must have walked back across the road still unaware of any traffic and at this point I felt the presence of a soldier next to me carrying the rifle.
>
> This soldier was in Army gear but had an unusual style of epaulettes. I could not see the soldier's face and felt that I myself did not exist below my neck. I felt as though I was the observer of the other fellow. I felt as though we had crossed the "start line" as in combat and had the impression in my mind that the ground in front of me was a short length of flat and then it started to go up like a parabolic curve and it wasn't grass but like plasticine, smooth and slippery but wavy. All I could see was the rifle barrel pointing to the front at about hip height and there was a pair of legs underneath it and they were going like the piston rods of a train and I was just a "head" observing all of this. My whole body was just a head and it was about two feet above the shoulder – the right shoulder of the soldier. I do not remember seeing the deceased Nancy.
>
> I heard the rifle firing and it lasted just a couple of seconds. This soldier and I kept advancing until I bumped into the fence. I looked down and saw that the rifle was actually in my own hands and realised for the first time that it must have been me who had been doing the firing.

It was held that it should have been left to the jury to consider the issue of involuntariness and/or insanity. The original conviction was quashed.

Index

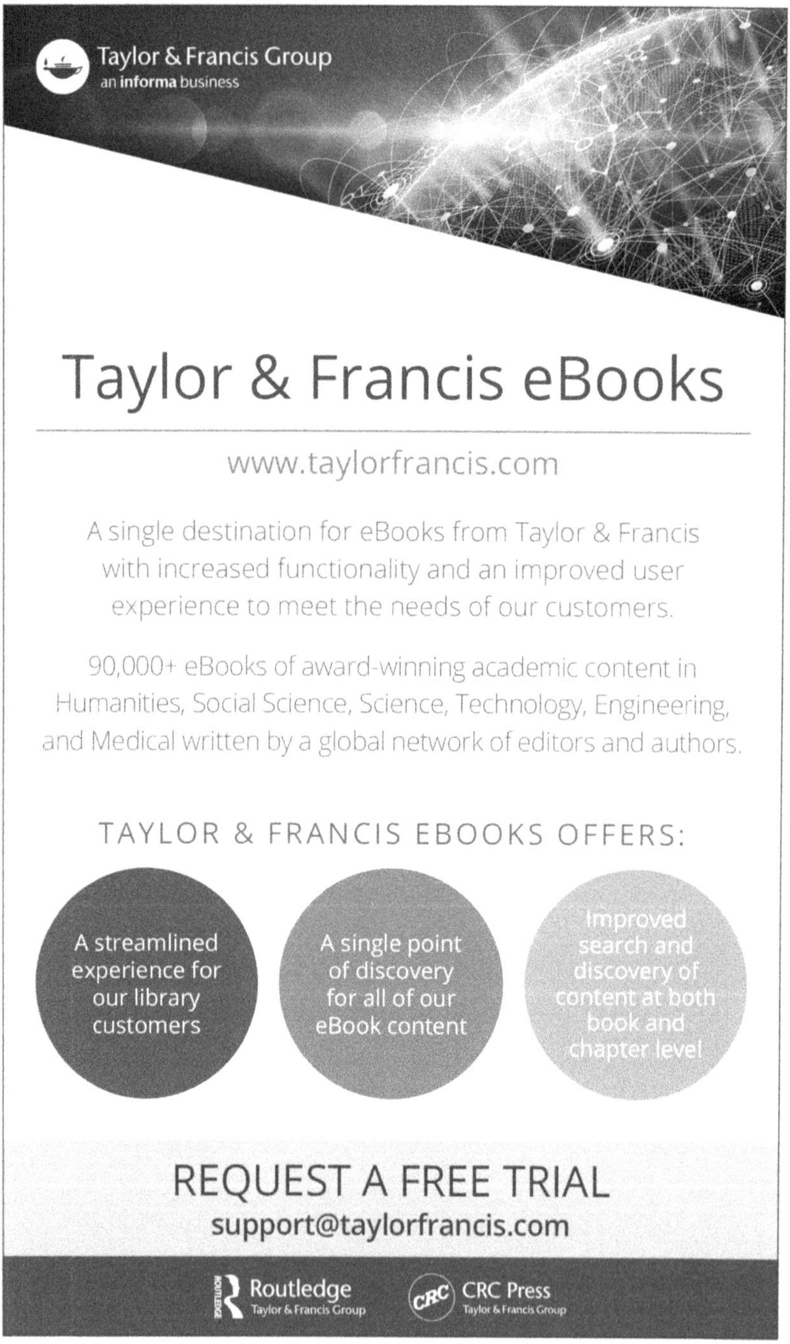
Taylor & Francis Group
an informa business
Taylor & Francis eBooks
www.taylorfrancis.com
A single destination for eBooks from Taylor & Francis with increased functionality and an improved user experience to meet the needs of our customers.
90,000+ eBooks of award-winning academic content in Humanities, Social Science, Science, Technology, Engineering, and Medical written by a global network of editors and authors.
TAYLOR & FRANCIS EBOOKS OFFERS:
A streamlined experience for our library customers
A single point of discovery for all of our eBook content
Improved search and discovery of content at both book and chapter level
REQUEST A FREE TRIAL
support@taylorfrancis.com
Routledge
Taylor & Francis Group
CRC Press
Taylor & Francis Group

For Product Safety Concerns and Information please contact our EU representative GPSR@taylorandfrancis.com
Taylor & Francis Verlag GmbH, Kaufingerstraße 24, 80331 München, Germany

www.ingramcontent.com/pod-product-compliance
Ingram Content Group UK Ltd.
Pitfield, Milton Keynes, MK11 3LW, UK
UKHW011014180926
475701UK00004B/738
* 9 7 8 0 3 6 7 5 8 5 6 4 8 *